CLICKER POLITICS

ESSAYS ON THE CALIFORNIA RECALL

REAL POLITICS IN AMERICA

Series Editor: Paul S. Herrnson, *University of Maryland*

The books in this series bridge the gap between academic scholarship and the popular demand for knowledge about politics. They illustrate empirically supported generalizations from original research and the academic literature using examples taken from the legislative process, executive branch decision making, court rulings, lobbying efforts, election campaigns, political movements, and other areas of American politics. The goal of the series is to convey the best contemporary political science research has to offer in ways that will engage individuals who want to know about real politics in America.

CLICKER POLITICS
ESSAYS ON THE CALIFORNIA RECALL

EDITED BY

Shaun Bowler
University of California, Riverside

Bruce E. Cain
University of California, Berkeley

PEARSON

Prentice
Hall

UPPER SADDLE RIVER, NEW JERSEY 07458

Library of Congress Cataloging-in-Publication Data

Clicker politics : essays on the California recall / edited by Shaun Bowler, Bruce E. Cain.
    p. cm.
    Includes bibliographical references.
    ISBN 0-13-193336-1
        1. Governors—California—Election–Case studies. 2. Recall—California–Case studies.
    3. Elections—California–Case studies 4. Political campaigns—California–Case studies.
    5. Direct democracy—California–Case studies. 6. Minorities—California–Political
    activity—Case studies. 7. California–Politics and government. I. Bowler, Shaun.
    II. Cain, Bruce E.

    JK87932003 .C55 2005
    324.6'8'09794090511—dc22

                                                                            2005048890

Editorial Director: Charlyce Jones Owen
Director of Marketing: Heather Shelstad
Marketing Assistant: Jennifer Lang
Director of Production and Manufacturing: Barbara Kittle
Managing Editor: Lisa Iarkowski
Production Liaison: Joe Scordato
Production Assistant: Marlene Gassler
Manufacturing Buyer: Sherry Lewis
Manufacturing Manager: Nick Sklitsis
Cover Design: Kiwi Design
Cover Art Director: Jayne Conte
Cover Illustration/Photo: Getty Images, Inc
Full Service Management: Andrea Clemente/Cadmus Professional Communications

This book was set in 10/11 Palatino by Cadmus Professional Communications and was printed
by R. R. Donnelley & Sons, Inc. The cover was printed by Phoenix Color Corp.

Credits and acknowledgments borrowed from other sources and reproduced, with permission,
in this textbook appear on appropriate page within text.

Pearson Education Ltd   Pearson Education Australia PTY, Limited
Pearson Education Singapore, Pte. Ltd   Pearson Education North Asia Ltd
Pearson Education, Canada, Ltd   Pearson Educacion de Mexico, S.A. de C.V.
Pearson Education—Japan   Pearson Education Malaysia, Pte. Ltd

10 9 8 7 6 5 4 3 2 1
ISBN 0-13-193336-1

CONTENTS

PREFACE

The "Clicker" in the title is the clicker for the TV remote. When we are bored with watching a program we click the remote and find another channel, then another and another. The recall lets us do that to politicians but with potentially far more damaging consequences than stopping watching *CSI: Miami* and starting watching *The Apprentice*.

The basic narrative of the 2003 California Recall is familiar to many people around the world. This is largely due to Arnold Schwartzenegger's star power, but that is not the whole story. It is rare in American politics for voters to remove a governor in mid-term. But in 2003, California voters essentially changed the gubenatorial "channel" before the Gray Davis show was supposed to finish. This book reflects on the causes and implications of this extraordinary event. To what degree was California's resort to the recall mechanism a function of institutional features like its low signature requirement and unusual ballot structure? How did the traditional and alternative media frame the election? Why does the recall pose such serious legal challenges to campaign finance law and to ballot mechanics? Was the recall a rejection of the man (Gray Davis) or of representative government? How did issues of race and gender play in the recall? Based on original research but written for a general audience, this book attempts to probe questions about the causes of this unusual event and the operation of the recall process.

ACKNOWLEDGMENTS

The Editors would like to thank those who reviewed the manuscript for this book and provided helpful suggestions: Christine Day of University of New Orleans–Lakefront, Ken Goldstein of University of Wisconsin–Madison, Rodney Hero of University of Notre Dame, Karen O'Connor of American University, Kelly Patterson of Brigham Young University, John Pitney of Claremont McKenna, Darrell West of Brown University, and Clyde Wilcox of Georgetown University.

The Editors would also like to thank Marc Levin, Jerry Lubenow, and the Institute of Governmental Studies for their support in organizing the conference on the recall out of which this project grew (http://www.igs.berkeley.edu/events/recall.html/).The conference was underwritten by a generous grant from the Pew Charitable Trusts. Additional financial support was provided by the Departments of Political Science at the University of California–Davis, University of California–Irvine, and University of California–Riverside.

Jack Citrin and Jonathan Cohen acknowledge the assistance of Kimberley Curry and Michael Murakami in preparing Chapter 5.

The authors of Chapter 7, Matt A. Barreto and Ricardo Ramírez, would like to thank Shaun Bowler and Bruce Cain for their review and helpful suggestions on an earlier draft of this chapter. They also benefited from discussions with Louis DeSipio, Janelle Wong, Gary Segura, and Nathan Woods about minority voters in California and are grateful for their suggestions.

Richard L. Hasen filed an *amicus curiae* brief on his own behalf supporting the American Civil Liberties Union's position in the punch card litigation described in Chapter 12. He thanks Nicole Drey for research assistance and Beth Garrett and Dan Tokaji for valuable comments and suggestions.

Shaun Bowler
University of California, Riverside

Bruce E. Cain
University of California, Berkeley

1

Introduction

Shaun Bowler

UNIVERSITY OF CALIFORNIA, RIVERSIDE

Bruce E. Cain

UNIVERSITY OF CALIFORNIA, BERKELEY

In October 2003, Gray Davis became only the second governor in U.S. history to be recalled. On a succession of issues, most notably those concerning the state's energy and budget problems, voters saw the governor to blame. After a petition drive and recall election, 55% of the voters answered "yes" to the question, "Shall Gray Davis be recalled (removed) from the office of Governor?" Bodybuilder turned movie-star Arnold Schwarzenegger won the contest to replace Gray Davis with a decisive 48% of the vote, more than 17 points ahead of his nearest rival in a crowded field. Gray Davis accepted defeat, telling supporters voters had decided "it was time for someone else to serve and I have accepted their judgment."

Democratic Governor Davis had come into office the previous November as the unenthusiastic choice of voters faced with a less appealing alternative, Bill Simon. As one preelection poll reported, "voters continue to be unsatisfied with the choice of candidates for governor (57%) and with the amount of attention the candidates are paying to the issues that matter to them (66%)." (PPIC survey October 7–17, 2002). Many of those who voted for him found Davis to be wanting in many dimensions, but better than the Republican candidate. The more moderate GOP candidate (Los Angeles Mayor Richard Riordan) was defeated at least in part because Davis had spent a good share of his $10 million campaign money running advertisements that attacked Riordan at the time of the GOP primary. In this way, Davis cleverly ensured that his Republican opponent at the general election would be the more conservative and hence vulnerable candidate, Bill Simon. The unusual audacity of a Democratic candidate running negative advertisements in a Republican primary campaign angered many Republicans and set the tone for the general election. Bill Simon repeatedly made a series of unfounded allegations of corruption while

> [s]trategists for Davis, who was widely unpopular heading into his reelection campaign, made no secret of their strategy: Destroy his opponent so that voters, however grudgingly, would see the incumbent as a preferable alternative.

Garry South, the mastermind of Davis' campaign, called the contest "damaged goods versus defective product." So the governor and his strategists "bludgeoned Simon with a blunt object, and it was not a pretty sight," South said. (Negative Campaign Repelled Some Voters, *LA Times*, November 11, 2002).

Such astonishingly negative campaign tactics may have seemed to be all part of the game for campaign professionals, but they left a decidedly nasty aftertaste so far as voters were concerned. Voters grudgingly gave Davis the win in an election in which turnout—at just over 50% of registered voters, 36% of eligible voters showed up at the polls—was the lowest recorded in a statewide election. Manifesting the lack of enthusiasm for the winner, turnout rates were low in the Democratic Party strongholds of Los Angeles, San Francisco, and Alameda counties. Gray Davis began his second term not much liked even by his own party. His troubles were only just beginning.

In the winter of 2002 and spring 2003, problems over state finances mounted further. The size of the state budget deficit grew with every press conference and produced a strong suspicion that its true size had been deliberately hidden during the election, eroding popular regard for politicians in general and the governor in particular. As demands for a recall began to build, Governor Davis further angered voters by unilaterally raising tax rates on cars. Republicans had more than an ample supply of failures to help motivate voters into signing the petition and demanding a recall.

Dissatisfaction with the state's political leadership and mistrust of the government's ability to address critical problems were amply demonstrated by polls taken during the first half of 2003. The political leadership of California was registering record low approval ratings. By July 2003—after yet another missed deadline for signing the state budget—only 19% of voters approved of the job the state legislature was doing, while a marginally larger 23% approved of the job Gray Davis was doing (California Poll, July 1–13, 2003). These were historically low approval figures that even exceeded the previous low recorded in April. By autumn of 2003, surveys showed that overall levels of trust in government had reached unusually low levels. Not only was the state facing a series of fiscal and policy problems, voters had little confidence in the ability and willingness of their political leaders to do anything about it. Rightly or wrongly Governor Davis was seen to be either a prime cause of that dissatisfaction or the most obvious lightning rod for discontent, even among Democrats. In the event, exit polls later showed that as many as a quarter of registered Democrats voted to recall Davis (*LA Times* exit poll).

Arnold Schwarzenegger's campaign gained considerable popularity from its attacks on "the politicians" who had failed to do their job. His campaign was based in large part on attacking Sacramento, a theme that resonated with voters. In his swearing-in remarks, the new governor highlighted the importance of this dissatisfaction for motivating the recall in pledging to restore trust in state government:

My fellow citizens: Today is a *new* day in California. I did not seek this office to do things the way they've *always* been done. What I care about is restoring your *trust* in your government.

When I became a citizen 20 years ago, I had to take a citizenship test. I had to learn about the history and the principles of our republic. What I learned–and what I've *never* forgotten is–that in a republic, sovereignty rests with the *people*, not the government.

In recent years, Californians have lost *confidence*. They've felt that the actions of their government did *not* represent the will of the people.

This election was *not* about replacing one man or one party. It was about changing the entire *political climate* of our state.

Everywhere I went during my campaign, I could feel the public hunger for our elected officials to work *together*, to work *openly*, and to work for the greater *good*.

The election was the people's *veto*, of politics as usual. (Swearing-in remarks of Governor Schwarzenegger, Sacramento, CA, November 17, 2003; emphasis in original).

As his first act, the new governor repealed the car tax that had generated such hostility toward Gray Davis. In the year following his election, the "anti-system" sentiment greatly worried members of the Assembly and helped to ensure that the new governor faced fewer difficulties in dealing with the legislature than his predecessor. Not surprisingly, the recall election attracted a good deal of attention. Partly, this was due to the novelty value of a recall in such an important state as California. But partly, it was the celebrity status of the eventual winner—Arnold Schwarzenegger. His entry brought the total number of candidates to 134. Those candidates ranged from ex-celebrities, pornographers, and cranks to ordinary citizens with sincere beliefs and a desire to fix the state through rigid principled ideologues. They provided TV and newspapers from around the world with seemingly endless raw material for stories, especially ones that seemingly illustrated the craziness of the California circus. By the end of the campaign, the recall's media coverage was so extensive that even the media coverage became a story.

In this volume, we step back from the recall's "circus" aspects to look at the election and the process itself in a broader perspective. For observers of direct democracy or state politics more generally, the 2003 California recall election was a fascinating event. But the California recall election also opened a window to a number of broader questions, questions that are often pushed to one side by more familiar contests, such as presidential elections. For example, given the prevailing immigration and migration patterns, minorities will be a growing portion of the California and the nation's electorate in the coming years. The recall allows us to look in some detail at minority voters, especially Latinos and Asian Americans.

The recall also allows us to look more closely at the citizen's role in the democratic process: how do citizens deal with complex vote choices and what does the recall say about citizens' evolving attitudes toward government. California voters were, during the autumn of 2003, greatly disillusioned with their government and mistrustful of it. Understanding why this was so and whether they had just cause to be disillusioned helps us to understand what it is that governments should be doing to be seen as trustworthy. Finally, the recall helped shed light on the election processes: how the media covered the election and how the actual voting mechanisms helped shape this election as they did in Florida in 2000 and will again. Although there are some unique features to the recall that limit the lessons we can learn from it, there are also ways in which California's recall can help shed light on wider political processes that often remain in the shadows at other times.

HISTORY OF THE PROCESS

Recall elections are usually categorized alongside the initiative and referendum as one of the instruments of direct democracy. Their first introduction into state politics was typically packaged with a series of reform efforts. It occurred around the time of World War I and was associated with the Progressive Movement. The initiative and referendum give voters a say on specific policy or constitutional questions; the recall is different, however, in that it allows voters to address incumbent politicians directly by subjecting them to another election.

The recall process was initially introduced in the city of Los Angeles in 1903 and then used successfully for the first time to recall Los Angeles Councilman Davenport in 1904. By 1911, when it was adopted for state politics in California as part of a package of reforms including the initiative and referendum, its use at the local level had expanded to 25 cities, and by the 1920s, it was in frequent use in local politics (Bird and Ryan 1930). Up until 2003, the only governor to be recalled was also from that period—Lyn Frazier of North Dakota who was recalled in 1921. Since then, the process has been used very infrequently at the state level. At present, eighteen U.S. states have some form of recall process but they vary widely in institutional features. The process is more common at the local level in which thirty-six states allow its use. In some states, such as Texas, the recall is not an option at the state level, even though it exists at the local government level. More than 2000 local political units in the United States use the process. In a five-year period, approximately one in ten political units will experience an attempt to recall a local official.

Before the Gray Davis recall election, there were 117 attempts to recall state-elected officials in California, including 31 attempts to recall the governor. The first gubernatorial recall of California was a 1936 attempt to remove Governor Merriam. Of all the previous attempts at recall, only seven, all aimed at members of the legislature, made the ballot and only four of these succeeded. All Davis' immediate predecessors had been subject to recall attempts; four attempts against Pete Wilson, nine attempts–a record–against George Deukmejian.

Like all direct democracy processes, recall elections are a product of reforms from the Progressive Movement era, which markedly changed the face of American democracy around the time of World War I. On its first introduction at the state level in Oregon in 1908, the recall was heralded as the "final crowning act to complete the temple of popular government." (Barnett 1912, 41). The majority of recall laws were adopted as part of a package of Progressive reforms in the early twentieth century that aimed to lessen the power and corruption of political bosses and party machines. The anti-corruption motivation is still alive today in some of the more recent recall adoptions, such as Rhode Island in 1992, which took place against a backdrop of a series of wide-ranging and massive corruption scandals in state politics. Some Progressives had doubts about the virtues of the recall, believing it to be "reform run mad" (Mowry, 140–141). However, the most serious doubts concerned the recalling of judges rather than legislators or executives. In the face of thoroughly corrupt political machines and "boss" politics in turn of the century America, institutional reforms that gave citizens a greater voice seemed to be the answer. Progressives believed the recall for legislators and executives would help restore honesty into politics by holding office-holdings immediately accountable for malfeasance in office.

As with many political processes in the U.S. federal system, the exact institutional details vary from state to state or from city to city in important ways, but all recall processes follow the same basic pattern. A petition is circulated and, if enough voters sign the petition, a special election devoted to the single subject of recall is called out of the normal electoral cycle. If the official loses, he or she is removed from office and a replacement elected. Sometimes, as in the California case, the election to replace the incumbent is held at the same time as the recall. The major hurdle in all recall efforts—as in all initiative elections—is, however, the same: the need to gather sufficient numbers of signatures to force a recall. All previous attempts to recall former California governors failed at this point.

Modern recall campaigns try hard to make it a 'grass roots' effort, but the obstacles to genuine amateur efforts are formidable at the state level. In the case of the Davis recall, the campaign began with a telephone conversation between two long-time activists in state politics, Mark Abernathy and Ted Costa, discussing their disappointment over the November election when one of them spoke the phrase, "Maybe we ought to recall him?" But there is a long step between saying such things and actually making them happen, as the long record of failed recall attempts showed. Costa and Abernathy attempted to harness new technologies in order to overcome the qualification hurdle and gather signatures. Their campaign, for example, designed petitions that could be downloaded from the Internet and submitted from home, and these Web sites were publicized over talk radio. But in the end, the major motor for the success of the signature drive was the contribution of nearly $1.7 million from the Republican Congressman Darrell Issa to bankroll professional signature gatherers. Paid signature gatherers are, and have always been, both a prominent and controversial feature of direct democracy. Standing outside stores and shopping malls, signature gatherers are paid a sum of approximately $1 for each registered voter they get to sign the petition. Over the years, an industry of signature gatherers has grown up in which companies contract with campaigns to raise signatures and then, in turn, subcontract with local persons who hire the signature gatherers to stand outside the store. The sums involved in the process can be huge and can account for a huge share of expenditures. For example "Rescue California," one of the major players in the recall attempt, spent $2.4 million in the recall effort, out of which nearly half, $985,000, went to a single firm, Bader and Associates, a firm of professional signature gatherers. Conventional wisdom has it that a million dollars can ensure that an initiative proposal in the state gathers enough signatures to make the ballot. In the words of one Democratic campaigner describing his initial reaction to the recall, "It's real if there's money [to qualify the proposal]"; Issa's money made it real.

CAMPAIGNS AND CAMPAIGNING

The recall of Governor Davis was not just a new kind of election. It also offered new opportunities and challenges for campaign strategists and strategies. Any campaign that spends close to $80 million in a matter of a few weeks, as this one did, offers clear financial opportunities, and California's political consultants were quick to seize upon them. Arnold Schwarzenegger's candidacy was also a boon to the recall effort. His larger than life persona was ready-made fodder for campaign advertisements and stories; hence, the frequent references to Schwarzenegger's movie roles, not just the titles (*Total Recall, The Terminator*), and famous lines from the movies ("Hasta la vista, baby"). Mainstream and entertainment media from around the world picked up the Schwarzenegger story and ran with it. Spin doctors and image consultants had brand new venues to practice their craft when *Entertainment Tonight* and *The Tonight Show* began showcasing candidates. The anti-Davis campaign, in particular, used the Internet and talk radio as a means of raising signatures for the petition and subsequently maintained voter interest in their campaign. In retrospect, none of this was so surprising since political campaigns, especially in California, have always made use of the latest technologies. Campaigns in the 1930's, such as Upton Sinclair's bid to become governor in 1936, used radio, cinema, and even sky writers to convey a campaign message. The Internet, talk radio, and the chat show are the modern successors to that history.

One new campaign tactic is the use of court challenges. Initiative proposals, if they pass, are often subject to lawsuits as a means to prevent them from being implemented, but this election was unusual in that the lawsuits preceded the election. Four federal and eleven state suits were filed during the course of the recall. Many of them concerned the potential disadvantages of various voting technologies and hence a justification for delaying the recall. The Lawyers Committee for Civil Rights, for example, filed a suit on behalf of minority voters in Monterey County, charging that the county needed to obtain preclearance to change balloting standards or procedures, *Oliverez et al. v. State of California; Monterey County; Kevin Shelley; Cruz Bustamante* (U.S. District Court, Northern District of California, filed August 5, 2002[3]). The American Civil Liberties Union filed suit on behalf of minority voters in counties where punch card voting was in use, leading to a temporary but nevertheless dramatic stay of the election. In other suits, the campaigns took a more obvious direct involvement. A July suit filed by Taxpayer's Against the Governor's Recall tried, and failed, to challenge the recall effort by challenging the credentials of petition signature gatherers. Later on, lawsuits were threatened over the use of campaign dollars in the Bustamante campaign and, later still, on the validity of loans to the Schwarzenegger campaign. Clearly, litigation has become a common campaign tactic. U.S. elections generally offer rich pick-ings for lawsuits; cases involving campaign finance or the Voting Rights Act are commonplace in America but not in most advanced democracies. This trend is partly about the prevalence of litigation in America, but also about the continuation of political struggles by any means and in new venues.

As well as opportunities, the recall also presented serious challenges to the campaigns and their campaign managers. The short campaign meant that both campaigns and campaign strategies had to be developed quickly. Unlike the drawn-out campaigns of the standard cycle of primary and general elec-tions that can last for months at a time, this election campaign had a short fuse. Standard elections with dates permanently fixed on the calendar can often resemble chess games. There is typically a lot of time to think through and prepare advertisements, press releases, photo opportunities, and all the other plays in a standard campaign. But a recall campaign is more like a video game, demanding instant real-time responses. As the timeline below shows, every couple of days a major event occurred during the course of the cam-paign. For example, candidates dropped out of the race, including several of the most notable candidates—Issa, Simon, and Huffington. Each withdrawal had implications for campaign strategy and for the vote share of remaining candidates. The rapid entry into and exit from the campaign that character-ized the recall resembled the U.S. presidential primary process in this sense, but even so, it did not unfold over a sequence of separate elections.

The recall ballot structure presented voters with a complex decision. Aside from the choice of voting for or against Gray Davis, there was the additional problem of choosing a challenger candidate to vote for. The ballot was lengthy due to the extraordinary number of candidates. No doubt some voters felt like throwing up their hands in frustration and disposing the ballot in the trash. Even excluding the fringe candidates, many credible choices remained. The political parties from whom voters could be expected to take their cue also faced difficult choices. Was having a Democrat on the second part of the bal-lot a sensible precaution or self-defeating trap? The Bustamante and the Davis campaign managers held sharply differing views on whether it was prudent or a mistake to run a Democrat on the second ballot. As Garry South put it, hav-ing a Democrat on the second ballot meant it was difficult to portray the move as a Republican power grab. Hence, he did not want a prominent Democratic candidate on the ballot. For the Bustamante campaign people, a ballot without a credible Democratic alternative meant that a Davis defeat, as seemed likely, necessarily meant a GOP win.

Republican Party strategists also faced strategic complications. Without coordination on a single candidate in order to avoid splitting the GOP vote, the recall might replace Davis with an even more liberal Democratic candidate. Prior to Arnold Schwarzenegger's entry, there was no consensus candidate. Winnowing down the field of candidates was a crucial problem for the GOP party, which was ultimately solved by the entry of Arnold Schwarzenegger. In addition, GOP campaign managers were constrained from running too negative a campaign for any of their candidates. Early on, concerns about the "puke politics" of Gray Davis seemed to sensitize the Democratic campaign against "going negative" and constraining the Davis campaign in particular.

But, even among GOP challengers, it was not obvious, given the public's mood, whether anything other than the mildest, obligatory criticisms of the incumbent would help. Dissuading voters from supporting Gray Davis was one thing, but having them support your candidate was another. It was not clear where votes would flow to as a result of negative campaigning. The recall campaign was for this reason a much cleaner and less negative race than the governor's race of the previous year.

THE RECALL: A "STORM IN A JAR"

Any election in California has consequences beyond its borders because it is home to nearly one in eight Americans and the world's fifth largest economy. Politically, too, California is important. Its state delegation is far and away the largest in the U.S. Congress and the state is typically a major source of campaign donations to both political parties. The state, thanks to its user-friendly initiative process, is an important political and policy trendsetter. For example, the Reagan-era tax revolt and the world's first professional firm of campaign advisors, Campaigns Incorporated, started in California. Commentary on the recall suggested that the 2003 effort, too, might be the start of a national trend, and a possibly worrying trend at that. To what extent is the 2003 recall election an exception or a sign of things to come?

Before saying too much about the lessons from the recall, it is worthwhile to take a moment to outline aspects of the recall that are either idiosyncratic to the particular recall or, alternatively, common to any election. As the chapter by Cain, Anderson, and Eaton shows, the possibility of state office recalls traveling much beyond the West Coast and becoming a frequent feature of state political life is limited by the fact that California's recall process is one of the easiest to use. The recall is common at the local level and Schwarzenegger's highly publicized success may well encourage even greater use there, but legal and constitutional limitations restrict how far and how fast recall fever can spread to other states.

If the recall had idiosyncratic components that make it hard to draw general lessons, it also had a number of familiar themes, especially insofar as voter behavior is concerned. The chapter by Drew Linzer shows that patterns of voter behavior and the outcome itself are readily understood in terms of standard approaches to voter behavior. This was a referendum election in which partisanship strongly colored vote choice. It was an election decided in large part by assessments of incumbent performance and influenced by long-standing party loyalty, as are most gubernatorial elections. Similarly, the chapter by Thad Kousser emphasizes that we should not claim that the election resulted in a major shift or realignment from being a blue (Democratic leaning) state to a red (Republican leaning) state. To be sure, elections mark the constitutional, orderly, and peaceful replacement of one leader by another. But the recall proved to be just another election and does not seem to have realigned California's politics. The highly personal success of Schwarzenegger's victory means that this will not likely be a turning point for GOP fortunes in the state any time soon. As the 2004 elections clearly illustrated, California is still a blue state.

The 2003 recall illustrated some other familiar themes not far below the surface. One of the more seemingly 'unique' features was Arnold Schwarzenegger's candidacy. When it comes to star power, size matters. Megastars dominate lesser ones. Schwarzenegger's victory owed something to lucky circumstance because it allowed him to become a moderate Republican candidate without running in a primary race dominated by conservatives. This also illustrated a familiar lesson that closed primary elections tend to produce relative extremists as nominees, extremists who have a hard time reaching out to mainstream voters. The experience of the previous year suggested that Gray Davis would have had a harder time beating Richard Riordan (a moderate Republican) than Bill Simon (a very conservative Republican) in the general election. Yet, GOP primary voters chose Simon over Riordan and lost the subsequent general election. Schwarzenegger's victory confirmed the conventional wisdom in California that moderate candidates have electoral appeal in the state; yet, the system of primaries pushes candidates to the extremes.

Similarly, money was as important in this election as it is in many U.S. elections. Every textbook on California politics at some point restates the phrase from an old-time Assembly Speaker Jesse Unruh, "Money is the mother's milk of politics." The recall experience gives us yet another opportunity to roll out that phrase. Congressman Issa's financial support during the signature-gathering phase and the millions of campaign dollars spent after the recall underscore the importance of cash to campaigns. Where there is so much money to be made, one might think campaign firms are sure to follow, but actually they are ahead of the curve. The direct democracy industry has already put in place the kind of firms that could run recall campaigns.

Another familiar theme in this campaign was the reluctance of most candidates to seriously address issues of state finance. Voters in California, much like voters everywhere, prefer to have both high quality state services and very low taxes. Unfortunately, this combination is an unrealistic one. There is a trade-off between the two preferences that most voters, and most candidates, remain unwilling to probe. Of the more prominent candidates, only Tom McClintock (Republican) and Peter Camejo (Green party) were willing to state clear positions on the trade-off: McClintock favoring lower taxes and fewer services, and Camejo favoring better services and higher taxes to pay for them. The remaining candidates, including the winner, stayed faithful to the standard political script of fudge and more fudge, claiming that some mix of getting rid of "waste" and supposedly painless bond debt would allow Californians to have their cake, eat it, and have someone else pay the bill.

Finally, the recall confirmed that voters are capable of figuring out whom to vote for in reasonable ways, even when the ballot has more than two choices on it. Concerns over voter confusion are raised whenever there are more than the customary two choices. Critics of direct democracy or, in this case, the recall, fuss over ballot complexity and potential citizen confusion. In the recall, the multiplicity of candidates (a total of 134) and the two-question format of the ballot, shall the governor be recalled followed by a second vote on who shall replace him, made for a more complex ballot than usual. Such complexity, some feared, would stump the average voter. Hence, the recall was needlessly demanding. Those who do not believe voters are so readily flummoxed point to everyday life for evidence that voters can manage. Super-markets stock a dozen kinds of toothpaste, spaghetti sauce, and soda. Lunchtime options for fast food do not stop at the choice between McDonalds and Burger King, and the average TV set now has several hundred channels instead of a handful of networks. There are even more than two music chan-nels. Evidence from everyday life suggests that voters can cope with choice, and evidence from this recall election confirmed that voters can cope with choice in a political setting too. The chapter by Alvarez, Kieiwiet, and Sinclair underscores this point.

What we learned from the recall campaign confirmed many things that we already knew and necessarily limit how much we can learn from the 2003 recall. Nevertheless, despite all that is familiar, it does help to shed light on some other topics that get lost in the details of more common elections. U.S. presidential campaigns, on which much of the academic understanding of elections is based, last months and months even after the primary season is over. It can be hard to sort out the events associated with the election from those associated with external events that happen during the campaign. From that perspective, the recall marks a 'storm in a jar': a chance to study an election within a contained setting and see how it fits into the broader picture.

What the chapters in this volume do is place the recall in a broader con-text by focusing on a number of themes that will recur in both state and fed-eral elections but are often overlooked or understudied. One of the most important of these themes is that of racial and immigrant politics. Racial and immigrant issues were relevant to the campaign in a number of ways. There were, for example, two Latino candidates running, most notably, Cruz Bus-tamante for the Democrats and Peter Camejo for the Greens, as well as two first generation immigrants (Arnold Schwarzenegger, a native of Austria, and Ariana Huffington, a native of Greece). Issues of race and immigration appeared in the campaign, most plainly in the decision to issue driver's licenses to illegal immigrants/undocumented aliens.

Underlying these bullet points from the recall campaign are the funda-mental shifts in California's demographic makeup that have taken place over the past generation, shifts that will take place in the rest of the U.S. over the next few years. California is now a majority-minority state (i.e., one in which minorities form the majority of the population). Whites no longer form a majority in the state but instead comprise a dwindling plurality. This trend will come to the rest of the U.S. in stages as the twenty-first century progresses, beginning in the southern and western states. Clearly, how minority popu-lations are or are not incorporated into the political system has enormous consequences for the pattern of U.S. democracy as a whole. Often minority issues and concerns are relegated to a side role in any study of elections in part, perhaps, because in the United States, Latinos and Asian Americans still constitute a relatively small share of the electorate. This means that minority politics remain understudied nationally, and since California is a majority-minority state, it is not easy to bracket minority politics as a secondary interest. Demographic trends mean that in future years we cannot so readily downplay minority politics nationwide, especially as the economic engine of the coun-try continues to shift south and west. For these reasons, several chapters take a serious look at these issues, especially in relation to the Latino community. Latinos are often called the "sleeping giant" of California politics because they comprise around a third of the population. The chapter by DeSipio and Masuoka examines Cruz Bustamante's candidacy while the chapter by Barreto and Ramirez examines Latino voting patterns generally. More specifically, the chapter by Scola and Garcia-Bedolla look at the interrelationship between gender and minority status in the context of the recall election.

The chapter by Masuoka and HoSang extends our understanding of minority politics by examining Asian Americans. This label is, as they note, an oversimplification since it embraces peoples whose family originated from the region ranging from Pakistan to Japan and so lumps together people with sharply different cultures, languages, and sensibilities. The growth in the Asian-American population of the state has often been overshadowed by the larger numbers of Latinos. Yet, Asian Americans comprise an increasingly important share of the state's population; approximately 12% of the state's population according to the 2000 census. This group, on average and speaking in very general terms, possesses many of the demographic advantages of political action. On average, members of this community, if we can speak in such broad-brush terms, possess higher levels of educational attainment and income than other minority groups, and these attributes are usually seen to be important in facilitating political action. But many within the Asian-American community are not as politically active as their income and education suggest they could be. Matsuoka and HoSang consider what kinds of political action a minority group should pursue when it is in such a relatively small minority.

Minority politics also came to the foreground in lawsuits over ballot format. Different methods of counting votes, optical scanner, machine, or punch card, have different rates of error. Some counties, especially those with large minority populations, used techniques for counting ballots that had high error rates. This raises the question of whether these votes would be systematically undercounted and goes against the underlying democratic premise that all votes be counted and weighted equally regardless of race, ethnicity, religion, or gender. Vote counting mechanisms, however, are similar to household plumbing in the sense that we tend not to think about them unless things go wrong, as happened in Florida in 2000. Whether or not someone's vote is accurately recorded is central to the integrity and legitimacy of the electoral process.

Within the recall, this issue generated several lawsuits and led to a brief but very dramatic court-ordered postponement of the election on September 15 that was overturned just over a week later by the Ninth Circuit Court of Appeals. The chapter(s) by Rick Hasen and Henry Brady discuss this episode in the recall race, drawing the broader lessons both voting technologies and the intervention of courts have for the electoral process.

The chapter by Citrin and Cohen considers what the 2003 recall tells us about trust in government, the public's attitude to their government, and to the process itself. A considerable disenchantment with those in power provided fuel for the recall effort. Some criticisms of the recall vote echoed a familiar criticism of all direct democracy processes: what was supposed to be a grass roots effort was not really grass roots. A small group of well-heeled conspirators fund professional signature gatherers and so help undermine the 'original intent' of the Progressives. But whatever the motivations of actors such as Darrell Issa or Ted Costa, the success or failure of their action depended upon the recall resonating with voters, and it did. In this chapter, Citrin considers why it was that voters so mistrusted their government.

At some point almost every political campaign has someone cry out "media bias"; the 2003 recall was no exception. Within the last week of the campaign, allegations of sexual harassment were made against Arnold Schwarzenegger, denied by the candidate himself, and were dismissed by his campaign as a carefully timed plot by the *Los Angeles Times* to derail his campaign. The chapter by Martin Johnson and others considers the role of the media and media bias in a very general sense: was the recall, for reporters, just a silly season story and a chance to poke fun at a California circus, or was something more profound going on? Was the recall "all about Arnold" or something else? They find that for California newspapers the recall was a serious story and not a circus. That label was one that especially was favored by out-of-state newspapers, but for Californians, as the papers by Linzer and Citrin show, the recall was a serious issue of judging government failure.

TRUSTEE VERSUS DELEGATE

One important feature of the recall is that as an institutional device it leads us to ask more directly how accountable our political leaders should be. Academic conceptions of representation often set up the representative's role as serving as a 'trustee' or 'delegate.' Trustees, once elected, are supposed to be given great leeway by voters to exercise their own judgment and express their own opinions. As Edmund Burke, an especially eloquent champion of the trustee model, stated:

> Your representative owes you, not his industry only, but his judgement; and he betrays, instead of serving you, if he sacrifices it to your opinion. (Burke, Address to the Electors of Bristol, 1774).

In his less well-known address at the next election in 1780, Burke elaborated on the argument,

> ... if we do not permit our members to act upon a very enlarged view of things, we shall at length infallibly degrade our national representation into a confused and scuffling bustle of local agency.... If the people should ... choose their servants on the same principles of mere obsequiousness and flexibility, and total vacancy or indifference of opinion in all public matters, then no part of the state will be sound; and it will be in vain to think of saving it. (Burke, Speech to the Bristol Voters, 1780).

The alternative model of representation, the delegate model, sees the job of elected representatives to reflect the views of voters, and not to express their own views. As eloquent as Burke was, it is worth recalling that even as Burke made this appeal in favor of a trustee model, the electors themselves preferred the delegate model. In the 1780 election, the gap between Burke and the opinion of his electorate led him to believe he would not be reelected and so he withdrew from the race. Nevertheless, even though the electors of Bristol were unmoved by Burke's eloquence, his argument in favor of a trustee model remains persuasive to many.

But recall elections imply an unusually robust version of delegation. Under the recall it is not enough that the electorate hold elected officials accountable for their actions every four or five years. After all, in between elections, incumbents may exercise their own judgments and simply hope voters forget transgressions, and incumbents can usually rely on the short memories of most voters. Recall elections imply not just that a public official is a delegate or agent of voters but that he or she "is a *continuously* responsible agent of the electorate" (Bird and Ryan 1930, 346, emphasis added). The recall thus implies that an elected official is always a delegate, even between elections, and should always be mindful of that. If, in between elections, the representative does not show the proper regard for the views of voters or is shown to be incompetent or corrupt, then, absent the recall, voters have to simply grin and bear it. Voters have to wait until the next election. But with the recall process voters do not have to wait until the next election to vote out the politician; instead, they can hold the representative directly accountable for specific actions.

Elections allow voters to reward and punish incumbents for their behavior and let them choose people they think are going to do a good job. But voters make mistakes. Sometimes, people are elected who are corrupt or simply incompetent. Moreover, most voters know or at least believe that elected officials will not make strenuous efforts to punish their colleagues. Many scandals are hushed up altogether or result in only minor punishments. Recall elections thus allow voters to correct their mistakes, mistakes the voters believe that the parties or the legal system will not correct for them.

The attempt to recall Governor Meacham of Arizona in 1987[1] gave as its rationale:

> In the first 180 days as Governor of the state of Arizona, Evan Meacham has demonstrated his lack of knowledge, vision and unifying leadership to govern the citizens of this state. He has embarrassed Arizonans nationally through his insensitive and demeaning statements about women and minorities as well as his appointment of individuals who are not qualified and whose backgrounds are at best questionable. He has failed to appropriately respond to the state's severe environmental problems. As a direct result of the Governor's actions and inactions, the state's economy has suffered dramatic loss (McClain 1988, 632-633)

In the California recall, the accusation was that Davis had engaged in "gross mismanagement of California finances by overspending taxpayer's money, threatening public safety by cutting funds to local governments, ... and failing

---

[1]Governor Meacham was eventually impeached rather than recalled.

in general to deal with the state's major problems" (petition to Recall Governor Davis 2003).

For critics of the process, recall elections make too many demands on incumbents. We, the public should not want our politicians to slavishly follow polling data in order to decide what to do, especially if they think that public opinion is wrong. We should, so the argument goes, want our representatives to exhibit leadership and we would like to respect leaders of principle. A constitutional mechanism such as the recall, which can force an official from office for doing what he or she thinks is right, skews incentives for representatives and makes them too timid, even cowardly.

The recall also skews the incentives of representatives who have lost on election day by providing them with an immediate means of revenge. Rather than waiting until the next election, poor losers can simply mount a recall election and run, or re-run, the election until the 'right' result is produced. To many this seems unfair in and of itself. Supporters of California's Governor Davis, for example, argued that the recall effort is being made by a "handful of right-wing politicians ... attempting to overturn the voters' decision." These people "couldn't beat him fair and square, so now they're trying another trick to remove him from office.... We should not waste scarce taxpayers' dollars on sour grapes." ("The answer of the officer sought to be recalled" on the petition to Recall Governor Davis, State of California, 2003).

It can also lead to a preoccupation with campaigns rather than with the job of governing. The campaigns themselves can easily become highly personalized and splenetic. Supporters of Arizona's Governor Meacham, for example, dismissed his would-be recall opponents as "homosexual agitators" and listed "lesbians, militant homosexuals, the Rev. Jesse Jackson, and the Communist party" as being part of the conspiracy (McClain 1988, 633). Not only are such campaigns wastes of time, they also generate unhelpful and hard to heal divisions.

Those who like direct democracy processes sometimes mention the value of the implied threat—the "gun behind the door"—that keeps politicians in line. But in the heat of recall elections that gun "becomes a thundering blunderbuss in the unsteady hands of a citizenry sufficiently irritated to blaze at any suspicious target" (Bird and Ryan 1930, 160). As with the TV remote, the recall allows voters to change the channel—dump politicians—simply because they feel like it and not for any substantive reason. In some states, voters recalling a politician need to show cause. In Minnesota, for example, the grounds for recall are "serious malfeasance or nonfeasance during the term of office in the performance of the duties of the office" or "conviction during the term of office of a serious crime" and the charges, at least those leveled against statewide officials, are reviewed by the state Supreme Court before a petition drive is begun (http://www.house.leg.state.mn.us/hrd/pubs/recall.htm #GRDS). But in California any statement will serve that purpose and it is not subject to review. California is not alone in that—British Columbia's recall process, for example, requires no set criteria. The only requirement is that the applicant provides a statement of 200 words or less, of why, in the opinion of the applicant, the legislator should be recalled. This means, however, that even minor complaints can become the basis of a recall effort. Even accepting that a recall process is a reasonable and appropriate tool of popular sovereignty, perhaps there should be some limits introduced so that it is at least used for serious reasons. Voters should not be allowed to get rid of politicians "just because" but should have to show some serious failing ("just cause") before proceeding.

But what did California voters themselves think of the recall? Just over 60% of registered voters (43% of eligible voters) turned out for the election: higher than the previous election in November but lower than the usual turnout level in presidential years. Given the mix of novelty value, media attention, and campaign spending, this figure might seem on the low side. But the recall did present a number of opportunities for direct citizen engagement similar to the politics of direct democracy and quite distinct from the politics of states in which there is no initiative process. The recall drive itself obviously marked a very direct way in which California's citizens could do more than simply grumble about their political leaders and hold them directly accountable for their actions, and—as we noted above—voters did think their leaders had something to be accountable for. Did this mean, then, that voters warmly supported the recall process?

Polling data showed that voters supported the recall process, in fact more people tended to support the process than voted for the governor's recall, but not without some serious reservations. One survey showed support for having a recall process as part of the Constitution at a remarkably high 76%, matching attitudes toward support of the initiative process, but this figure masks some serious reservations. When asked about the use of the recall in this case, support in the same survey dropped to 52%, a figure more in line with other survey results. Democrats, not surprisingly, had more misgivings about the process than Republicans and a majority of voters thought the recall process needed major (32%) or minor (25%) changes (PPIC survey 2003, http://www.ppic.org/content/pubs/JTF_RecallElectionJTF.pdf).

The kinds of reasons people offered for liking or opposing the recall shed some light on how much of a trustee or a delegate people want their representative to be. Those who opposed the recall were not as upset by the idea of the GOP trying to overturn the election or the threat of instability so much as concerns over cost of the election and the possibility that a replacement candidate could win with relatively few voters. One of the possible scenarios of this recall, especially with so many candidates, was that Davis could lose the recall yet still gain more votes than the replacement. In the event, this did not occur. Davis received 45% of the vote and Schwarzenegger 49%. But this possibility clearly bothered people. For supporters of the recall, the benefit was clear—the firing of a bad governor and the hiring of a new one who could, hopefully, do a better job.

One feature of the recall process is that it is a major shift into 'delegation' rather than 'trusteeship.' The two terms mark the idealized end points of a continuum and most people, if pushed, would rather not be at the end point but in some middle ground. But how to find that middle ground—when and how often should politicians ignore us—remains unresolved.

One of the more general consequences of the recall is that it asks us to be more precise about defining the proper relationship between voters and their government. This is both a fundamental relationship in democratic politics and also one that scholars have yet to resolve. Not only does this mean being more precise about where we want our representatives to be in this mix of trusteeship and delegation, it also means we need to be more precise about just what is supposed to happen when our political leaders disappoint us. One question here, of course, is how much disappointment ought we, the voters, to bear. We should presumably exercise patience over the smaller failings of office and take care not to blame politicians for things that are not their fault. But if it is indeed the case, as recent research suggests that voters simply don't understand politics very well, then we are likely to lose our patience too readily and over the wrong things. When looking at politicians we, as voters, are too quick to judge, too ready to criticize, and too willing to be uncharitable. In the ordinary run of things, the smaller grievances are forgotten before the next election and the more serious ones inform our vote but the recall gives us the chance to act on those grievances right away. On the other hand, the current mechanisms of representative government seem to work to insulate many politicians from voters; super-safe seats, the importance of money, and the tone of campaigns all seem to leave a small role for what the voters want and a much larger one for what campaign professionals, interest groups, and the politicians want.

BIBLIOGRAPHY

Bird, Frederick and Frances Ryan. *The Recall of Public Officers.* New York: Macmillan, 1930.

McClain, Paula, "Arizona High Noon: The Recall ad Impeachment of Evan Mecham,"

PS:Political Science and Politics 21 (1988): 628-638.

Mowry, George. *The California Progressives.* Berkeley, CA: UC Press, 1951.

2

Barriers to Recalling Elected Officials:

A Cross-State Analysis of the Incidence and Success of Recall Petitions

Bruce E. Cain

Melissa Cully Anderson

Annette K. Eaton

University of California, Berkeley

The 2003 California election to recall Governor Gray Davis thrust California's recall laws into the national and international spotlight. It would be a mistake, however, to think that election recalls operate the same way in every state. Recall rules vary widely across the states, and these variations shed light on how often and under what conditions recalls have been used in the past and will be used in the future. These recall rules also highlight the prospects of candidates to defeat incumbents by means of recall. In its variation, the recall is similar to other direct democracy mechanisms. The rules that govern initiatives and referendums also vary by state in terms of the number of required signatures, the subject matter that they can cover, the degree to which they can be amended, and the like. These same forces of federalism operate with respect to recall rules.

As political scientists have noted in other contexts, institutions contribute to the incentives and constraints that political actors face. Whether a recall law even exists determines whether there is an opportunity to use it. But if the rules make it more difficult to use the recall opportunity, then they impose greater costs on those who would use the recall and, on average, deter usage. Conversely, user-friendly laws encourage higher use. If this is true, it poses a political design question: How high should a political jurisdiction set the usage threshold? That is, how much of a threat should the recall pose to officeholders in the interest of greater responsiveness?

In the sections of the paper that follow, we do several things. First, we review the origins of the recall laws in the United States; second, we review the state variations in the laws; and third, we look to see whether the thresholds affect the level of recall usage.

ORIGINS OF THE RECALL LAWS

The wave of support for the recall that swept the country in the early decades of the twentieth century was part of a larger revolt against the political establishment. Beginning at the end of the nineteenth century and continuing through the 1920s, during what has been termed the Progressive Era, citizen groups and individuals sought to change the way government at all levels was managed. Advocates of so-called good government, labeled *goo-goos* or *mugwumps*, pressed for numerous reforms. Among these reforms were measures that took power away from elected officials and gave it to the voters; these measures conferred on the electorate a more direct form of democracy.

The recall mechanism, or the ability of voters to remove elected officials from office, was one such measure. Its adoption was concentrated most heavily in the period from 1908 to 1914, but states continued to adopt provisions for the recall of state-level officials well into the 1990s. As one might expect, the recall mechanism is available to states mostly in the Midwest and west because of the concentration of progressivism in those regions. Of course, there are always exceptions: Among the states with state-level recall provisions are Louisiana, Georgia, New Jersey, and Rhode Island.

While the recall is available in many states for a variety of different government functions—including city council members, judges, and appointed administrative officials at the local level—this text focuses on states with constitutional or statutory provisions for the recall of elected or appointed state-level officials only. There are eighteen states with state-level recall measures, and the adoption of these measures spans the twentieth century (see Figure 2.1).[1]

RECALL PROVISIONS: VARIATION BY STATE

While the states in this study share the characteristic of offering their voters the ability to recall state-level officials, the parameters guiding the actual use of the recall mechanism vary widely.[2] For example, some states allow for the recall of appointed state officials or judges, while others permit only the recall of elected statewide officers. Some states provide only narrow windows (for example, some time after the first six months but not after the beginning of the last six months) during which a recall may be attempted. Others restrict the maximum number of times recalls may be attempted against a particular individual. The grounds for a recall vary as well: States' provisions range from permitting a recall for any reason to permitting it only in the case of criminal action.[3]

A range of parameters also guides the actual execution of a recall attempt and election. In particular, states vary in the signature thresholds[4] required to put a recall attempt on the ballot and in the permitted time in which a petition for recall may be circulated among the voters. Moreover, penalties for violating these parameters differ by state.

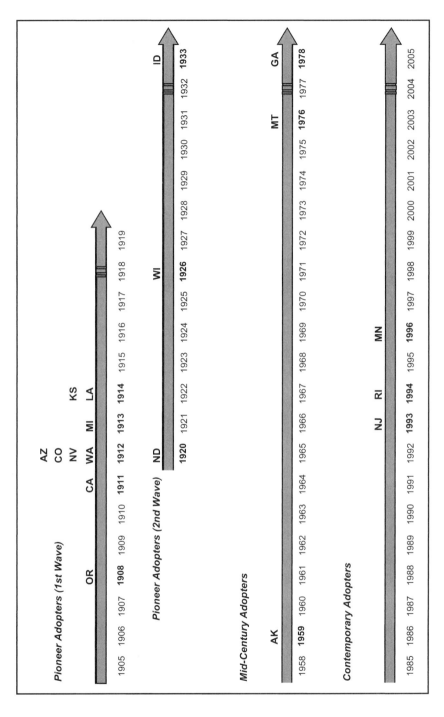

FIGURE 2.1 Timeline of adoption of state-level recall provisions.

Recall elections take a number of different forms. Some states provide for a single ballot, as in California, where a voter is asked two distinct questions: Should the elected official be recalled? And if so, who should replace him or her? Other states, such as Washington, require two separate elections: one for the recall question, and another to select among the replacement candidates. Apart from the structure of the election, states differ in their treatment of the incumbent. In Colorado, the incumbent is not permitted to run on the replacement ballot. Conversely, in Wisconsin, the incumbent is listed among a series of challengers, and the voters are asked to select their preferred candidate. No separate recall question is posed.

Because these differences can deter or encourage prospective recall sponsors and guide the actions of voters and recall targets in all stages of the recall process, we suspect that the differences among these states may contribute to the rates of success of recall attempts and elections. For example, one might expect that states whose regulations permit recalls on any grounds would experience more recall attempts than those that restrict recall attempts to incumbents who act illegally. Similarly, we might anticipate that states with a lower signature-gathering threshold would have more recalls on the ballot, because it is easier (and less costly) for proponents to gather the necessary signatures.

In this chapter, we hope to gain some empirical understanding about the relationship between these features (or institutional parameters) and the success of recall attempts and elections. For this purpose, we distinguish between two stages of the recall process: first, the decision on the part of prospective sponsors to pursue a recall attempt and the effort to place a recall attempt on the ballot for voters' evaluation; and, second, the effort, after the petition has cleared the qualification barrier and the recall will be presented to the voters, to negotiate a successful recall. Among our cases are recall attempts against statewide officers (governors or state legislators) and against mayors.

DESCRIPTION OF CASES

We have gathered data for as many recall attempts as possible, and, as such, our distribution of cases is likely influenced by the fact that information from the recent past is more readily available than information for cases that occurred in the earlier parts of the twentieth century (Table 2.1). We also suspect that information for cases in larger locales was more readily available than those in smaller locales, and the tendency of the press to cover more high-profile events may also bias our data. Notwithstanding these limitations, we have found evidence of approximately 150 cases among thirteen[5] of the eighteen states that have state-level recall provisions, and we have gathered complete data for nearly 60 of those cases. Most of the recall attempts in our study occurred after 1990. Although recall efforts against state-level officers were confined largely to that decade, there has been a flurry of activity in recent years against mayoral targets as well.

As discussed, the grounds permitted to justify a recall vary considerably by state. For the most permissive states, there are no grounds criteria; just

TABLE 2.1　Incidence of recall efforts, by decade.

	STATEWIDE OFFICERS		MAYORS		TOTAL	
1900s	0	0%	1	1%	1	1%
1910s	0	0%	3	3%	3	2%
1920s	3	10%	4	4%	7	6%
1930s	2	7%	8	9%	10	8%
1940s	0	0%	2	2%	2	2%
1950s	0	0%	1	1%	1	1%
1960s	3	10%	3	3%	6	5%
1970s	2	7%	2	2%	4	3%
1980s	4	14%	2	2%	6	5%
1990s	13	45%	27	29%	40	33%
2000s	2	7%	39	42%	41	34%
Total	29	100%	92	100%	121	100%

about any reason imaginable is sufficient to pursue a recall attempt. As you might expect, particularly in smaller towns where political propaganda is commonplace, enraged citizens have used some interesting rationales to justify recall attempts. For example, individuals and resident groups have tried to oust their leaders for such reasons as increasing the streetcar fare,[6] choosing unpopular locations for a town building or dumpsite,[7] or simply being "aloof."[8]

In the tiny town of Minto, North Dakota, home to 660 individuals, a group of neighbors residing on Kilowatt Drive took frivolity to even greater heights. Because North Dakota requires the number of signatures to be gathered to equal or exceed 25 percent of the number of eligible voters in the last election for the official being pursued, the sponsors needed only 39 signatures to get the recall attempt on the ballot. The recall attempt survived the first barrier and easily made it onto the ballot. The proponents' grievance? The mayor had refused to consider Kilowatt Drive a residential street in the context of a neighbor's purchase of town land for personal use. As the primary sponsor of the recall remarked to the press upon the attempt's ultimate defeat at the polls, "It's hard to explain. It's a multi-complicated issue."[9]

In other locales, long-standing family disputes provide the setting for recall attempt, after recall attempt, after recall attempt. For example, in North Bergen, New Jersey, the political activities of Mayor Angelo Sarubbi precipitated a series of contested elections, criminal charges, and recall elections that endured through the next two decades. Although Sarubbi survived a recall attempt in 1969 in a replacement election against the sponsor, Peter Mocco, Mocco was undaunted. In the next general election, Mocco beat Sarubbi and created a political machine alleged to be worthy of a great crime family that endured for the next decade. Surviving charges of ballot fraud in 1976 and a recall attempt by another political aspirant, Anthony DeVincent, several years later, Mocco finally retired in 1980. Anthony DeVincent, the recall challenger in 1979, took over as mayor, only to be recalled (successfully) in an act of vengeance by Joseph Mocco, Peter's brother, several years later.[10]

In another tale of small-town scandal, Mayor Koleen Brooks of George-town, Colorado, turned heads when it became known that she had once pursued a less illustrious (and scantily clad) career in a nightclub. The truth was disclosed when Mayor Brooks had a bit too much to drink at a local bar and proceeded to remove her shirt for the presumed enjoyment of the other patrons. When a group of appalled residents sought her recall and succeeded in gaining enough signatures to get the effort on the ballot, she sought the sympathy of the voters by revealing that she had recently been physically attacked by an acquaintance. To substantiate her claim, she sued the alleged perpetrator. The case went to trial, but the evidence on her behalf was flimsy (or, perhaps, not flimsy enough). The attorneys for the attacker rested their defense after demonstrating that her long fingernails would have sustained considerable damage in any attack that occurred as Mayor Brooks had described. Needless to say, the recall election went along as scheduled and Koleen Brooks was again compelled to make a career change.[11]

While these stories provide an amusing backdrop for any investigation of the recall, they also illustrate the frivolity with which an instrument intended to protect the democratic operation of the political process, when taken to extremes, can be utilized. From the perspective of political science, we ask whether there is a proper role for the recall process, one that is neither too permissive nor too restrictive. Are recall mechanisms without guidelines or criteria too lenient? Do particularly high signature thresholds deter recalls that might be altruistic?

In the following sections, we present some descriptive statistics concern-ing the cases for which we have gathered data, the outcomes of which are summarized in Table 2.2. Again, we wish to emphasize that these data are neither complete nor necessarily representative of all cases of recall.[12] They represent what could be found. In particular, we have not been able to unearth (or generate complete data for) a notable number of recall attempts against state-level elected officials. As such, while we distinguish state-level recall attempts from mayoral recall attempts to acknowledge the different contexts surrounding each level of office, we are reluctant to generalize conclusions from any of the patterns we discern.

Among our cases, several interesting patterns emerge. First, the statewide cases we identified successfully qualified for the ballot at a lower rate than the mayoral recall attempts. While almost 60 percent of the mayoral cases achieved enough signatures to qualify for the ballot, only about one-third of the state-level recall efforts made it to the ballot stage. This pattern is not surprising; while on a percentage basis, the number of signatures required for state-level recalls compared with mayoral recall attempts should be equally onerous, in some cases, the number of required signatures was as low as seven.[13] In addition, the geographic challenge of gathering signatures in a statewide recall effort is relatively substantial compared with a more compact locale.

However, while the state-level recall attempts were less likely to achieve success at the signature-gathering stage, the pattern is different for recall

TABLE 2.2   Outcome of recall efforts: An overview.

	STATEWIDE OFFICERS		MAYORS		TOTAL	
All Cases:						
Failed to get to ballot	18	67%	30	41%	48	47%
On ballot, but failed	3	11%	24	32%	27	27%
On ballot, then succeeded	6	22%	20	27%	26	26%
Total	27	100%	74	100%	101	100%
Stage I (petition):						
Failed to get to ballot	18	67%	30	41%	48	48%
Made it to ballot	9	33%	44	59%	53	52%
Total	27	100%	74	100%	101	100%
Stage II (on ballot):						
Recall unsuccessful	3	33%	24	55%	27	51%
Recall successful	6	67%	20	45%	26	49%
Total	9	100%	44	100%	53	100%

elections once the petition qualifies. In particular, approximately two-thirds of our state-level cases resulted in a successful recall once the effort qualified for the ballot. In contrast, just under half of the mayoral recalls that qualified for the ballot ultimately ousted the elected official. For recall proponents at the state level, then, perhaps getting the petition qualified is more than half the battle. This could suggest that the difficulty of the first barrier for state officials signals a greater discontent and, hence, a greater likelihood of success in the second period.

FINDINGS: HOW INSTITUTIONAL VARIABLES RELATE TO OUTCOMES

As suggested earlier, the ability to get a recall petition on the ballot may be influenced by institutional factors and thresholds. In this section, we compare recall efforts that succeed in getting on the ballot with those that do not, and we evaluate three factors: (a) the identity of the sponsor, (b) the grounds used to justify the recall, and (c) the signature thresholds imposed by state law. First, we ask whether recall efforts sponsored by institutionalized interests, which typically have more organizational strength compared with individual citizens or resident groups, would be more successful at signature gathering and have a higher likelihood of qualifying for the ballot. Second, we explore whether the grounds for each recall petition might relate in some way to the success rate; more concrete or convincing claims perhaps generate more signatures than frivolous claims.[14] While not attempting to operationalize frivolity, we question whether there is a relation among the reasons for recalling

TABLE 2.3   Stage I: Getting onto the ballot, by sponsor.

	STATEWIDE OFFICERS		MAYORS		TOTAL	
Failed to get to ballot						
Individual cititzen	6	35%	11	39%	17	38%
Resident group	7	41%	12	43%	19	42%
Institutionalized interest	4	24%	5	18%	9	20%
Total	17	100%	28	100%	45	100%
Made it to ballot						
Individual citizen	3	38%	17	44%	20	43%
Resident group	2	25%	14	36%	16	34%
Institutionalized interest	3	38%	8	21%	11	23%
Total	8	100%	39	100%	47	100%
All Cases						
Individual citizen	9	36%	28	42%	37	40%
Resident group	9	36%	26	39%	35	38%
Institutionalized interest	7	28%	13	19%	20	22%
Total	25	100%	67	100%	92	100%

officials and successful qualification and whether this varies between the two levels of office. Finally, as we suggested earlier, we expect higher signature thresholds to increase the rate of failure for recall petitions seeking to qualify for the ballot.

Table 2.3 and Table 2.4 are the most useful if we use "all cases" as the base scenario against which we compare the outcome. Looking at sponsorship in Table 2.3, we can see that the distribution of all cases among the three groups does not differ markedly between state-level recall attempts and mayoral recall attempts, except perhaps that individual citizens seem to play a stronger role in mayoral recall attempts at the expense of organized interest groups.

Among the state-level cases, recalls sponsored by individual citizens constitute a similar proportion of failed and successful petitions. Resident groups and institutionalized interests, however, show opposite patterns. While resident groups seem to make up a lower proportion of successful petitions, institutionalized interests had greater success among these cases, lending tentative support to our hypothesis. Among mayors, with lower levels of sponsorship by institutionalized interest groups overall, no clear pattern emerges. The cases pursued by institutionalized interests more often than not succeeded, but they included the same proportion of both successful and failed qualification attempts.

Concerning the grounds used to justify each recall, most cases, as we noted earlier, were pursued for either specific or general political reasons. Not

TABLE 2.4   Stage I: Getting onto the ballot, by grounds.

	STATEWIDE OFFICERS		MAYORS		TOTAL	
Failed to get to ballot						
Specific policy behavior	12	75%	15	50%	27	59%
General political behavior	2	13%	14	47%	16	35%
Personal behavior/crime	2	13%	1	3%	3	7%
Total	16	100%	30	100%	46	100%
Made it to ballot						
Specific policy behavior	2	25%	19	40%	21	38%
General political behavior	6	75%	19	40%	25	45%
Personal behavior/crime	0	0%	10	21%	10	18%
Total	8	100%	48	100%	56	100%
All Cases						
Specific policy behavior	14	58%	34	44%	48	47%
General political behavior	8	33%	33	42%	41	40%
Personal behavior/crime	2	8%	11	14%	13	13%
Total	24	100%	78	100%	102	100%

many recalls in our study were pursued for personal reasons, either at the state or mayoral level. However, the political grounds for state-level recalls were associated with quite different outcomes: While general political behavior tended to be more successful (six of eight such cases made it to the ballot), recall petitions pursued for a specific policy choice much more often failed to qualify (twelve of fourteen cases). Both recalls pursued for personal reasons at the state level also failed to qualify for the ballot. In contrast, while political (either specific or general) grounds at the mayoral level reveal no distinct patterns, mayoral recalls pursued for personal reasons were successful much more often than not (ten of eleven cases).

SIGNATURE THRESHOLDS

Regarding institutional factors, we expected signature thresholds to exert a particularly strong influence on the success of recall petitions. We have created a rough gauge of signature thresholds that accommodates several different measurements of this variable. In some states, signature thresholds are a fixed percent of the number of registered voters. In others, the required number of signatures is a fixed percent of the number of voters who appeared at the polls in the last general election for the office for which the recall is being pursued.

It is difficult to create a scale that compares the ability to qualify under requirements based on turnout with those based on registration percentages.

Doing so requires standardizing thresholds based on turnout data with those based on registered voter data. As a simplifying assumption, we peg turnout thresholds as 0.5 of the registration. For example, California's requirement that petitioners gather signatures in the amount of 12 percent of the prior election's turnout for the race in question is captured as 0.06 whereas another state that requires 12 percent of the registered voters would be captured as 0.12. In effect, this measure assumes that thresholds based on turnout are approximately 50 percent less than those based on registered voters. One might think that cases with a lower signature threshold by this measure should be more likely to get on the ballot.

Table 2.5 stratifies the cases in our study by the level of office and by the outcome of the recall effort at the petition stage. The cases are characterized as having a low threshold (less than 0.10), a medium threshold (between 0.10 and 0.20), and a high threshold (between 0.20 and 0.30).

Table 2.5 shows that most cases in our study (48 percent) have a low threshold, but that figure varies considerably by level of office. While the majority of mayoral recall efforts (55 percent) occurred under low signature thresholds, high thresholds characterize more than half (50 percent) of recall efforts against state-level incumbents. Contrary to our predictions, the number of cases that made it to the ballot while facing a low signature threshold was less than (state-level recalls) or equal to (mayoral recalls) the number of cases that failed. The high threshold cases were similarly unpredictable: Many more statewide recall attempts facing high signature thresholds made it to

TABLE 2.5   Stage I: Getting onto the ballot, by signature threshold.

	STATEWIDE OFFICERS		MAYORS		TOTAL	
Failed to get to ballot						
Low threshold (<0.10)	2	33%	12	67%	14	58%
Medium threshold (<0.20)	3	50%	1	6%	4	17%
High threshold (<0.30)	1	17%	5	28%	6	25%
Total	6	100%	18	100%	24	100%
Made it to ballot						
Low threshold (<0.10)	1	17%	12	46%	13	41%
Medium threshold (<0.20)	0	0%	9	35%	9	28%
High threshold (<0.30)	5	83%	5	19%	10	31%
Total	6	100%	26	100%	32	100%
All Cases						
Low threshold (<0.10)	3	25%	24	55%	27	48%
Medium threshold (<0.20)	3	25%	10	23%	13	23%
High threshold (<0.30)	6	50%	10	23%	16	29%
Total	12	100%	44	100%	56	100%

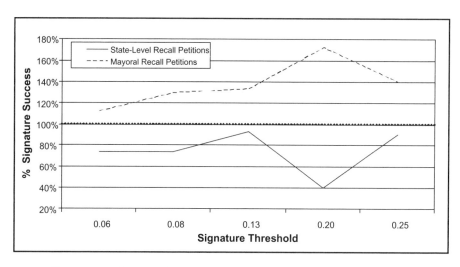

FIGURE 2.2 Average signature success rates, by signature threshold.

the ballot than did not, and the number of mayoral recall cases facing a high threshold was divided evenly between successes and failures.

Additionally, there was no relation between threshold levels and the level of signatures that were, on average, gathered. Figure 2.2 maps the average percent of signatures achieved relative to the threshold by the level of threshold for both state and mayoral races.

While one might expect the lowest signature thresholds to have the highest average levels of signatures, this is not really the case. Moreover, the trends seem to differ for state and mayoral offices. Consistent with the higher level of success of recall attempts at the mayoral level, local recall campaigns achieve a higher percentage of their thresholds across the board.

THE SUCCESS OF MEASURES THAT ARE ON THE BALLOT

After the recall petition makes the ballot, we expect additional constraints to influence whether the recall is successful. In addition to the substantive issues that form the basis for each recall election, captured in part by the sponsor groups involved in the effort and the grounds used to justify it, we suspect that ballot format, including whether the incumbent can run in the recall election and the type of ballot and election, might play a role in the outcome of recall elections (Table 2.6).

As in the earlier section (see Table 2.3), we examined the distribution of cases according to their sponsors and the grounds used to justify the recall effort. By sponsor, we see that successful state-level recalls are relatively evenly distributed among the three categories of sponsors. In contrast, successful mayoral recalls were most often pursued by individual citizens or resident

TABLE 2.6   Stage II: Outcome of the recall election, by sponsor.

	STATEWIDE OFFICERS		MAYORS		TOTAL	
Failed recall						
Individual citizen	1	5%	11	22%	12	17%
Resident group	0	0%	8	16%	8	11%
Institutionalized interest	1	5%	4	8%	5	7%
Total	2	11%	23	45%	24	36%
Successful recall						
Individual citizen	2	4%	6	13%	8	17%
Resident group	2	4%	6	13%	8	17%
Institutionalized interest	2	4%	4	9%	6	13%
Total	6	13%	16	34%	22	47%
All Cases						
Individual citizen	3	12%	17	25%	20	22%
Resident group	2	8%	14	21%	16	17%
Institutionalized interest	3	12%	8	12%	11	12%
Total	8	32%	39	58%	47	51%

groups and not by institutionalized interests. For state-level cases, which are low in number, there is no discernible pattern that characterizes failed as compared with successful efforts. Even for mayoral recall elections, while resident groups tended to be somewhat more successful than individual citizens in achieving recalls, the pattern is weak.

Table 2.7 displays the number of recall elections in our study by the grounds used to justify the effort. Most cases at the state level were pursued as complaints regarding the incumbent's general political behavior (no statewide cases in our study qualified for the ballot using personal behavior as the primary justification); mayoral recalls were split evenly between general and specific political behavior and, to a lesser extent, personal behavior. Because so few state-level cases made it to the ballot, even descriptive comparisons held little weight. For mayoral recalls, it is interesting to note that, while personal behavior seemed to create quite a stir at the signature-gathering stage, these cases more often than not failed at the election stage.

BALLOT FORMAT

Among the states that have recall mechanisms, election formats fall into three categories. The first is the format used in California and Colorado: a single two-question ballot that first asks whether the incumbent should be recalled and then asks which candidate (the incumbent is not listed) should replace him or her (that is, recall and placement format). The second format simply

TABLE 2.7   Stage II: Outcomes of the recall election, by grounds.

	STATEWIDE OFFICERS		MAYORS		TOTAL	
Failed recall						
Specific policy behavior	0	0%	8	29%	8	27%
General political behavior	2	100%	13	46%	15	50%
Personal behavior/crime	0	0%	7	25%	7	23%
Total	2	100%	28	100%	30	100%
Successful recall						
Specific policy behavior	2	33%	11	55%	13	50%
General political behavior	4	67%	6	30%	10	38%
Personal behavior/crime	0	0%	3	15%	3	12%
Total	6	100%	20	100%	26	100%
All Cases						
Specific policy behavior	2	25%	19	40%	21	38%
General political behavior	6	75%	19	40%	25	45%
Personal behavior/crime	0	0%	10	21%	10	18%
Total	8	100%	48	100%	56	100%

presents a list of candidates (including the incumbent) from which the voter chooses; this format is used in Arizona, Nevada, North Dakota, and Wisconsin. The third format has two separate elections: The first election determines whether the incumbent is to be recalled, and the second election, if necessary, determines the incumbent's replacement. This format is most common,[15] but these states are divided as to whether the incumbent is permitted to run in the second election.[16]

Based on our institutional costs model, the recall-and-replacement format should favor recall challengers because it forces the incumbent to garner at least 50 percent support on the first question to preserve his or her post. Moreover, because recall-and-replacement elections do not allow the incumbent to run again, there is no chance for the incumbent to lose on the recall question and then regain the post in the second question or second election.

In the states in which there are two separate elections, we expect the constraints to be similar to those in the recall-and-replacement election, with two important exceptions. While the recall-and-replacement elections, as noted, do not allow the incumbent to run, about half of the states providing for two separate elections do allow the incumbent to run in the second election. Moreover, the recall-and-replacement format presents some strategic challenges that differentiate it from the two separate-election formats. In particular, recall and replacement forces recall proponents and opponents to make decisions about putting forth challengers who could have a significant impact on the outcome of the recall portion of the election. Conversely, holding two separate

TABLE 2.8   Stage II: Outcomes of the recall election, by type of election/ballot.

	STATEWIDE OFFICERS		MAYORS		TOTAL	
Failed recall						
Recall and replacement	2	100%	7	41%	9	47%
List of candidates	0	0%	1	6%	1	5%
Two separate elections	0	0%	9	53%	9	47%
Total	2	100%	17	100%	19	100%
Successful recall						
Recall and replacement	3	75%	7	78%	10	77%
List of candidates	1	25%	2	22%	3	23%
Two separate elections	0	0%	0	0%	0	0%
Total	4	100%	9	100%	13	100%
All Cases						
Recall and replacement	5	83%	14	54%	19	59%
List of candidates	1	17%	3	12%	4	13%
Two separate elections	0	0%	9	35%	9	28%
Total	6	100%	26	100%	32	100%

elections allows those groups to withhold the selection of challengers until the recall question has been decided. In short, the recall-and-replacement format, which then-Governor Davis had to contend with, should be less favorable to the incumbent than the separate-election format. The most favorable format for the incumbents should be the one that provides a list of candidates, because it requires only that the incumbent in office obtain a plurality of votes.[17]

The evidence from Table 2.8 suggests that holding two separate elections is the most favorable format for incumbents, although these cases derive from mayoral recalls. On the opposite end of the spectrum, the list-of-candidates format seems to favor incumbents the most, but the number of cases is too small to have confidence on this point. Thus, evidence suggests that there is a weak correlation between format and the success of recall elections. This point is reinforced to some degree by the average vote for recall that is achieved under these different formats. Figure 2.3 identifies cases by the type of election that took place (including whether the incumbent was allowed to run), and the average percent vote to recall in the recall election.

Figure 2.3 shows a weak distinction between the votes garnered for recall and format. The distinction between separated and nonseparated elections is evident. If, encouraged by the California example, we are on the cusp of more recalls, we may find more cases in the near future that allow us to identify patterns more clearly. For the moment, there is some evidence that format matters

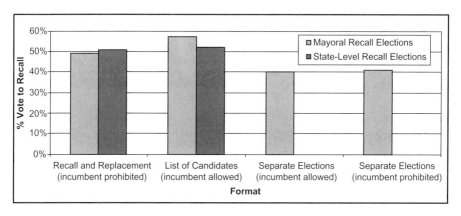

FIGURE 2.3 **Average percent vote to recall, by election type.**

to the success of the incumbent facing recall, and that states that separate the task into two separate elections make the process somewhat less user-friendly.

CONCLUSIONS

We can put the California recall into perspective. Given the professionalization of the signature-gathering process and the lack of any relation between signature gathering and the incidence of qualification across the states, the signature phase was not the critical obstacle. Someone had to provide the money, but once provided, the qualification process was not a difficult problem to overcome. More importantly, the recall-and-replacement format helped to seal then-Governor Davis' fate. Precluded from running on the second part of the ballot and forced, in essence, to get a majority vote, the odds were stacked against him (particularly given his job approval ratings and these rules). Moreover, the strategic dilemma for the incumbent's party—whether to stand by their man or run a replacement candidate—proved to be a further complication. The mixed message confused some voters (vote no on the recall and yes on Cruz Bustamante), and Democratic Party voters, particularly Latinos, who supported Bustamante had an incentive to vote for the recall. If the replacement election had been held separately, that incentive would not have existed, and voters would not have been as confused by the no, no and no, yes options.

But should recalls be user-friendly? Each state will have to decide, and that in turn may depend on how frequently recalls are used in the wake of the California example. To date, most of the action has been at the mayoral level, for which the costs of qualification and of campaigns are less. If one adds in the cost to the state of holding a special election, there are strong disincentives to overusage at the state level. For state legislative and local elections, however, one suspects that the trend will continue to be upward unless the institutional barriers are raised.

BIBLIOGRAPHY

Associated Press State and Local Wire, "Elevator Expansion Leads to Feud," October 5, 2001.

——, "Mayor's Opponents Turn In Petitions to Remove Her from Office," January 7, 2002.

——, "News in Brief from the San Joaquin Valley," June 19, 2003.

Ferguson, Dean. "Mayor Says Dumpsite's OK Now; But Lapwai Woman Continues Recall Attempt." *Lewiston Morning Tribune*(Lewiston, ID), March 10, 2003, 5A.

Gonzales, Manny. "Council Faces Recall Vote: Petitioners Get Signatures Against Mayor, Five Others." *Rocky Mountain News*, August 14, 1999.

Laura, Joseph. "North Bergen: The 'Sin City' Label Persists." *New York Times*, January 4, 1981.

New York Times, "San Francisco Drive Asks Mayor's Recall," April 7, 1946.

Weller, Robert. "The Case of the Undamaged Fingernails and Breast Implants." Associated Press State and Local Wire, January 11, 2003.

Zimmerman, Joseph F. *The Recall: Tribunal of the People*. Westport, CT: Praeger, 1997.

NOTES

1. Joseph F. Zimmerman, *The Recall: Tribunal of the People* (Westport, CT: Praeger, 1997).

2. The state-by-state parameters for the use of the recall are summarized in Zimmerman, *The Recall*, cited above. In addition, we consulted the secretary of state Web sites for each of the recall states to confirm the relevant guidelines regulating recall petitions and elections in each state.

3. While eleven states (Arizona, California, Colorado, Idaho, Louisiana, Michigan, Nevada, New Jersey, North Dakota, Oregon, and Wisconsin) have no standards for the grounds upon which a recall must be based, other states have rules restricting prospective sponsors from using frivolous justifications for a recall. For example, Alaska and Montana require that the recall justification be limited to an explicit lack of fitness for the office, neglect of duties, or corruption. Even more restrictive, the laws in Minnesota and Rhode Island permit recalls only in the case of serious malfeasance or conviction of a crime.

4. The signature thresholds are the number of signatures that must be collected by the sponsors before the recall will be allowed on the ballot. These thresholds vary by state, and are usually either set at a certain percent of the registered voters in the state, or a certain percent of the voter turnout at the prior statewide election. In addition, some states require that signatures be collected from a certain distribution of counties or locales to be certified.

5. The cases in our study are drawn from the District of Columbia (one case) and the following thirteen states: Alaska, Arizona, California, Colorado, Georgia, Idaho, Louisiana, Michigan, New Jersey, North Dakota, Oregon, Washington, and Wisconsin.

6. Roger Lapham, mayor of San Francisco, survived a recall election for this purpose in 1946. "San Francisco Drive Asks Mayor's Recall," *New York Times*, April 7, 1946.

7. Only recently, in 2003, James Angle, the mayor of Lapwai, Idaho, incited a recall attempt for refusing to move a town dump out of proximity of the irate sponsor's home. "Mayor Says Dumpsite's OK Now; But Lapwai Woman Continues Recall Attempt," *Lewiston Morning Tribune* (Lewiston, ID), March 10, 2003.

8. In 2003, Hilda Plasencia was successfully recalled from her mayoral post in Huron, California for what the sponsors characterized as "aloofness" and an "indifference to the public." "News in Brief from the San Joaquin Valley," Associated Press State and Local Wire (French Camp, CA), June 19, 2003.

9. Paul Koehmstedt, mayor of Minto, North Dakota, faced a recall attempt at the hands of the outraged Kilowatt Drive residents in 2001. "Elevator Expansion Leads to Feud," Associated Press State and Local Wire (Minto, ND), October 5, 2001.

10. "New Twist in North Bergen Politics," *New York Times*, April 29, 1979; "North Bergen: The 'Sin City' Label Persists," *New York Times*, January 4, 1981.

11. "Mayor's Opponents Turn In Petitions to Remove Her from Office," Associated Press State and Local Wire (Georgetown, CO), January 7, 2002; "The Case of the

Undamaged Fingernails and Breast Implants," Associated Press State and Local Wire (Eagle, CO), January 11, 2003.

12. The most useful sources of information for our cases have been contemporaneous newspaper and journal accounts. More than 750 articles were consulted to compile the data used in this chapter; as we mentioned, we suspect the availability of these articles has influenced the geographic and temporal distribution of our cases, perhaps producing a systemic bias concerning case selection. While Lexis-Nexis provides nationwide coverage of local newspapers and journals, it only covers the past few decades, depending on the state. In addition, while the *New York Times*, the *Wall Street Journal*, and the *Los Angeles Times* have historic indexes that cover the entire twentieth century, their coverage is no doubt more comprehensive for regional news.

13. As an example, the attempted recall of mayor Al Parker (Castle Rock, CO) qualified for the ballot with 20 signatures, 286 percent of the required 7. "Council Faces Recall Vote: Petitioners Get Signatures Against Mayor, Five Others," *Rocky Mountain News* (Denver, CO), August 14, 1999.

14. We acknowledge that the distinctions we make on the basis of sponsor and grounds are subjective. Concerning sponsor, we considered whether the sponsor of the recall was identified most often as an individual (for example, "Bill Cannon"); a resident group, which we considered to be any local, organized interest (for example, "Supporters of Mayor Fawcett"); or a non-local interest group (for example, "White Panther Party"). Concerning grounds, we considered whether the target was being pursued for personal reasons (for example, "lacked education" or "sexism"); general political behavior (for example, "wanted control of council" or "abused voter trust"); or a specific political action (for example, "waste management issue" or "support for gun control").

15. Alaska, Georgia, Idaho, Kansas, Louisiana, Michigan, Minnesota, Montana, New Jersey, Rhode Island, Washington, and Oregon use this format.

16. The incumbent is prohibited from running in the second election in all recall elections in Louisiana, Michigan, Minnesota, Montana, Rhode Island, and Oregon. In Kansas, the incumbent may run in statewide and legislative elections but not in local elections. In New Jersey, the incumbent is only prohibited from running in legislative elections. In Washington, the incumbent may run regardless of the level of the election.

17. States vary in their approach to runoff elections. Some states, like Alaska, have a "recall primary" if the first election calls for a recall. We expect that this format, however, would continue to favor the incumbent by allowing him or her to survive the primary with less than 50 percent of the vote.

3

STATISTICAL REGULARITIES IN THE RECALL RESULTS

DREW LINZER

UNIVERSITY OF CALIFORNIA, LOS ANGELES

Because of its historic rarity and the fact that fully 135 candidates—many quite colorful personalities included—appeared on the replacement gubernatorial ballot, the recall election and the campaign leading up to it were portrayed in the news media as "bizarre," a "circus," and a "mockery of democracy." California Governor Gray Davis himself asserted that the recall effort was "part of an ongoing national effort to steal elections Republicans cannot win" (quoted in Noah 2003). But despite its high political theater, empirical analysis of the November 2002 general election and the October 2003 special (recall) election results reveals that the election turned out to be a fairly normal case of retrospective voting in a partisan context.

The recall of Davis passed by a very wide margin: 55.4 percent to 44.6 percent. The victory by Arnold Schwarzenegger to replace Davis as governor was equally clear-cut—he won with 48.6 percent of the vote under the recall election's plurality rule, fully 17.1 percent ahead of the second-place finisher. These were decisive elections.

The outcome of the 2003 recall election must be understood in relation to the unusual circumstances of Davis' reelection less than one year earlier. In 2002, Davis began his second term after defeating conservative Republican businessman Bill Simon 47.3 percent to 42.4 percent. This victory was surprisingly close, given California's Democratic leanings. Most observers had expected Davis to win by a much greater margin—especially after he contributed to an unexpected late surge by Simon in the Republican primary election by campaigning against the Republican front-runner, moderate former Los Angeles Mayor Richard Riordan, widely seen as better poised to defeat Davis in the general election.[1] The results in this chapter suggest that, had Republican voters nominated Riordan instead of Simon to oppose Davis in 2002, Davis would not have been reelected and the recall would never have occurred.

Davis was profoundly unpopular in California at the time of the recall election. Considering the reluctance with which so many Californians voted to reelect Davis, his removal from office in 2003 and the subsequent election of Schwarzenegger as governor gave a great many Californian voters an outcome much closer to what they would have likely preferred in 2002.

This chapter provides a detailed account of where the votes came from to expel Davis from office and replace him with Schwarzenegger. Empirical data come primarily from three sources: county-level election returns from the California secretary of state, county-level demographic data from the *California Statistical Abstract*, and exit poll data from the *Edison Media Research/Mitofsky International California Recall Election Exit Poll*. The Edison/Mitofsky exit poll was based on interviews with 3,814 randomly selected voters leaving polling places across California, as well a sample of 400 absentee voters interviewed by phone before the election.

The recall election was an exceptional historic event, but it should not be viewed as a travesty of the democratic process. Its outcome was no fluke occurrence. At the county level, partisanship, economics, geography, and, to a lesser extent, ethnicity explain both the withdrawal of support from Davis between 2002 and 2003, and the voters' choice of Schwarzenegger to replace him. Except for a small but highly wealthy Democratic area surrounding the San Francisco Bay, voters across California overwhelmingly endorsed a new direction for the state when they cast their ballots in the 2003 recall.

DAVIS' FIRST TERM AND REELECTION

The easy answer to why Davis was recalled is that Californians held an extremely unfavorable opinion of his job performance as governor (Figure 3.1). *The California Field Poll*, which tracked Davis' approval ratings throughout his two terms, reported in August 2003 that Davis' 70 percent disapproval rating was "the largest proportion of Californians disapproving any state or national office holder as measured by *The Field Poll* in its fifty-six year history." Moreover, Davis' 22 percent approval rating was even lower than the 24 percent "which Californians gave to Richard Nixon in early August 1974, just prior to his resignation as President" (*California Field Poll* 2003).

Despite Davis' unpopularity in 2002, however, voters still chose to reelect him, while in 2003 they voted to remove him from office. It is because of just how reluctantly voters reelected Davis in 2002 that this turnaround is less paradoxical than it at first appears.

Trial heats run in September 2001 by *The California Field Poll*—a full year before the 2002 elections—showed Riordan beating Davis, 45 percent to 42 percent (*California Field Poll* 2001). At this time, Riordan led the hypothetical Republican primary with 46 percent to Simon's 5 percent. By January 2002, Riordan was still well ahead of his Republican primary opponents, and was opening his lead against Davis, 47 percent to 40 percent. Against Simon, however, Davis fared much better, winning 46 percent to 37 percent (*California Field Poll* 2002a).

But by late February 2002, Simon had remarkably surged ahead of Riordan in the polls and led the Republican primary matchup with 37 percent to Riordan's 31 percent. As noted in the pollsters' report, "strongly conservative Republican voters who represent about 41% of [likely Republican voters],

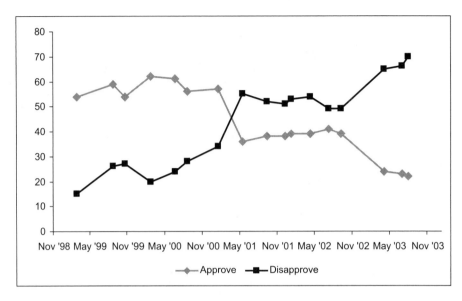

FIGURE 3.1   Trend of Job Approval Rating of Gray Davis as Governor.

SOURCE: *California Field Poll* 2003.

overwhelmingly prefer Simon over Riordan—52% to 27%" (*California Field Poll* 2002b). Over the same time span, Riordan's unfavorable rating among Republicans increased from 12 percent to 35 percent. Among strongly conservative Republicans in particular, Riordan was viewed favorably by 44 percent, compared with 41 percent who viewed him unfavorably. In contrast, Simon was viewed favorably by 74 percent of strongly conservative Republicans, versus only 5 percent unfavorably. Although a clear majority (56%) of Republican voters believed that Riordan had "the best chance of defeating Davis in the general election," Republican pluralities also agreed that Simon "best represents the views of the Republican Party," and "would make the best Governor." Simon even led a trial heat against Davis at this time, 44 percent to 42 percent. So it was that in March 2002, Simon defeated Riordan in the Republican primary 49.5 percent to 31.4 percent. Republican voters sided with Simon's ideology over Riordan's electability.

The sudden turnaround in the last weeks of the Republican primary was largely the result of a massive, negative television ad blitz organized by the Davis campaign to "get" Simon as a general election opponent, instead of the moderate Riordan (Lucas 2002; Marinucci 2002). Knowing that Simon's more conservative views would make him by far the weaker candidate head-to-head with Davis, the Davis campaign spent approximately $10 million on a negative ad campaign designed to portray Riordan as inconsistent on abortion issues, crime, and taxes. Meanwhile, Simon spent nearly $5 million of his own money on the primary campaign, attacking Riordan repeatedly for his moderate record and past donations to Democratic candidates.

The attack advertising did not cease once the Republican primary election had ended, and the highly negative tone of the campaign took its toll on Californian voters: Turnout on Election Day was only 30 percent of the voting-age population, the "worst turnout ever for a statewide general election" (Wildermuth 2002). The greatest declines in voter turnout occurred among the Democratic base—African Americans and Latinos in particular. Candidate approval also suffered, as "Davis and Simon both ended the campaign disliked by roughly six in ten of those who bothered to vote" (Barabak 2002).

California voters did not want to have to reelect Davis. A *California Field Poll* survey conducted just a week before the election found that approximately 18 percent of the Californian electorate in 2002 voted for Davis largely because they felt they had no other choice. This would have been more than sufficient to swing the election away from Davis, had a less ideologically extreme candidate—namely, Riordan—been nominated by the Republicans. In fact, polling just before the election found that "if Republican former Los Angeles Mayor Richard Riordan were the GOP nominee instead of Simon, he would be preferred over Davis among likely voters by a huge 15-point margin—49% to 34%" (*California Field Poll* 2002c). The evidence points to a disengaged electorate that reelected Davis in 2002 only as the far lesser of two evils.

2003 RECALL ELECTION RESULTS

The results of the 2003 recall election did not leave much ambiguity about voters' desire to remove Davis from office. And despite concerns that the recall would be antidemocratic and enable a minority of Californians in 2003 to overturn the 2002 election, it turned out that nearly 1.5 million more votes were cast in favor of the recall than had been cast in favor of Davis' reelection. Moreover, large numbers of Democrats joined with Republicans to remove Davis from office and replace him with Schwarzenegger.

GEOGRAPHY AND DEMOGRAPHICS

The state of California includes fifty-eight counties, which vary greatly in size. Southern Californian counties are typically larger than northern Californian counties: Los Angeles County, with nearly 10 million residents is by far the largest, while Orange and San Diego Counties have nearly 3 million apiece. Many of California's counties are also very small: 23 have 100,000 residents or fewer. These population figures are roughly proportional to the number of registered voters in each county. Los Angeles again leads all counties with nearly 4 million registered voters, San Diego County has another 1.4 million, and Orange County has 1.3 million. California's 23 smallest counties have fewer than 50,000 registered voters apiece.

Most of California's voters are registered Democratic, with 44.6 percent statewide. Republicans represent 35.2 percent of all registered voters, and voters who have declined to state a party affiliation (declines, 15.2%) or are registered with other parties (others, 5.0%) make up the remaining amount.

COUNTY-LEVEL ELECTION RESULTS

The recall election followed a very particular geographic pattern, as is evident in Figure 3.2. Opposition to the recall was almost entirely confined to California's western coast, and it centered on the San Francisco Bay Area. Beyond the Bay Area, Los Angeles was the only noncontiguous county to have had a majority vote against the recall—and, even there, it was a slim majority with just 51 percent in opposition.

The second question on the recall ballot gave voters the opportunity to choose who would replace Davis if the recall succeeded. In this vote, Schwarzenegger's 48.6 percent victory was unambiguous. The rightmost map in Figure 3.2 shows that the geographic pattern of support for Schwarzenegger for governor closely mirrored the pattern of support for the recall. After Schwarzenegger, Democratic Lieutenant Governor Cruz Bustamante finished second with 31.5 percent of the vote, and conservative Republican State Senator Tom McClintock took third with 13.5 percent. Bustamante received a plurality in only eight of California's fifty-eight counties, all of which were tightly centered on San Francisco.

The recall vote and the gubernatorial vote were closely related; at the county level, voting in favor of the recall was an excellent predictor of voting for Schwarzenegger for governor. Across the state, counties that were most favorable to the recall also tended to vote most strongly for Schwarzenegger. Likewise, counties that opposed the recall also tended not to vote for Schwarzenegger (San Francisco was the most vivid instance of opposing both the recall and Schwarzenegger for governor). Between these two extremes, the relationship between the two votes was striking for its linearity (Figure 3.3).

The close links between geography, support for the recall, and support for Schwarzenegger suggests a quite obvious explanatory variable: the partisan composition of each county. The more Republican a county, the higher that county's vote in favor of the recall (Figure 3.4). Note, however, that in every county, the percent voting in favor of the recall usually exceeded the percent of registered Republicans in that county by anywhere from 10 percent to 25 percent, and sometimes even more. Thus, even if Republican support for the recall had been unanimous, there still must have been a certain number of Democrats, declines, and others who also voted in favor of the recall for the statewide recall vote to reach 55.4 percent—fully 20 points greater than the statewide proportion of registered Republicans.

INDIVIDUAL-LEVEL ELECTION RESULTS

The Edison/Mitofsky exit poll provides some answers to questions about how many Democrats voted for the recall, and how many recall opponents voted for Schwarzenegger. Because the overall sample size of the exit poll is large—3,814 voters interviewed—the poll results can be reported with some confidence. Yet despite the evident geographic patterns in the recall election, the percentages reported in the exit poll are all statewide averages, and do not explain geographic variation.

Not surprisingly, Republicans were more likely to support the recall than were Democrats. According to the exit poll, 88 percent of self-reported

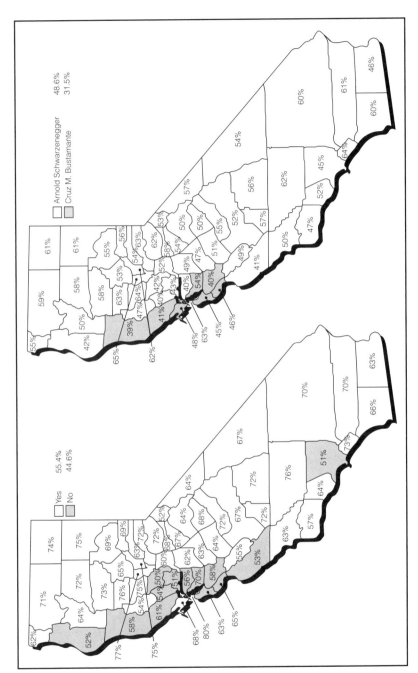

FIGURE 3.2 County maps of California, showing geographic distribution of votes for/against the recall (left) and vote for new Governor (right).

SOURCE: California Secretary of State.

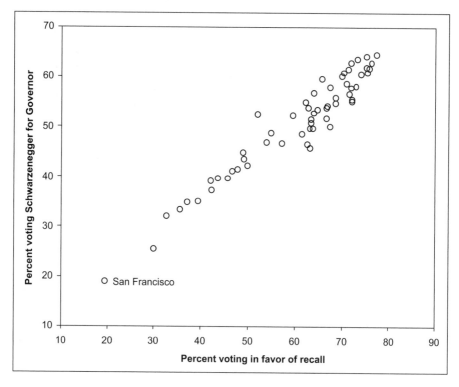

FIGURE 3.3 Scatterplot of percent voting for Schwarzenegger for Governor versus percent voting in favor of the recall for fifty-eight counties.

Republicans voted for the recall, while only 24 percent of self-reported Democrats voted. Roughly 53 percent of independents and other voters supported the recall. From a purely partisan perspective, then, the recall succeeded because, although independents split only slightly in favor of the recall, the percentage of Democrats who voted for the recall was twice as great as the percentage of Republicans who opposed it.

This pattern was evident again in the vote for governor, with Republicans nearly united in their support for the two leading Republican gubernatorial candidates. Schwarzenegger won 74 percent of the Republican vote, while McClintock took an additional 17 percent. That left a remarkably small 9 percent of Republicans who voted for any other candidate; only 6 percent of Republicans voted for Bustamante. On the Democratic side, less than one-fifth (18%) voted for Schwarzenegger. Independents and others combined preferred Schwarzenegger to Bustamante 43 percent to 28 percent.

For Californian voters, the decision to vote for both the recall and for one of the leading Republicans for governor—either Schwarzenegger or McClintock—was fairly consistent. So too was the decision to vote against the recall and for Bustamante. Among those who voted for the recall, 74 percent also

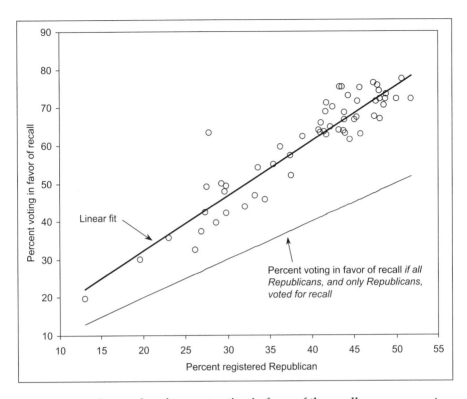

FIGURE 3.4   Scatterplot of percent voting in favor of the recall versus percent registered Republican for fifty-eight counties.

voted for Schwarzenegger and 16 percent voted for McClintock. Among those who voted against the recall, approximately 72 percent voted for Bustamante. Statewide, an estimated 42 percent of voters voted for both the recall and Schwarzenegger on Election Day. In comparison, 31 percent voted both against the recall and for Bustamante. The proportion of voters statewide who flip-flopped, voting in favor of the recall and for Bustamante, was just 3 percent, while the proportion who voted against the recall and for Schwarzenegger was 4 percent.

Looking beyond party identification (although, certainly, Republicans tended to view Davis much more unfavorably than did Democrats), voters' approval or disapproval rating of Davis' job as governor was an excellent predictor of voting for the recall. Voters who disapproved of Davis—of whom there were many—were quite eager to vote to remove him from office. Only 26 percent of recall voters either "strongly" or "somewhat" approved of Davis' job performance and, within this group, 90 percent voted against the recall, in favor of keeping Davis in office. Another 23 percent only "somewhat" disapproved of Davis' job performance, and these voters also tended to oppose the recall, 64 percent to 36 percent. But fully 48 percent of voters "strongly" disapproved of Davis' job performance and, of these, 90 percent voted for the recall, versus just 10 percent against.

Why did Californian voters hold such a poor opinion of the job Davis was doing as governor? A leading reason was the perceived state of California's economy and, in particular, of Davis' handling of it. Voters who took a more pessimistic view of the state of the economy were more likely to back the recall effort. Of the 33 percent of voters who thought the condition of California's economy was "poor," 71 percent voted for the recall. Another 50 percent thought the condition of the economy was "not so good," and these voters were split evenly on the recall.

Thus, far from being a bizarre outcome, the recall election of 2003 followed logically from a combination of partisan opposition to Davis and a widespread, highly negative, retrospective evaluation of California's economy under Davis' leadership. These findings do not merely represent the effects of a hard-fought and highly negative election campaign: The exit poll found that fully two-thirds (67%) of voters had "finally decided how to vote" in the recall "more than a month" before the actual election. Another 15 percent decided "within the last month." Evidence from the exit poll reveals a Californian electorate deeply displeased with the Davis administration and eager to take advantage of the opportunity provided by the recall election to put the moderate Schwarzenegger into office in Davis' place.

EXPLAINING THE ABANDONMENT OF GRAY DAVIS

The empirical data in the preceding section paint a tidy picture of the primary factors that produced the outcome of the 2003 recall and gubernatorial special elections. But the question remains: What happened between 2002 and 2003 to explain the *falloff* in electoral support for Davis? In 2002, Davis was reelected to a second term, but less than 12 months later, he was resoundingly defeated at the polls.

To identify the conditions that led many voters who had supported Davis in 2002 to abandon him in 2003, we turn to a series of straightforward statistical models to estimate the precise effects of various partisan, demographic, and economic variables at the level of California's fifty-eight counties. Models of this sort also enable us to entertain a number of hypothetical "what if?" scenarios and draw inferences about how the election might have turned out differently had some of these county-level variables been different than they actually were.

HOW MANY 2002 DAVIS SUPPORTERS VOTED FOR THE RECALL?

For each of California's fifty-eight counties, we know the percentage of registered voters who voted for Davis in 2002, as well as the percentage of registered voters who voted for the recall in 2003. We can use this aggregate county-level data to estimate the statewide proportion of voters in favor of the recall, given that they voted to reelect Davis in 2002.[2] We estimate this proportion of voters to be approximately 16.1 percent.[3] That is, statewide, approximately 16.1 percent of the 47.3 percent who voted for Davis for governor in 2002 voted to recall him in 2003. Multiplying these two proportions indicates that approximately 7.6 percent of California voters abandoned Davis between 2002 and 2003.

This number, 7.6 percent, represents a large swath of the electorate. It is roughly twice as large as the proportion who reported that they voted inconsistently on the recall and the gubernatorial vote. Because Davis' margin of victory over Simon in 2000 was only 5 percent, had just 2.5 percent of voters switched their vote (much less, 7.6%), Davis would not have been reelected.

WHERE DID DAVIS' SUPPORT CRUMBLE?

In California's 2002 gubernatorial election, 7,476,311 votes were cast for governor, of which Davis won 3,533,490. In the 2003 "replacement" gubernatorial election, 8,652,659 votes were cast for governor, of which the Democratic frontrunner, Davis' Lieutenant Governor Bustamante, won 2,723,768. In comparison, Schwarzenegger received 4,203,596 votes for governor in 2003; 670,106 more than Davis received in 2002. Thus, although more than 1 million additional votes were cast in 2003 than in 2002, 809,722 fewer Californians voted for the leading Democrat in the race.

Neither Davis nor Bustamante were generally well-liked by Californian voters on Election Day. According to the Edison/Mitofsky exit poll, only 36 percent of California voters held a favorable opinion of Bustamante, while even fewer—26 percent—approved of "the way Gray Davis [was] handling his job as governor." It is most likely safe to assume that had Davis appeared on the ballot instead of Bustamante, he would have received even fewer votes than Bustamante did. If this assumption is correct, then the difference in votes received by Bustamante in 2003 and Davis in 2002 is a conservative measure of the magnitude of the withdrawal of voter support from Davis and his administration. Because the total number of votes cast in 2003 exceeded those cast in 2002 by more than 1 million, we scaled back the number of votes cast for Bustamante in 2003 in proportion to the total number of votes cast for governor in each county in 2003 before subtracting Davis' votes in 2002. The "adjusted" statewide Bustamante vote—that is, the number of votes cast for Bustamante had turnout in each county in 2003 been identical to 2002—is 2,378,406; this corresponds to an increased falloff of 1,155,084 votes.

Where did these 1 million "lost" votes come from? The culprits are clear: Los Angeles, Orange, and San Diego Counties—California's three largest counties, all in the southern part of the state—combined to account for nearly half of the Davis/Bustamante falloff. The California counties that withdrew the most support from Davis/Bustamante, sorted both by net change (top) and percentage change (bottom), are listed in Table 3.1. The percentage decline was greatest in some of California's smallest counties: Lassen, Tehama, Sutter, and so on. But remarkably, Orange County tops both lists, with Bustamante receiving fewer than half the votes Davis received in 2002, assuming equal turnout in the two elections. San Bernardino, Riverside, and Ventura Counties—all large southern counties—also rank highly on both lists.

Another way to view this decline is to calculate the difference in each county between the percent voting for the recall in 2003 and the percent voting

TABLE 3.1   Counties in which the Davis/Bustamante administration suffered
its worst losses between 2002 and 2003.

COUNTY	BUSTAMANTE '03 VOTES (ADJUSTED) MINUS DAVIS '02	PERCENT OF REGISTERED VOTERS IN COUNTY	PERCENT CHANGE
Sorted by Net Votes Lost			
Los Angeles	−313519	−7.90%	−32.9%
Orange	−114345	−8.80%	−51.5%
San Diego	−112207	−7.90%	−41.8%
Riverside	−56717	−8.70%	−46.5%
Santa Clara	−55636	−7.60%	−27.9%
San Bernardino	−55566	−9.00%	−47.6%
Sacramento	−45352	−7.90%	−35.1%
Contra Costa	−39328	−8.10%	−27.9%
Ventura	−37745	−9.60%	−45.2%
Alameda	−32377	−4.90%	−15.0%
Sorted by Percent Change			
Orange	−114345	−8.80%	−51.5%
Lassen	−1246	−8.50%	−51.3%
Tehama	−2532	−9.40%	−50.6%
Sutter	−2884	−7.80%	−49.9%
San Bernardino	−55566	−9.00%	−47.6%
Riverside	−56717	−8.70%	−46.5%
Modoc	−415	−8.10%	−46.1%
Shasta	−6990	−8.20%	−45.7%
Amador	−2024	−10.60%	−45.6%
Ventura	−37745	−9.60%	−45.2%

Note: The number of votes cast for Bustamante for Governor in 2003 is adjusted as if countywide turnout
had been the same in 2003 as 2002.

against Davis in 2002. This is the countywide increase or decrease in the
percent of voters who opposed Davis between his reelection and recall. So,
for example, in Los Angeles County, 56 percent voted for Davis in 2002 and
49 percent voted for the recall in 2003. Thus the percent of voters opposed to
Davis increased in Los Angeles County by 5 percent. If we compare this
"change in opposition" variable with Davis' vote share in 2002, the pattern is
a decreasing trend: Counties that supported Davis more strongly in 2002 were
less likely to withdraw that support in the 2003 recall (Figure 3.5). In this sense,
the recall election essentially "amplified" the existing tendencies of counties
to vote for or against Davis between 2002 and 2003.[4]

Unfortunately for Davis, among the counties that withdrew their support
were some of California's largest, including a majority of the ten southern

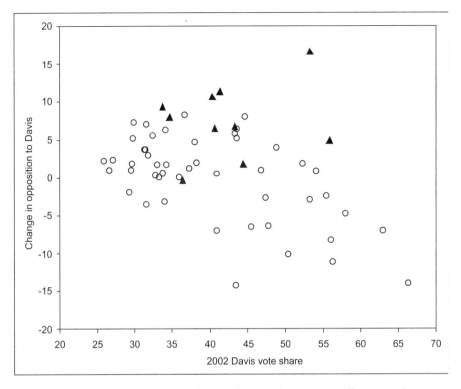

FIGURE 3.5   Scatterplot of percentage difference between recall support in 2003 and Davis opposition in 2002 versus percent voting for Davis in 2002 for fifty-eight counties. California's ten southern counties are denoted with solid triangles.

counties denoted in Figure 3.5 with solid triangles. Given Los Angeles County's relatively high level of support for Davis in 2002, its 5 percent increase in opposition to Davis in 2003 is unusually high. The other large southern counties that figured prominently in Table 3.1—Orange, Riverside, San Bernardino, San Diego, and Ventura Counties—also stand out as having large decreases in support for Davis in 2003, given their vote for him in 2002. There is no county in which Bustamante's adjusted 2003 vote exceeded Davis' 2002 vote. It was the southern part of the state, however, that inflicted, by far, the worst of the damage.

A MODEL OF COUNTY-LEVEL FALLOFF

Statewide, approximately 16.1 percent of those who voted for Davis in 2002 voted to recall him in 2003, with counties in Southern California accounting for the bulk of this falloff. There was substantial variation, however, in counties' tendencies to continue to support or abandon Davis in 2003. What county-level characteristics account for these differences?

TABLE 3.2   OLS (ordinary least squares) estimation.
Dependent variable is logit-transformed estimated percent
of 2002 Davis voters who voted in favor of the recall in 2003,
by county (standard errors in brackets).

VARIABLE	COEFFICIENT ESTIMATE
Constant	4.020
	[1.448]
Percent Republican	0.032
	[0.004]
Income 2001 (ln)	−0.714
	[0.129]
Percent Latino	0.009
	[0.002]
South	0.442
	[0.092]
Number of Obs.	58
R^2	0.850

The estimation routine not only estimated the statewide proportion of voters who voted for the recall in 2003 after having voted for Davis in 2002 (that is, the 16.1%), but also it returned county-level estimates of this quantity. As expected, these estimates are highly correlated with the county-level measure of "change in opposition to Davis" plotted on the vertical axis in Figure 3.5. Both variables measure the increase, for a given county, in voters' opposition to Davis between 2002 and 2003.

Taking the logit-transformed[5] countywide proportion of 2002 Davis voters who were estimated to have voted for the recall in 2003 as the dependent variable to be explained, we fit a linear regression model;[6] results are given in Table 3.2.[7] This model explains 85 percent of the county-level variation in the proportion of 2002 Davis voters who voted for the recall in 2003. Explanatory variables are as follows: **Percent Republican** is the countywide proportion of registered voters who are Republicans. **Avg. income, 2001 (ln)** is the logit-transformed per capita personal income by county in 2001 (the most current year available), as reported by the *California Statistical Abstract*, table D-9. **Percent Latino** is the percentage of each county's population identified as Hispanic or Latino in the 2000 Census, as reported by the *California Statistical Abstract*, table B-5.[8] **Southern County** is a dichotomous variable equaling 1 for southern counties Imperial, Kern, Los Angeles, Orange, Riverside, Santa Barbara, San Bernardino, San Diego, San Luis Obispo, and Ventura; 0 otherwise.

The coefficients in this model offer a clear picture of the factors that contributed to removing Davis from office in 2003. Once again, the model confirms that partisanship played the most significant role. Counties with larger Republican populations tended to abandon Davis in greater numbers between 2002 and 2003. A hypothetical countywide increase in Republican voter registration from 40 percent to 50 percent—slightly larger than one standard deviation—predicts an additional 4.7 percent of 2002 Davis voters voting for the recall, all else equal, holding the other explanatory variables constant at their mean.

That said, even controlling for partisan effects, the effect of per capita income on withdrawal of support from Davis remains strong. Had a county's 2001 per capita income been $35,000 rather than $25,000, Davis would have retained 3 percent more of his supporters in that county. As county-level per capita income is highly correlated from one year to the next, it does not matter much that 2001 is the most recent year available. The poorer the county, the less likely it was to continue to support Davis between 2002 and 2003.

Counties with larger Latino populations tended to withdraw more support from Davis at the recall. The Edison/Mitofsky exit poll found that Latinos just barely opposed the recall in 2003, although they had been very strong in their support of Davis' bid for governor in 2002. But although the effect of having a larger Latino population is statistically significantly non-zero, it is not of great substantive significance. A one standard deviation increase from 20 percent to 35 percent of the population predicts 1.8 percent greater desertion from Davis between his reelection and recall.

Finally, even after controlling for county partisanship, income, and a measure of ethnic composition, there remains a strong and significant positive effect of "south-ness" on the tendency of a county to vote to recall Davis in 2003 despite its support of him in 2002.[9] The model predicts that, on average, simply by virtue of living in the southern part of California, 6.3 percent more voters in any given southern county who had voted to reelect Davis in 2002 subsequently voted to recall him in 2003.

EXPLAINING SCHWARZENEGGER'S VICTORY

Evidence from the recall election exit poll indicated that Californian voters were behaving highly consistently in first voting for the recall and then voting for Schwarzenegger for governor. As further evidence of this regularity, the same county-level factors that predicted Davis' recall also explain well the voters' choice of Schwarzenegger as Davis' successor.

The gubernatorial election to replace Davis followed a plurality rule, and although 135 candidates appeared on the replacement ballot, just four candidates accounted for nearly all of the votes cast. These were Republican Schwarzenegger (48.6%), Democrat Bustamante (31.5%), Republican McClintock (13.4%), and Green Peter Camejo (2.8%). All other candidates combined received just 3.7 percent of the vote. Among counties, however, there was significant variation in these mean values. The standard deviation of Schwarzenegger's countywide vote share was 10.2 percent, Bustamante's was 10.6 percent, McClintock's was 3.9 percent, and Camejo's was 1.8 percent.

To explain the large cross-county variation in candidates' vote shares, we apply a seemingly unrelated regression (SUR) model of multicandidate elections (Tomz, Tucker, and Wittenberg 2002; Zellner 1962).[10] A model of the gubernatorial election outcome as a function of the same four independent variables used to model the recall in the previous section fits the data extremely well

TABLE 3.3   SUR (seemingly unrelated regression) estimation, fifty-eight observations. Dependent variables are log-ratios of countywide vote shares for all candidates, calculated with respect to Bustamante's vote shares.

Schwarzenegger ($R^2 = 0.899$)	Coef.	Std. Error	t	$p > t$
Constant	2.757	1.167	2.36	0.018
Percent Republican	0.054	0.004	15.20	0.000
Avg. income, 2001 (ln)	−0.405	0.104	−3.88	0.000
Percent Latino	−0.005	0.002	−2.74	0.006
Southern County	0.163	0.074	2.20	0.028
McClintock ($R^2 = 0.852$)	**Coef.**	**Std. Error**	***t***	***p > t***
Constant	0.005	1.442	0.00	0.997
Percent Republican	0.057	0.004	13.00	0.000
Avg. income, 2001 (ln)	−0.262	0.129	−2.04	0.042
Percent Latino	−0.005	0.002	−2.04	0.041
Southern County	−0.001	0.091	−0.01	0.992
Camejo ($R^2 = 0.637$)	**Coef.**	**Std. Error**	***t***	***p > t***
Constant	−6.665	2.040	−3.27	0.001
Percent Republican	−0.004	0.006	−0.71	0.477
Avg. income, 2001 (ln)	0.484	0.182	2.65	0.008
Percent Latino	−0.024	0.003	−7.17	0.000
Southern County	0.000	0.129	0.00	0.999
Others ($R^2 = 0.384$)	**Coef.**	**Std. Error**	***t***	***p > t***
Constant	3.267	1.741	1.88	0.061
Percent Republican	0.005	0.005	1.02	0.307
Avg. income, 2001 (ln)	−0.507	0.156	−3.25	0.001
Percent Latino	−0.011	0.003	−3.69	0.000
Southern County	0.046	0.110	0.41	0.679

(Table 3.3). For each coefficient estimate, high levels of statistical significance indicate that a variable is effective in explaining the vote differential between a candidate and Bustamante. The model explains nearly 90 percent of the variation in Schwarzenegger's log-vote ratio, more than 85 percent of McClintock's vote ratio, and 64 percent of Camejo's vote ratio.

As expected, increases in a county's percentage of registered Republicans predict an increased vote share for Schwarzenegger and McClintock at Bustamante's expense. The model predicts that, in an average northern county, Schwarzenegger would beat Bustamante if but 28 percent of a county's voters were registered Republicans. In southern counties, this number falls to just 26 percent. On average, northern counties have 39.2 percent registered Republicans, and southern counties have 40.7 percent. In fact, there are only eight counties statewide with fewer than 28 percent registered Republicans (incidentally, Los Angeles, at 27.6 percent Republican, is one of them). And of the eight counties in which Bustamante received a plurality of the vote, all had fewer than 30 percent registered Republicans. The model once again confirms the strong county-level effect of partisanship on the outcome of the gubernatorial election.

What of the effect of income? Calculating predicted vote shares as above, we find that, holding party registration constant, Bustamante's vote share increased in wealthier counties. The poorer a county, the more votes Schwarzenegger received. Only five counties in California exceed an average annual income of $40,000, all of which happen to be located in the northern part of the state (Marin is the wealthiest at $63,083). In the bulk of California's northern counties, at mean levels of Republican registration, the variation in income levels predicts Schwarzenegger victory margins of 20 percent to 30 percent over Bustamante. This gap is even greater in southern counties.

That Bustamante won pluralities in any counties at all is only due to a confluence of counties being northern, very wealthy, and very Democratic. Of course, there are relatively few counties in which all three factors are present, and these counties happen to be located in the San Francisco Bay Area. In this respect, this statistical model simply confirms the intuition gathered from Figure 3.2: The continued support of Davis in the counties surrounding San Francisco was unique. The 2003 special gubernatorial election was a major Schwarzenegger landslide, arising from both party and wealth at the county level, plus an added boost in the southern part of the state.

CONCLUSION

For all of the excitement and fanfare surrounding California's 2003 recall election, careful empirical analysis of the election results demonstrates that voters behaved consistently and rationally in replacing Davis with Schwarzenegger as governor. For the most part, voters simply followed their partisan inclinations, while factoring into their vote options their typically unfavorable retrospective evaluation of Davis' performance in office.

When Davis was reelected to a second term as governor of California in 2002, exit polls indicated that, despite Davis' victory, his support in the electorate was extremely weak. A large percentage of voters chose Davis over Simon largely because Simon's politics were too conservative for their liking. At the time, it seemed plausible that because of his widespread unpopularity—with a job approval rating well on its way to reaching historic lows—Davis would not have been reelected had his Republican opponent been the more moderate Riordan, instead of the conservative Simon. But there was no way to know for sure just how heavily voters weighed Davis' unpopularity against Simon's ideological misalignment with the Californian electorate. What was clear, however, was that neither candidate represented much of a desirable option to most voters statewide.

The recall election of 2003 gave a great many Californians the choice they had wanted in 2002: a moderate alternative to Davis for governor. Davis' unpopularity was a necessary condition for his recall, but as the election of

2002 showed, it was not sufficient. Only once the California Republican Party put forth a moderate—Schwarzenegger—were voters willing to remove Davis from office. As it happened, the joint decisions to vote to recall Davis and elect Schwarzenegger in his place were highly consistent. Overall, an estimated 16.1 percent of Davis' supporters in 2002 voted to recall him in 2003, corresponding to 7.6 percent of all voters statewide. Had even half this number voted against Davis in 2002, as is reasonable to expect had Riordan been the Republican nominee that year, Davis would never have even been reelected.

The outcome of the 2003 recall election was decisive. Certainly a large part of the opposition to Davis was partisan, but the recall would never have succeeded without the support of large numbers of Democratic voters who had grown displeased with Davis—especially in southern California. Poorer counties and counties with fewer Latinos and more whites also tended to abandon Davis in favor of Schwarzenegger. Given the combined effect of all of these factors, Davis (and Bustamante after him) stood little chance of victory in 2003 in the face of voters' desire for new leadership in the state of California.

BIBLIOGRAPHY

Barabak, Mark Z. "Negative Campaign Repelled Some Voters; A Times Exit Poll Finds Alienation of Latinos and African Americans Also Kept Turnout Low." *Los Angeles Times*, November 11, 2002.

Benoit, Kenneth and Gary King. EzI: An (Easy) Program for Ecological Inference. Version 2.7 for Windows, 2003.

Berke, Richard L. "Novice Wins G.O.P. Primary for Governor of California." *New York Times*, March 6, 2002.

California Field Poll. Release #2081, August 15, 2003. http://field.com/fieldpollonline/subscribers/RLS2081.pdf.

California Field Poll. Release #2061, November 1, 2002d. http://field.com/fieldpollonline/subscribers/RLS2061.pdf.

California Field Poll. Release #2051, September 5, 2002c. http://field.com/fieldpollonline/subscribers/RLS2051.pdf.

California Field Poll. Release #2032, February 27, 2002b. http://field.com/fieldpollonline/subscribers/RLS2032.pdf.

California Field Poll. Release #2023, January 29, 2002a. http://field.com/fieldpollonline/subscribers/Rls2023.pdf.

California Field Poll. Release #2011, September 26, 2001. http://field.com/fieldpollonline/subscribers/Rls2011.pdf.

California Secretary of State. http://vote2003.ss.ca.gov/index.html.

California Statistical Abstract. 44th ed. December 2003. http://www.dof.ca.gov/HTML/FS_DATA/stat-abs/sa_home.htm (accessed February 2005).

Edison Media Research/Mitofsky International California Recall Election Exit Poll. http://www.mitofskyinternational.com/ca-recall.htm (accessed February 2005).

King, Gary. *A Solution to the Ecological Inference Problem: Reconstructing Individual Behavior from Aggregate Data*. Princeton: Princeton University Press, 1997.

Lucas, Greg. "Attack Ads the Big Winner in Mudslinging Primary; Riordan Suffered Most in Statewide Trend." *San Francisco Chronicle*, March 7, 2002.

Marelius, John. "Simon Passes Slumping Riordan in GOP Race, Poll Finds; Davis Ads Contribute to Gubernatorial Surprise." *The San Diego Union-Tribune*, February 27, 2002.

Marinucci, Carla. "Simon Catapults over Riordan in Poll; Stunning Rebound for Businessman." *San Francisco Chronicle*, February 27, 2002.

Noah, Timothy. "Does the GOP Subvert Democracy? Gray Davis May Be onto Something." *Slate.com*, August 21, 2003. http://slate.msn.com/id/2087297/.

Stone, Walter J., and Monti Narayan Datta. "Rationalizing the California Recall." *PS: Political Science and Politics* 37, no. 1 (2004): 19–21.

Tomz, Michael, Joshua A. Tucker, and Jason Wittenberg. "An Easy and Accurate Regression

Model for Multiparty Electoral Data." *Political Analysis* 10, no. 1 (2002): 66–83.

Wildermuth, John. "Worst Turnout Ever for a California General Election." *San Francisco Chronicle*, November 15, 2002.

Zellner, Arnold. "An Efficient Method of Estimating Seemingly Unrelated Regressions and Tests for Aggregation Bias." *Journal of the American Statistical Association* 57, no. 298 (1962): 348–368.

NOTES

1. See, for example, Berke (2002), Marelius (2002), and Marinucci (2002).
2. The estimation technique used here is an application of King's (1997) "solution to the ecological inference problem," as implemented by the software package EzI (Benoit and King 2003). Those interested in the ecological inference "fallacy," why it applies (as opposed to simple linear regression) in this case, and how the EzI software estimates parameters of interest, are advised to consult King (1997).
3. The standard error of this estimate is 1.9 percent.
4. Note that many of the large apparent increases in support for Davis by this measure are, in part, an artifact of voters in left-leaning counties such as Mendocino and Marin choosing the Green Party candidate, Peter Camejo, over Davis in 2002.
5. The logit (or log-odds) transformation is used in this instance because the estimates of the countywide proportion, p, of Davis 2002 voters who voted for the recall in 2003 is bounded by 0 and 1. For each county, the transformed measure is equal to $\ln\left(\dfrac{p}{1-p}\right)$.
6. Stone and Datta (2004) take a similar ordinary least squares (OLS) regression approach to explain the countywide percentage of votes in favor of the recall; they find that at the county level, the 2002 percentage voting for Davis for governor accounts for 92 percent of the between-county variation in support for the recall.
7. When interpreting regression results from Table 3.2, remember that all coefficient estimates apply only to the *county* level—not the individual level. Saying that more heavily Republican *counties* were more likely to abandon Davis between 2002 and 2003 does *not* necessarily imply that Republican *individuals* were more likely to abandon Davis than were Democrats, declines, and

others. That said, the regression models are highly effective in pinpointing county characteristics that determined Davis' fate.
8. The decision to use the "Latino" measure rather than a measure of each county's percentage white is arbitrary. The two variables follow a pronounced linear relationship and are correlated at −0.87. Both variables measure a county's ethnic makeup; the use of either returns nearly identical coefficient estimates on the other control variables and does not alter the substantive interpretation of the model.
9. Although southern counties tend to be larger than northern counties, the "south" dummy variable is not acting as a proxy for population size; and even if it were, there is no apparent theoretical link between larger populations and greater withdrawal of support from Davis. If we add to the right-hand side of this model the log-transformed estimated 2002 county populations from the *California Statistical Abstract*, table B-3, the "south" variable remains statistically significant, while the effect of the population variable is not significant.
10. This model satisfies the constraint that the dependent variable—the countywide vote shares of the four leading candidates and "others"—must all sum to 1 in every county. The candidates' countywide vote shares are therefore not independent (knowing any four automatically determines the fifth), and they are bounded by 0 and 1. We designate (arbitrarily) Bustamante's vote share in each county as a reference, and calculate the log-ratio of each of the candidate's vote shares with respect to Bustamante's. This transformation retains all of the information of the five-candidate outcome, but returns four unbounded log-vote ratios that can be modeled as a linear function of some set of explanatory variables.

4

RECALLING THE REALIGNMENT LITERATURE

DID OCTOBER 2003 BRING A CRITICAL ELECTION?

THAD KOUSSER

UNIVERSITY OF CALIFORNIA, SAN DIEGO

Beginning with V.O. Key's pioneering work, a venerable body of literature in political science defines critical elections and studies the partisan realignments that they appear to bring. As recent critics have pointed out, many famously critical elections do not stand out among a larger set of contests that have brought lasting but moderate changes. While the realignment literature's consensus on the crucial turning points of American political history seems to have collapsed, the accumulation of definitions and statistical standards in this field still can serve a more modest task: showing what is *not* a critical election.

Applying the classification schemes and quantitative tests of the realignment literature to California's October 2003 recall rules it out as a critical election. First, comparing the size of the recall electorate with participation rates in recent history shows that it did not generate intense interest. Second, the tight correlation of the geographic distribution of the vote in the recall with 2002 patterns shows that it did not reshuffle party supporters, but instead brought an across-the-board Republican surge. Analyses of registration levels, party mobilization, and vote shares in the March 2004 primary election all suggest that this surge was not durable, marking the recall as a deviating rather than critical election.

Did the historic recall of a once-popular governor and the runaway victory of a novice outsider really change anything in California politics? Many of those who covered the race for state, national, and international media outlets answered that question in the affirmative, ever more loudly. The *Boston Globe* declared it a "landslide election that set the stage for a massive political realignment in the nation's most populous state." Pollster Frank Luntz declared that "it means California is in play for the presidential" and Bob Novak predicted that it "could exert overriding political significance nationally."[1] Perhaps a better way to reflect on this crucial question is to ignore the hyperbole of current journalism and punditry in favor of the historic context and methodological tools provided by a venerable body of political science literature.

Works seeking to identify critical elections that produce realignments in American politics, while flawed in important ways, still supply a useful lens through which to view California's 2003 recall contest. This essay borrows the definitions and methods of the realignment literature to make two arguments. First, although recent works have shown that famously critical elections may not be as periodic, national in scope, and important to policymaking as was once supposed, this well-developed concept is still helpful in determining what is *not* a critical election. Second, Gray Davis' recall, shocking and entertaining as it was, does not appear to be a critical contest that will deliver a durable realignment of California politics.

V.O. Key's 1955 article, "A Theory of Critical Elections," first defined the concept and illustrated it by showing how the 1896 and 1928 presidential elections changed New England voting patterns. Schattsneider followed with broader claims of how the pro-Republican swing in 1896 and Roosevelt's "revolution of 1932" fundamentally altered partisan alignments and national policies. After scholars developed further classifications of elections (Campbell et al. 1960) and quantitative methods for spotting them (Pomper 1967), the landmark works of Burnham (1970) and Sundquist (1973) argued that periodic realignments marked the borders between a set of distinct "party systems." While today's political scientists are often taught to view American political history through this lens, few are engaged in active research on realignments. The flow of work on the subject began to diminish at about the time that Arnold Schwarzenegger's film career took off. By 1991, Shafer's edited volume asked, "Is Realignment Dead?" Mayhew's 2002 work reviewed the realignment literature not to praise it but to bury it.

While Mayhew's critique is powerful, the body of work built up by so many of the founders of the modern study of political behavior can still be useful to scholars today. The body of work provides clear definitions of a concept like a critical election, a standard set of quantitative measures to know one when we see it, and examples of how realignments can shift electoral fortunes and influence party strategies. This essay reviews a small portion of the realignment literature to show how critical elections have been defined and identified, while noting the limits of the concept pointed out by Clubb, Flanigan, and Zingale (1980) and Mayhew (2002).

I then apply these standards and tests to see whether California's 2003 recall election qualifies as a critical election. First, I look at participation rates to see whether or not it captured enough interest from voters to meet the "high intensity" criterion set forth by Key (1955). When put in historic context, the recall appears to signify a return to the normal turnout rate experienced after the 2002 gubernatorial contest brought a deviation below the recent path of California political participation. The next section examines shifts in county and assembly district vote shares to determine which process—either a uniform surge or a reshuffling of party strongholds—brought defeat to Davis and victory for Schwarzenegger. I find clear evidence for an across-the-board swing away from Democratic candidates. Because a one-election change does not qualify as a critical contest, in the final empirical section I search for signs of a durable effect. Looking at the composition of voter registration, patterns in party mobilization, and electoral returns in the 2004 primaries, I find none. It may be too soon to tell, but all of the evidence available today indicates that the impact of this "landslide" has already eroded after six months. I conclude by discussing the policy effects of replacing California's governor, arguing that substituting Schwarzenegger for Davis has not led to a major shift in the direction of state government.

THE REALIGNMENT LITERATURE AND ITS CRITICS

In Key's work, which initiated the search to identify, explain, and explore the effects of critical elections, he begins by outlining what defines these momentous events. Critical elections are ones "in which the depth and intensity of electoral involvement are high, in which more or less profound readjustments occur in the relations of power within the community, and in which new and durable electoral groupings are formed" (1955, 4). Voting patterns in these elections make it clear that the process has been realigned. The works of Schattsneider (1960), Burnham (1970), and Sundquist (1973) claimed more explanatory power from critical elections, arguing that their periodic occurrence separated distinct party systems that brought different modes of political interaction and changed the direction of national policy. They did not, however, depart from Key in their basic definition of the concept. The realignment literature progressed with works that proposed quantitative methods for identifying critical elections (Pomper 1967) and that used these tools to conduct comprehensive analyses of patterns in U.S. presidential and congressional contests (Burnham 1970; Clubb, Flanigan, and Zingale 1980).

Even in the heyday of this field, critics pointed out that the division of American political history into a neat set of five "party systems" was imperfect. Political historians questioned the accuracy of the way in which the critical election label had been bestowed (Lichtman 1976) and attacked the concept as having "no clearly stated macro- or micro-theoretical underpinning" (Kousser 1981, 23–24). Clubb, Flanigan, and Zingale's reassessment of the evidence supporting previous categorizations of elections found that famously critical elections such as the 1896 presidential race were in fact "little more than a momentary disruption in a continuing pattern of relative partisan strength," and thus "deviating rather than realigning" (1980, 100–02). These authors, along with McCormick (1986), stressed that realignments should bring policy changes and called for other scholars to study this link. While Brady (1988) has contributed in this area, interest in critical elections and their effects has generally waned over the past twenty years.

In fact, the major recent work on realignment is Mayhew's 2002 critique of the genre. After taking a propositional inventory of the literature, Mayhew outlines the fifteen points that it makes and seeks to refute each in turn on empirical grounds. He argues convincingly that there is not a handful of critical elections that stand out in American history, and thus that the emphasis that Burnham and Sundquist put on periodicity and party systems was misplaced. Perhaps most damaging to the literature's legacy is Mayhew's claim that it is not "illuminative," adding nothing to our "baseline knowledge" of American politics (2002, 35).

Mayhew's critique is sound. Only the election of 1932 brings a national electoral realignment that fits the ideal type identified in the literature. The next level of what might be termed "major elections," the fifteen to twenty that bring some form of permanent realignment in presidential politics, do not occur at regular intervals. He shows that many of the political and policy shifts spotted by scholars may be influenced by their reliance on the organizing principle of the party systems idea. But at least, and perhaps at most, the literature is useful in that it provides a way to judge what is clearly *not* a critical election. This can be seen an improvement on our baseline knowledge, as represented by the conventional wisdom of political journalists. The concepts and statistical techniques developed by the realignment scholars delineate the signals that must be observed for a contest to be considered a potentially critical election. Whether the presence of one or more of these signs is sufficient to bring about an important political realignment is another question. If none exist, however, we can definitively rule out the election as part of the critical category.

Although we do not know what is a critical election, one might reasonably ask how we can know what is not a critical election. If no distinctions can be drawn among elections, the categorization scheme becomes meaningless. Yet Mayhew's critique on this point, based mainly on Clubb, Flanigan, and Zingale's evidence, does not go this far. It merely shows that the "specified dates of the realignment calendar" (2002, 47)—that is, the presidential contests of 1800, 1828, 1860, 1896, and 1932—do not bring especially dramatic realignments compared with other major elections. Clubb, Flanigan, and Zingale (1980, 92–93) identify seventeen presidential elections between 1836 and 1964 in which there was some sort of permanent change in the fortunes of either the Democratic or Republican Parties. This set of more or less equally major elections is larger than the set of critical elections identified in the literature, casting doubt on the traditional taxonomy. Recognizing this makes the critical election concept less useful as a starting point for discussions of periodicity, party systems, and policy change. But the major contests are indeed distinct from the other half of presidential elections, which showed no quantitative evidence of realignment. These are manifestly not critical elections.

While Mayhew's work should destroy the consensus that five critical elections are the mainsprings of American politics, systematic distinctions among types of elections can still be drawn. This is Key's essential insight, and his eye was drawn not only to the cases of change. After showing the changes in New England vote shares that persisted long after the 1928 election, he allowed that "Melancholy experience with the eccentricities of data ... suggests the prudence of a check on the interpretation of 1928. Would the same method applied to any other election yield a similar result?" (1955, 8). He showed what voting patterns in a noncritical election would look like, returning to their previous patterns after a one-time deviation. This sort of minor departure from a stable pattern, as the remainder of this essay shows, appears to be the legacy of California's 2003 recall.

POLITICAL PARTICIPATION IN CALIFORNIA'S RECALL

To meet the first standard that Key sets forth, a critical election must attract the intense interest of voters, bringing them into the system or turning them out at record rates. By comparing current exit polls and participation figures with historic data, I investigate how much the recall enlarged California's electorate and why it may have done so. I began by exploring the number of new voters brought into the system. Although I did not have a historic base-line to compare it with, this figure is small, and first-time voters were not par-ticularly supportive of the recall. Then I turned to voter registration. While registration levels were high for an odd year, the percentage of eligible voters who were registered at the time of the recall was the lowest it had been for a general election in more than a decade. Finally, I looked at how many people voted on Election Day. At 61 percent of eligible voters, turnout in the 2003 recall was just about average for a contemporary California governor's race. Overall, the recall fails to meet the intensity criterion of a critical election.

It seemed reasonable to predict that an action movie hero who commu-nicated through novel media channels might pull a sizable group of first-time voters into California's electorate. Such an expansion of the electorate can have a profound impact on the balance of political power. Anderson's (1979) exploration of the mechanism behind the Roosevelt-era realignment showed that the "new Democratic majority" was created more by the mobilization of new voting groups than by the conversion of regular participants. In October 2003, however, few new voters showed up at the polls. The *Los Angeles Times* exit poll, conducted at polling places, found that 4 percent of recall voters were first-time participants. The Edison Media Research/Mitofsky inter-national exit poll, which sampled absentee voters in addition to those at precincts, estimated this number at 3 percent. Because 29.5 percent of participants voted absentee in this election (Shelley 2003a), and because these are the voters most familiar with the voting process, taking their composition into account is an important consideration when answering this question. Consequently, 3 percent seems to be the best guess at the percentage of first-time voters. Unfortunately, I could not locate any previous California exit poll containing this question, which prevented me from putting the data in a historic context.

Looking at how these voters behaved suggests that, regardless of whether or not 3 to 4 percent is a significant figure, their participation made no big difference to the election outcome. First-time voters cast their ballots 57 to 43 percent in favor of the recall, while electoral veterans supported it by a 55-to 45-percent margin.[2] Half of these voters supported Schwarzenegger, just slightly above the 49 percent of experienced voters who backed him (*Los Angeles Times* 2003). Unlike the blue-collar voters that Franklin Roosevelt brought into the system (Andersen 1979) or the young males who flocked to support Jesse Ventura in Minnesota (Sifry 1998), first-time voters here displayed no extraordinary allegiance to the recall or to Schwarzenegger.

Turning to registration levels, the effect of the recall was small and con-sistent with past patterns. Because California's population steadily grows, the absolute number of registered voters has increased over time from nearly 1 million in 1912 to 10 million in 1972 to more than 15 million today. Fluctu-ations around this secular trend are usually the result of three factors. First, presidential contests drive registration higher than is typical during guber-natorial races. Second, registration tends to dip in the odd years following both types of contests. Third, registration is lower in the spring of election

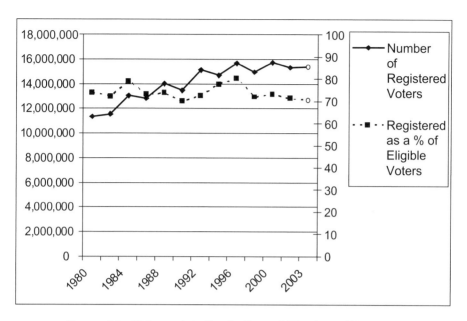

FIGURE 4.1   Voter registration in General Elections, 1980–2003.

SOURCE: Figures appear in Shelley (2003b).

years than it is in the fall, when general elections approach. Figure 4.1, which presents even year registration figures since 1980, illustrates the impact of this first factor and shows that recall registration was typical, and perhaps a bit low, for gubernatorial elections.

The solid line in Figure 4.1 tracks the absolute number of registrants across time. It rises as California's population grows, and is always higher in presidential election years than when the governor's office is up for grabs. The line flattens as it gets to the open circle marking the 2003 recall. About the same number of eligible voters registered for this election as had registered for the 2002 general election. The dotted line shows that the rate at which they registered actually declined. This line, showing the percentage of eligible voters who are signed up in time for any given election, dips slightly as it reaches the recall. At 70.46 percent, the percentage of eligible voters who were registered in September 2003 was lower than it had been during any general election since 1990. This figure was high for the fall of an odd numbered year, but by the spring of 2004, it returned to its usual low level at the beginning of a presidential campaign. Put in the context of registration for past elections, the recall looks like a gubernatorial contest that did not attract particularly much attention.

Many observers have pointed to Election Day turnout as evidence that the recall dramatically increased the size of the electorate. Indeed, with 61.2 percent of registered voters casting a ballot, turnout in October, 2003 surpassed the 50.6 percent level recorded in the 2002 governor's race.[3] However, a closer look at typical turnout rates over a longer time period again shows that this contest was a return to past patterns. Turnout for California gubernatorial and presidential contests since 1980 indicates that participation, whether measured as a percentage of registered voters or of eligible voters, has declined slightly over this period and is always higher in presidential years. This fact also highlights what an anomaly Davis' 2002 reelection was, posting what is by far the lowest turnout of any regularly scheduled election for at least 90 years (Shelley 2004). More typical are the governor's races in 1986, 1990, 1994, and 1998, all of which had turnout levels that were approximately 60 percent of registrants. Judging by these figures, Schwarzenegger's candidacy did not thrill and mobilize California voters any more than the campaigns of George Deukmejian, Pete Wilson, and even, in 1998, Davis.

THE RECALL AND DEVIATIONS FROM PAST BEHAVIOR

Even if the recall electorate was not any larger than recent history would lead one to expect, voters' behavior patterns could have diverged so sharply from the past in this election that it would merit the label "critical." A standard set of measures developed in the realignment literature can tell us whether the election passes this test. One measure—the correlation from election to election in the vote totals that one party captures across states, counties, or cities—can demonstrate a "differential change" in party fortunes.[4] When voters from different areas shift in opposite directions, the correlation between vote totals for a critical election and totals in the preceding contest will be weak. This was the primary type of realignment envisioned by Schattschneider (1960) and by Sundquist (1973). A critical election occurs when a new political cleavage emerges to swing some Republican voters into the Democratic camp, with the number of Democrats converting to Republican support being either larger or smaller and thus shifting the balance of political power. Pomper (1967) provided the quantitative methods to demonstrate such a shift and its stable aftermath by using correlation coefficients.

Another type of critical election, a second subspecies existing alongside contests that bring differential change, is conceptually and empirically distinct. Key's pioneering work devotes equal attention to elections that create new party divisions and to those in which one party "succeeded in drawing new support, in about the same degree, from all sorts of economic and social classes" (1955, 12). To illustrate a critical election marked by such a "surge," Key points to the 1896 presidential race. He shows that after the Panic of 1893, Democrats suffered in all types of Connecticut and New Hampshire cities, moving all towns to "a lower plateau of Democratic strength" (1955, 13). This parallel shift, however, will be invisible in an analysis that relies solely on correlations, because it does not cause the relative strengths of parties across cities or states to change. Clubb, Flanigan, and Zingale (1980, chap. 3) point this out. They resurrect Key's notion of the critical election that brings an across-the-board surge, and show how to measure it. By looking for changes in the level of electoral support as well as geographic correlations, the authors are able to detect both surges and differential changes and to assess their permanence.

Applying their approach[5] to California's recall allowed me to test for the presence of either variety of critical election. I looked at vote shares in counties and in assembly districts. Perhaps the contest tilted recent lines of political cleavage, pushing conservative, blue-collar Democrats in the Central Valley and Inland Empire across party lines, while affluent Republicans in urban and coastal areas recoiled at the thought of a celebrity governor and shifted their support. If so, the correlation between vote shares in the 2002 governor's race and in the recall will be low. Another possibility is that Democratic replacement candidate Cruz Bustamante fared well, and the recall did poorly, in the areas that have traditionally been Democratic strongholds, but that the Democratic advantage dropped across the board in 2003. If so, an intercept shift would be apparent in a regression that uses 2002 results to predict recall replacement vote shares. Of course, neither a weak correlation nor a significant intercept shift is proof that the election has brought permanent change and thus qualifies as critical. The durability of effects will be explored in the next section, but here I identify which subspecies of realigning event may possibly have occurred.

California's fifty-eight counties vary greatly in their size and demographic compositions, from urbanized Los Angeles with its 9.5 million diverse residents to Alpine and its 1,208 mostly white residents. This mixture of sizes creates some estimation issues. Still, the socioeconomic differences across counties makes them ideal units for indicating changes in not only the geographic but also the social bases for parties during potential realignments. Another advantage is that county borders have been stable in recent years, providing a way to gauge patterns in correlations over multiple elections. This is not true of California assembly districts, which were redrawn between the 2000 and 2002 elections. Their lack of continuity is made up for by the fact that all eighty districts have nearly equal numbers of residents, making comparisons of districts reliable indicators of state trends. Additionally, a bipartisan gerrymander in the last round of redistricting has made districts relatively homogenous in their party balances. Looking at aggregate trends in San Francisco's thirteenth assembly district, where Democrats hold a five-to-one registration advantage, or Orange County's seventy-first district, where Republicans have a two-to-one edge, provides a good look at possible shifts in the behavior of each party's members (Shelley 2004b).

Figure 4.2 uses both counties and assembly districts to explore the relationship between voting patterns in California's humdrum 2002 gubernatorial race and outcomes in the 2003 recall replacement contest. Arbitrarily, I chose to look at the fortunes of Democrats.[6] These charts plot the percentage of the vote won by Davis in 2002 in counties or assembly districts on the horizontal axis, while the vertical axis shows the share captured by Bustamante, the major Democrat in the race to replace Davis. In both counties and districts, past Democratic performance is an excellent predictor of what happened in 2003. Correlations between these figures are very high, yielding coefficients of 0.94 in counties and 0.96 in assembly districts. This indicates that the recall race[7] brought little differential change in the fortunes of Democrats. How high are these correlation coefficients? In their historic analyses of presidential and congressional elections, Clubb, Flanigan, and Zingale (1980, 55–61) found correlations of between 0.2 and 0.7 in critical elections and took

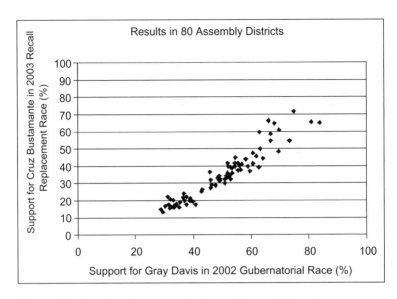

FIGURE 4.2   Recall voting shifts, by Assembly districts and by counties.

SOURCE: Vote shares appear in Shelley (2002c, 2003a).

coefficients of 0.9 or larger as evidence that an election maintained the status quo partisan divide. Using counties to provide a historic California comparison case shows that the correlation between Davis' vote shares in 1998 and in 2002 was 0.96, only two ticks higher than the county correlation in the recall. It is clear that the recall did not reshuffle Democratic and Republican voters across counties or assembly districts.

This does not mean, though, that it could not have been a critical contest. There may have been an across-the-board shift away from Democratic candidates and, in fact, that appears to be the case. All of the districts and counties in Figure 4.2 fall below a 45 degree diagonal, indicating that Bustamante fared worse in 2003 than Davis had in 2002 everywhere. The clearest way to measure this consistent Republican surge is by examining the intercept term from a regression of 2003 vote shares on 2002 figures. The term shows where regression lines drawn onto Figure 4.2. would have intersected the vertical axis, revealing the uniform shift in support levels.

Table 4.1 presents the results of these regressions that use the percentage of the vote captured by Davis to predict Bustamante's percentages, both in assembly districts and in counties. An ordinary least squares regression using data from the eighty assembly districts yields a strongly significant intercept term of −18.53 percentage points, with a confidence interval of about 4 percentage points in either direction. A coefficient of about 1 percentage point for Davis' vote share again indicates a tight correlation in Democratic strength across districts, meaning that there was little differential change. Davis' fortunes explain 91 percent of the variation in Bustamante's performance.

TABLE 4.1   Models predicting Bustamante's vote share in the recall replacement race.

	ASSEMBLY DISTRICT COEFFICIENT ESTIMATE (CONFIDENCE INTERVAL)	COUNTY COEFFICIENT ESTIMATE (CONFIDENCE INTERVAL)
Vote share won by Davis in November 2002	1.06 (0.99, 1.14)	1.07 (0.97, 1.18)
Intercept	−18.53 (−22.34, −14.72)	−18.93 (−23.91, −13.94)
Adjusted r-square	0.91	0.88

Note: The dependent variable in both models is the percentage of the vote won by Bustamante in the recall replacement race. N = 80 in the assembly district model, N = 58 in the county model. Confidence intervals are at the 95 percent confidence level.

In a regression on county data that is weighted by the number of votes cast in each county to account for the variance in errors, the intercept is −18.93 percent of the vote, give or take about 4 percentage points. Again, Davis' support level is a strong and nearly certain predictor of the share of the vote that Bustamante won in each county. No matter how the state is divided, there is no evidence of a differential change in the basis of each party's support; however, there is clear proof that the 2003 recall replacement race brought a Republican surge across California. Of course, this is not the only time that such a surge has occurred. A weighted least squares regression that uses Davis' 1998 vote share to predict his county totals in 2002 shows a Democratic decline of about 9 percentage points. Still, the Republican's recall surge was twice that size. Before labeling it a critical election, though, I had to determine whether the change that the recall brought has persisted or whether it was a one-year deviation from past patterns.

A RETURN TO POLITICS AS USUAL IN CALIFORNIA

A consensus in the realignment literature holds that a critical election must bring a change that is "both sharp and durable" (Key 1955, 11), and that consequently leads to a "stable phase in the alignment cycle" (Burnham 1970, 5). If the next election brings a reversion to the old patterns of allegiance, levels of support, and rules of the political game, then only a "deviating" election has occurred (Campbell et al. 1960, 532–33). There are obvious ways to test for durability, given sufficient historic perspective. For example, Key tracks patterns in the five presidential elections following the 1896 and 1928 contests to ensure that their effects persisted. Unfortunately, this method cannot be used to analyze an election held only one year ago. Clubb, Flanigan, and Zingale (1980) examine the durability of critical elections that bring differential change by making sure that their state-to-state patterns correlate closely with those in the next election. Because the recall did not bring any differential change, this method is ruled out. In the case of a surge election, the lack of a uniform decline in the next contest would provide evidence that it was permanent. While I cannot follow the exact methods of previous scholars here, I can use the logic behind their approaches and their criterion of permanence to show that the 2003 recall was a short-term deviation bringing effects that have faded quickly.

To do so before 2004's general election has taken place, I must shift my focus to the 2002 and 2004 primaries and the assembly districts in which they were fought. Before exploring voting patterns, I look at statewide party registration and party turnout figures. One way in which a critical election can have a lasting impact is if voters who cross party lines are so certain of their conversion that they switch their party registration. Alternatively, a larger than normal percentage of new registrants will choose to associate themselves with the surging party. Either form of behavior would lead to a permanent shift in the proportion of voters registered with each party. The recall did bring a trend in registration toward the Republican Party, but it does not appear to be permanent.

Party registration figures produced by the secretary of state from February 2002 through the recall to February 2004 reveals a subtle shift in the electorate's composition: Republicans rise and decline, Democrats fall, and those who do not affiliate with a major party make up a steadily increasing portion of potential voters. Shelley (2002b, 2003b, 2004b) reports that the Republican Party grew by approximately 75,000 voters by the deadline to register for the recall, but it then lost all but 11,000 of these new registrants by the eve of the 2004 primary. The Democratic Party fared even worse, losing 155,000 voters by 2003 and another 199,000 by 2004. Their losses, however, went to minor parties and independent voters, or were part of the typical drop-off in registration levels from one presidential election to the next. Democrats do not appear to have lost many voters to their rival party. In the spring of 2004, Republicans statewide do not look much better off than they did in the spring of 2002.

Although registration figures do not change dramatically, another possible explanation of the Republican surge at the polls in 2003 is differential mobilization. Perhaps Republican voters turned out at a higher rate than normal, allowing them to compose a larger proportion of the recall electorate. If this drove voting patterns during the recall, for 2003 to be considered a critical election, the Republican mobilization advantage must continue in 2004. Figure 4.3 compares a series of exit polls to examine the composition of the electorate during recent contests. It shows a significant boost in Republican turnout during the recall. Democrats held only a 1 percentage point edge on October 7, 2003, much smaller than the 6 to 12 percent advantage they had held in previous elections.

However, a glance at the 2004 primary shows that this pro-Republican shift has more than faded away. This March's contest saw the Democrats gain their biggest recent lead in the composition of Election Day voters, a 52 percent to 34 percent edge. Certainly, the Democratic primary featured more candidates, which may have drawn more Democrats than usual, but John Kerry's nomination victory was all but assured by the time Californians went to the polls. Although the 2004 general election rendered a more definite verdict, the lesson of this year's primary is that the recall's impact on the partisan composition of the electorate has already disappeared.

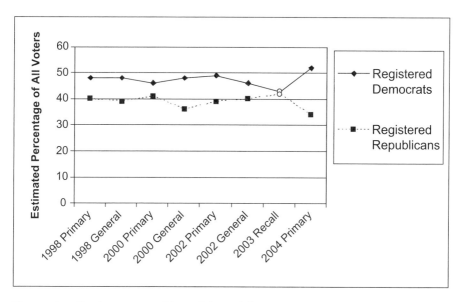

FIGURE 4.3   Partisan composition of the California Electorate (exit polls estimates).

SOURCE: Each partisan breakdown is taken from the appropriate report issued describing the *Los Angeles Times* exit poll and is archived at http://www.latimes.com/news/local/timespoll/state/.

Similarly, the pattern in assembly primary contests in March 2004 demonstrated the fleeting nature of the Republican surge. In short, the Republican surge in assembly districts in 2003 was outweighed by a slightly larger Democrat surge in 2004, leaving Democratic nominees a bit better positioned today than they were in 2002. Figure 4.4 displays this continuity. On the horizontal axis, it plots the share of the major party primary vote won by all Democratic candidates combined in each district. The vertical axis plots this vote share in the 2004 primaries. The correlation between the two sets of figures shows that Democratic strength in assembly districts today is about what it was two years ago. Regression results can demonstrate that the recall did bring a Republican surge in these districts, but that it was temporary.

First, notice that there are some outlying cases in Figure 4.4, that is, districts in which one of the major parties did not enter a candidate or put up only token opposition in one or both years. Because voters in these areas do not have enough options available to demonstrate the district's true level of support for one of the parties, I eliminated them from my analysis.[8] Removing districts in which one of the parties attracted more than 95 percent of the vote in either of the elections left me with sixty-four of the eighty assembly districts. The 0.94 coefficient of correlation between 2002 Democratic vote shares and Bustamante's level of support in 2003 demonstrates, yet again, that the recall did not bring a differential shift in the basis of Democratic power. The correlation between 2002 Democratic support and opposition to the recall itself was also tight (0.91). Regressing Bustamante's vote share on the 2002 primary

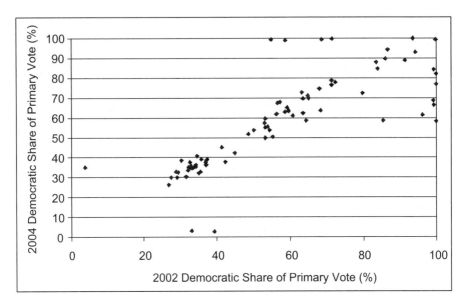

FIGURE 4.4   Vote shares in Assembly Primaries (before and after the recall).

SOURCE: Vote shares appear in Shelley (2002a, 2004a).

figures yields a statistically significant intercept of approximately 6 percentage points in the Republican Party's favor. This represents the magnitude of the Republican surge from the 2002 primary to the recall.

A similar analysis reveals a larger Democratic surge from the recall election to the 2004 primary. Again, a 0.96 correlation between vote shares in these two contests demonstrates that Democrats did well in 2004 in exactly the places where they had weathered the recall storm best. Regressing the combined vote shares of all of their primary candidates in each district on support for Bustamante confirms this close link and shows that Democrats recovered from their losses by surging ahead approximately 14 percentage points. The combined effects of these countervailing surges can be seen in Figure 4.4. Not much has changed in California politics, either in geographic patterns of Democratic strength or in the overall level of party support. Between 2002 and 2004, the average Democratic share of the major party primary vote increased by approximately 2 percentage points in the sixty-four districts analyzed here and by about half a point when all eighty districts are counted.

There are limits to using primary election results to gauge the impact of an event on the electorate as a whole. Perhaps the recall changed California politics only by converting swing voters in the middle of the ideological spectrum. Because few of these centrists participate in California's currently closed primaries, their shifts will not be picked up in an analysis of March voting patterns. The exit poll data, however in this section suggest that it was in fact differential mobilization that drove the vote swing during the recall. The persistence of this sort of effect can be gauged by looking at primaries. In March

2004, the Democratic base did not appear to be demoralized nor was the Republican base particularly energized. In fact, Democrats turned out in greater numbers than usual and their candidates did a bit better in 2004 than in 2002. For Republican and Democratic candidates fighting for votes in assembly primaries, it was as if the recall never happened.

CONCLUSIONS

According to Walter Dean Burnham, critical elections are "intimately associated with and followed by transformations in large clusters of policies" (Burnham 1970, 9). Although the empirical record of spotting postrealignment shifts in national policy is weak,[9] at least most works in the literature note that a critical election *should* be followed by policy change. Judged by this criterion, the 2003 recall again appears to fail. Replacing Davis with Schwarzenegger meant substituting one moderate pragmatist for another. Schwarzenegger, who has been prominently advised by former Governor Wilson, follows in the fiscally conservative, socially liberal tradition of Republican Wilson and his predecessor Deukmejian. Davis himself won the office by emulating their positioning, declaring himself to be "death on crime" and a centrist.[10]

All players have had their policy goals tempered by economic realities and an uncooperative legislature. When California's budget deficit grew in 2002 and 2003, Davis spent his summers negotiating with Democratic legislative leaders who objected to making deep service cuts and Republican leaders (empowered by the requirement of a two-thirds vote of each house to pass a budget) who opposed tax increases. To solve the budget standoff in time to fight the recall effort, Davis agreed to a deal that authorized $10.7 billion in deficit-reducing bonds. Faced with the same hard choices and intractable legislature when he replaced Davis, Schwarzenegger chose a similar stopgap strategy by restructuring Davis' debt and borrowing an additional $5 billion to cover the deficit in his first budget.[11] He was unable to convince Democrats to agree to a limit on state spending, and his feints toward a tax increase were strongly rebuffed by Republican legislators. Although he has negotiated moderate spending cuts in education and local government aid, Schwarzenegger has left the kindergarten through twelfth-grade education and children's health care programs that Davis championed largely untouched.[12] Perhaps because of the structure of government in California, or perhaps because Schwarzenegger's policy goals are not that different from those of the moderates who preceded him in the governor's office, the political switch brought by the recall has so far produced no radical policy changes.

This should not be surprising, given the lack of evidence that an electoral realignment has occurred. It may be too soon to tell, because critical elections are easier to observe with historic perspective. California's 2003 recall, however, appears to be a rare case in which the limited effects of a political surge fade quickly enough to categorize it as a temporary deviation from the path of normal politics. It did not turn out very many new voters or mobilize a larger-than-average electorate. It also did not change the traditional geographic bases of Democratic and Republican power. The recall did bring a Republican surge, but evidence of registration levels, party mobilization, and vote shares in the March, 2004 primary shows that this surge was not durable. For all of its flaws, the realignment literature still provides useful guidelines for evaluating political events. Applying these guidelines makes it clear that California's 2003 recall was not a critical election.

BIBLIOGRAPHY

Andersen, Kristi. *The Creation of a Democratic Majority, 1928–1936*. Chicago: University of Chicago Press, 1979.

Brady, David W. *Critical Elections and Congressional Policy Making*. Stanford: Stanford University Press, 1988.

Burnham, Walter Dean. *Critical Elections and the Mainsprings of American Politics*. New York: W.W. Norton and Company, 1970.

Campbell, Angus, Philip E. Converse, Warren E. Miller, and Donald E. Stokes. *The American Voter*. New York: John Wiley and Sons, 1960.

Chubb, Jerome M. William H. Flanigan, and Nancy H. Zingale. *Partisan Realignment: Voters, Parties, and Government in American History*. Beverly Hills, CA: Sage Publications, 1980.

Eu, March Fong. California Ballot Pamphlet, Special Statewide Election, November 2, 1993. Sacramento: California Secretary of State, 1993.

———. California Ballot Pamphlet, Special Statewide Election, November 6, 1979. Sacramento: California Secretary of State, 1979.

Key, V.O. Jr. "A Theory of Critical Elections." *Journal of Politics* 17 (1955): 3–18.

Kousser, J. Morgan. "Key Changes." *Reviews in American History* 9 (1981): 23–28.

Lichtman, Allan J. "Critical Election Theory and the Reality of American Presidential Politics, 1916–40." *American Historical Review* 81 (1976): 317–51.

Los Angeles Times. Los Angeles Times Poll #2003-490: California Recall Election Exit Poll. Los Angeles: *Los Angeles Times*, 2003.

Mayhew, David R. *Electoral Realignments: A Critique of an American Genre*. New Haven, CT: Yale University Press, 2002.

McCormick, Richard L. *The Party Period and Public Policy*. New York: Oxford University Press, 1986.

Murphy, George. *Proposed Amendment to Constitution, Initiative Constitutional Amendment, Together With Arguments*. Sacramento: California Secretary of State, 1973.

Pomper, Gerald M. "Classification of Presidential Elections." *Journal of Politics* 21 (1967): 535–56.

Schattschneider, E.E. *The Semi-sovereign People: A Realist's View of Democracy in America*. New York: Holt, Rinehart and Winston, 1960.

Shafer, Byron E., ed. *The End of Realignment? Interpreting American Electoral Eras*. Madison: University of Wisconsin Press, 1991.

Shelly, Kevin. *Statement of Vote, 2004 Presidential Primary Election*. California Secretary of the State, 2004a. http://www.ss.ca.gov/elections/sov/2004_primary/contents.htm (accessed April 2004).

———. *February 17, 2004 Report of Registration*. California Secretary of the State, 2004b. http://www.ss.ca.gov/elections/ror_0217 2004.htm (accessed April 2004).

———. *Supplement to the Statement of Vote, 2003 Statewide Special Election*. California Secretary of the State, 2003a. http://www. ss.ca. gov/elections/sov/2003_special/contents. htm (accessed April 2004).

———. *September 22, 2003 Report of Registration*. California Secretary of the State, 2003b. http://www.ss.ca.gov/elections/ror_0922 03.htm (accessed April 2004).

———. *Statement of Vote, 2002 Primary Election*. California Secretary of the State, 2002a. http://www.ss.ca.gov/elections/sov/2002 _primary/contents.htm (accessed April 2004).

———. *February 19, 2002 Report of Registration*. California Secretary of the State, 2002b. http://www.ss.ca.gov/elections/ror_0219 02.htm (accessed April 2004).

———. *Statement of Vote, 2002 General Election*. California Secretary of the State, 2002c. http://www.ss.ca.gov/elections/sov/2002_ general/contents.htm (accessed April 2004).

Sifry, Micah. "Body Slam: Jesse Ventura Turned Out Turned-off Voters on Election Day, and Upended the Nation's Political Elite." Salon.com, November 6, 1998, http:// www. salon.com/.

Sundquist[MODI]. 1973.

NOTES

1. The first quote is taken from Anne E. Kornblut, "Schwarzenegger is in , Davis Out in California on Landslide Vote, a Historic Change," *The Boston Globe*, A-1, October 8, 2003. Luntz is quoted in Adam Nagourney, "California Insurrection Puts Other Politicians on Notice," *The New York Times*, A-1, October 8, 2003. Novak's statement is taken from his editorial in *The Chicago Sun Times*, 37, October 9, 2003.

2. These figures are drawn from the Los Angeles Times exit poll. Because first-time voters are such a small group, the Edison-Mitofsky poll reported their behavior along with those who "rarely" vote. Combined, these voters supported the recall by a 65 percent to 35 percent margin, compared with the 54 percent to 46 percent margin among voters who claimed to "always" or "usually" vote.

3. Turnout in the recall also dwarfed the turnout rate in California's three previous statewide special elections, which averaged 40.5 percent. At first glance, this seems like spectacular proof that the recall really was "special," mobilizing a larger electorate than in comparable contests. However, the special elections held in 1973, 1979, and 1993 were all fought over ballot initiatives (Eu 1979; Eu 1993; Murphy 1973). Because no statewide candidates appeared on any of these ballots, they are not comparable to the recall with its one movie star, two adult entertainment stars, and 132 other candidates.

4. Burnham (1970, chap. 2) employs a "discontinuity coefficient" for a similar purpose.

5. While Clubb, Flanigan, and Zingale (1980) use an analysis of variance technique to explore both correlations and shifts in levels, the parallel and more familiar approach of regression analysis is sufficient to demonstrate these changes through the estimated intercept and the model's goodness of fit.

6. Clubb, Flanigan, and Zingale (1980), analyzing elections over a time period in which many third parties ran strong candidates, note the importance of tracking both Democratic and Republican fortunes. In analyses not presented here, I confirm that my findings do not change when I look at Republican vote totals. The reason appears to be that the minor parties were not a major factor

in either 2002 or 2003, and that the leading minor party candidate, the Green Party's Peter Camejo, ran in both races and thus drew similar patterns of support.

7. I correlate results from 2002 with the governor's replacement race, rather than the "yes or no" recall question, because these are the two most similar sorts of contests. However, the correlations between Davis' 2002 vote share and opposition to the recall (and thus support for Davis) were similarly high: 0.91 in counties and 0.92 in assembly districts. In all of the analyses presented here, parallel analyses using vote shares on the recall questions itself revealed the same substantive story.

8. Another set of factors that could make inferences across districts and years misleading is differences in the number of candidates running in each party's primary and the presence of incumbents. To hold these constant, I estimated all of the regression models discussed here with variables representing the number of candidates and the presence of incumbents in each party's primary in each appropriate year added to the specification. Because none of the substantive findings change, I report the more straightforward models.

9. See Chapter 6 of Mayhew (2002), which characterizes the search for policy change as "the third rail of the realignment genre. It has been unwise to touch it" (104).

10. See for instance Harriet Chang, "Davis, Lundgren Talk Equally Tough on Crime," *The San Francisco Chronicle*, A-1, October 5, 1998; and Martin Kasindorf, "Governor's Race Giving California GOP Unwanted Surprise," *USA Today*, 10-A, October 27, 1998.

11. For an analysis of both bonds, see the California Legislative Analyst's Office, "Proposition 57: The Economic Recovery Bond Act," December 2003.

12. For Schwarzenegger's tax policy statements, see Robert Salladay and Peter Nicholas, "Tax Opposition May Be 'Wishful,' Gov. Says," *The Los Angeles Times*, March 31, 2004. For examples of restorations of proposed spending cuts, see California Legislative Analyst's Office, "Overview of the 2004-2005 May Revision," May 17, 2004.

5

VIEWING THE RECALL FROM ABOVE AND BELOW

JACK CITRIN

UNIVERSITY OF CALIFORNIA, BERKELEY

JONATHAN COHEN

ABC NEWS POLLING UNIT

The recall is the least raced of the three horses pulling the troika of direct democracy, but it ran in a high-stakes contest in 2003. Like the initiative and referendum, the recall was introduced a century ago for the purpose of making government more responsive to the people by curbing the power of wealthy interests. Yet many contemporary critics argue that the promise is an illusion and that more direct democracy actually diminishes policymaking in the broader public interest. For Peter Schrag, a seasoned and respected observer of California politics, the wave of initiatives ushered in by Proposition 13 in 1978 has turned the state into "Paradise Lost," its government dominated by well-organized economic interests and unable to cope with the needs of a modern economy and changing population.[1]

During the 2003 recall campaign, most political scientists, pundits ranging from the conservative George Will of the *Washington Post* to the liberal Robert Scheer of the *Los Angeles Times,* and editorialists in major newspapers echoed the charge that direct democracy was the cause of, rather than a solution for, California's woes, portraying the recall as a Trojan horse aimed at overturning the legitimate result of a recent election. Writing after the voters' 2003 verdict, Shaun Bowler and Bruce Cain warned that if revenge and opportunism made use of the recall (as well as the initiative) a regular occurrence in California, fear would sap elected representatives of "their last ounce of political courage."[2]

The view from below, however, is quite different. Voters, unlike the experts, value the initiative process and want to retain it. The public also welcomes the ability to recall officials and, in 2003, swept aside appeals to vote against the recall of Governor Gray Davis on the nonpartisan ground that the recall process was unfair and inappropriate, a misuse of democracy. The purpose of this chapter is to document and explain the gap between expert and mass opinion. The chapter begins with a summary of the usual arguments for and against direct democracy and considers how these apply to specifically the recall. Next, it provides a content analysis of the editorial coverage of the 2003 California recall election in leading state and national newspapers. This account shows overwhelming opposition to the election as illegitimate, wasteful, and damaging. The next section of the paper describes public opinion and indicates that, despite reservations about how the process works, there is broad and persistent support for direct democracy. This attitude cuts across party lines and is rooted in a general mistrust of state government. In this context, arguments about the defects of the recall process made no impact on voters in 2003. With the election framed as an opportunity to replace an unpopular governor with a charismatic alternative rather than a referendum on the process per se, voters were not confused. They had their chance and took it. The chapter concludes by considering whether a potential consensus exists for reforms that would honor the public's demand for voice yet alter the rules governing the recall and initiative in ways that reduce the political constraints on elected officials.

DEBATING DIRECT DEMOCRACY

The framers of the U.S. Constitution considered and then rejected the idea of direct democracy, opting instead for a system of representation designed to protect the people from themselves. Direct democracy, like the direct election of the president, threatened the nation with a tyranny of the majority by exposing it to the power of an uninformed, gullible public who could be easily swayed by skilled demagogues. Deliberation and compromise in the legislature would simultaneously discipline majority sentiment and limit the selfishness inherent in "faction."

The Populist and Progressive reformers introduced direct democracy to state government in the late nineteenth and early twentieth centuries, in part, because they believed Madison's ideal of representation had failed. Their stated target was the incestuous marriage between party machines and well-financed selfish interests, an alliance that bred corruption while thwarting the will of most honest citizens. To the advocates of change, the initiative would translate majority opinion into public policy and the recall would be a catalyst to clean government by rooting out officials guilty of malfeasance.

Contemporary criticisms of direct democracy have concentrated on the initiative process in California. A dominant complaint is that most initiatives are not "grassroots" affairs, organized from below and promoted by committed volunteers. Rather, some claim the initiative process has become a device used by interest groups and policy entrepreneurs to advance their pet projects.[3] Professional political consultants dominate the process of preparing, qualifying, and campaigning for initiatives and have a vested interest in proposing them.[4] Conventional wisdom holds that $1 million paid to professional signature-gatherers guarantees qualification of an initiative for the ballot, regardless of its content.[5] Campaigns are increasingly expensive, underscoring the power of individuals and groups with deep pockets. What is billed as a device for popular control thus is converted into a tactic for organized interests to obtain benefits without having to bargain or compromise. And because the electorate in statewide elections is disproportionately white, elderly, and wealthy, some critics maintain that initiatives are a means, deliberate or inadvertent, of diminished responsiveness to the interests and rights of the poor and ethnic minorities.[6]

A second major complaint about California's direct democracy is that the electorate is asked to decide the complex policy questions that direct legislation is designed to address. Ballot propositions often are lengthy, technical, and complex. The details of these measures, how they would be implemented, and their intended and unintended consequences are difficult to identify and assess. When rival measures on the same general subject appear on the same ballot, additional confusion often arises. Yet decades of public opinion research shows that the average voter lacks basic political knowledge and often is uninformed about major public issues. When asked to make choices in domains where firm prior attitudes are lacking, average voters are heavily influenced by "top-of-the-head" responses to slogans and symbols rather than by careful analysis of issue relevant information.[7] In the case of initiatives, a large segment of uninformed voters decide late in the campaign when subjected to a flood of televised advertisements.[8] Accordingly, they respond to specific ballot measures on the basis of emotional reactions to horrific recent crimes, generalized sympathy for ethnic minorities, or feelings about the sponsors and opponents of the measures. The extent to which such choices are rational, in the sense of conforming to the voter's interests or underlying values, is controversial.[9] What is generally agreed is that many voters come to the polls with limited awareness and information about important policies that, once adopted, are difficult to modify or repeal in the future.

A third criticism of direct democracy in California is that it undermines the will and effectiveness of legislators. With the threat of initiatives (or recalls) hovering above them, elected representatives avoid necessary, if difficult, decisions. The disincentives for undertaking unpopular actions increase, and legislators are tempted to abdicate responsibility or, alternatively, to turn to the initiative process to promote pet policies or gain name recognition. This tactic obviously has greater appeal for the minority political party in the legislature, further highlighting the ways in which direct democracy can undermine electoral majorities.

Defenders of direct democracy downplay the significance of these arguments. While acknowledging the potent role of money, consultants, and interest groups in the process, these defenders say that such activities are no different in elections for candidates.[10] Grassroots initiatives remain possible, and if moneyed actors enlist in the cause, the ability of ordinary citizens to define the policy agenda only is enhanced. Moreover, by comparison with broad-based citizen groups, corporate interests are better able to ward off initiatives that regulate them than to succeed in passing their own proposals.[11] Voters use rules of thumb like party affiliation and approval or disapproval of sponsoring groups to help them make appropriate choices on complex matters such as insurance reform,[12] so worries about the political competence of ordinary citizens are overstated. Finally, the threat to minority rights also has been overstated. A recent study shows that, overall, the preferences of minority groups are just as likely as those of whites to win out on initiatives.[13]

The jury may still be out on the competence of voters to make reasoned decisions on initiatives, but the problem clearly is less acute in recall elections.

The recall is an up or down vote on the fate of a sitting politician. In the case of the 2003 California election, the target was a sitting governor with a long career in state politics, not an obscure, relatively unfamiliar official. Assessing the specific allegations against the recall's target may require more political knowledge than many voters possess, but this intellectual task requires about the same amount of effort required to choose among candidates in a normal election. Some critics of the 2003 California recall argued that the enormous number of nuisance candidates in the replacement election would confuse voters; however, this did not seem to occur and should not, in any case, have complicated voters' ability to make a reasoned judgment about the recall itself.

THE RECALL DAMNED FROM ABOVE

One way to envisage the recall is as a motion of no confidence on an incumbent leader. Yet this familiar feature of parliamentary government is a foreign tumor in the American system of fixed elections, making it outside the spirit of the constitution to resort to the process simply because a leader is unpopular or incompetent. (If that were the case, a political cynic might say, there would be daily recall elections.) The right analogy for a recall is impeachment, something generally used in instances of serious malfeasance, as the phrase "high crimes and misdemeanors" implies. California requires no demonstration of any kind of malfeasance on the part of the official to be recalled. Simply obtaining the required signatures—numbering 12 percent of the vote for the office in the last election, the lowest threshold of any state—is sufficient.[14]

As Bowler and Cain state, the petition recalling Governor Davis was essentially political in character.[15] He was accused of fiscal mismanagement for failing to adopt a budgetary approach that cuts taxes and spending and for failing "to deal with the state's general problems."[16] Recall opponents thus portrayed the effort as a postelection coup aimed at reversing the results of Davis' reelection. Those unhappy with his policies had their chance to oust him and failed. The democratic thing to do was to fight on in the legislature and wait for the next gubernatorial election. Searching for malfeasance, recall supporters condemned Davis for hiding the facts about California's fiscal deficit until after his election and for interfering in the Republican primary to assure the nomination of someone easier to beat. It is hard, however, for a detached observer to consider these hardball campaign tactics as warranting what amounts to the political death penalty.

According to political scientist John Ellwood, columnist Robert Scheer, and journalism professor Susan Rasky, the gubernatorial recall was populism run amok.[17] Its success would not solve the state's budget crisis but would encourage costly sequels. George Will reminded readers that the recall was made possible by a well-heeled contender for the office, Darrell Issa, and concluded that it was a "conservative travesty."[18] A *Washington Post* editorial printed just before the election termed the recall "appalling" and called on Californians to excise the provision from the state constitution and return to representative government.

The undemocratic character of the recall was a prominent theme in elite commentary. Another criticism was the preoccupation of both voters and mass media with just one of the candidates seeking to replace Governor Davis should the recall succeed: movie star Arnold Schwarzenegger. One review of media coverage indicated that more than three-quarters of all stories about the recall in the *New York Times, Los Angeles Times, San Francisco Chronicle,* and *San Jose Mercury News* reported on Schwarzenegger's candidacy.[19] A common accusation was that the actor's celebrity status created a political "circus" diverting attention from "the issues" and his lack of experience in government. For the *Washington Post,* "the colorless technocrat Gray Davis" was preferable to "a swaggering political neophyte." The *Los Angeles Times* moaned that the recall, with an actor as frontrunner and a bizarre group of 135 candidates on the replacement ballot, would make California a global "laughing stock."[20]

We undertook a content analysis of all opinion-editorial columns and editorials about the gubernatorial recall published in the following California and national newspapers between the day after the recall qualified for the ballot (July 24, 2003) and two days after the election (October 9, 2003): *Contra Costa Times, Los Angeles Times, Oakland Tribune, Sacramento Bee, San Diego Union-Tribune, San Francisco Chronicle, San Jose Mercury News, New York Times,* and *Washington Post.* Each article was coded by one of the authors and a research assistant as being either negative, positive, or neutral about the recall itself, with editorial recommendations about how to vote being classified as either positive or negative. (Because the concern here is with readers' exposure to these messages, if a syndicated column appeared in more than one newspaper each appearance was counted as an independent communication. In addition, we should emphasize that this is not a comprehensive set of opinion pieces. We did not include coverage from other California newspapers, for example, or coverage in the *Wall Street Journal,* an omission that probably weights the overall results in an antirecall direction. Still, the content analysis does subsume the California newspapers with the largest circulation in the main population centers of the state.)

The results are reported in Figure 5.1 and reveal the predominance of negative opinions. Of the ninety-one coded stories, fifty-nine were negative and only eleven positive. The *Los Angeles Times* published eighteen negative columns and editorials and only two positive ones; the comparable score for the *San Francisco Chronicle* was eight to zero. Only the *San Diego-Union Tribune,* known for its conservative editorial slant, has balanced coverage, and even here the count was eight negative, four positive, and eight neutral stories. The collective judgment of the editorial pages was unmistakable: No on the recall process and no on recalling Davis.

THE MORE POSITIVE VIEW FROM BELOW

The people of California, unlike the newspapers, generally favored the recall process and ultimately voted to oust Davis. For many years, California voters have supported the initiative process, and in 2003 there was significant support for the use of the recall to remove state officeholders deemed guilty of "mismanagement." Between 1979 and 2004, a series of field polls asked

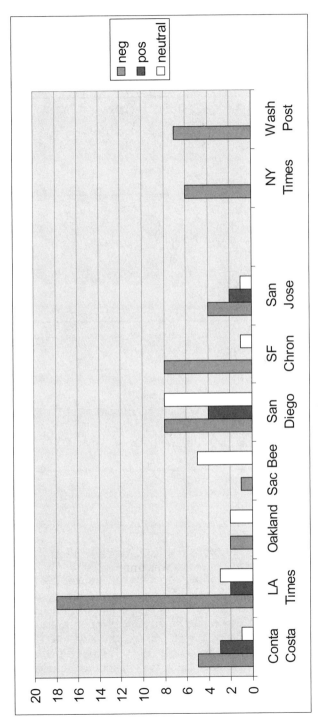

FIGURE 5.1 Editorial and op-ed characterization of the recall process.

Note: Ninety-one editorials and op-eds in major dailies from July 24, 2003, through October 9, 2003. Pieces are coded as either negative, positive, or neutral about the recall itself, with editorial recommendations about how to vote being classified as either positive or negative. Kimberly Curry coded these data.

TABLE 5.1   California opinion about direct democracy.

"Do you think that statewide ballot proposition elections are a good thing for California, a bad thing, or don't you think they make much difference?"*

	1979	1982	1985	1989	1990	1997	1999	2004
A good thing for California	83%	80%	79%	75%	66%	74%	62%	68%
No difference	11	9	10	12	23	17	25	17
A bad thing	4	6	5	6	8	7	8	9
No opinion	2	5	6	7	3	2	5	6

SPECIFIC REASONS FOR LIKING INITIATIVES**	1989	1997
Gives people a voice, a chance to express their opinions	50%	44%
Allows citizen groups to put things on the ballot	8	11
Voters are able to decide on things that legislators are either unable or unwilling to address	8	7
Takes power out of the hands of the few	7	11
Makes voters more aware of specific public issues	7	6

SPECIFIC REASONS FOR DISLIKING INITIATIVES		
They are too complicated, confusing, misleading	12	7
Voters aren't knowledgeable enough, don't have all the information to make a proper judgment	9	11
There are too many of them on the ballot	8	7
There are too many special interest group initiatives	7	5
Laws are not enforced after they pass/too easily overturned	6	14
They are poorly thought out, not good law, or unconstitutional	–	10
Ads used in campaigns are misleading, distorted/not restricted on funding	–	5

Notes: *Columns may not total to 100 percent because of rounding error.

**Respondents were allowed to state up to three likes or dislikes as answers to an open-ended question. Figures are based on all three mentions. Any items mentioned by less than 5 percent of respondents are excluded.

Source: Field Research Corporation, Field Polls, 1979–2004. All samples are representative cross-sections of California registered voters.

Californians whether statewide ballot propositions were good or bad for the state.[21] The results are reported in Table 5.1.

In 1979, soon after the passage of the notorious Proposition 13, 83 percent of registered voters in the state said having direct legislation was a good thing. By 1990, this proportion had dipped to 66 percent, but it rose to 70 percent in 1997 before declining again to 64 percent in 1999. Today, 68 percent think of Californians think that statewide ballot measures benefit the state. Throughout this period, the proportion of Californians regarding direct legislation as a "bad thing" varied less, ranging from 4 percent in 1979 to 9 percent today. The main shift in opinion, then, is that more people are saying that initiatives don't make much of a difference.

The desire for voice is the main reason for public support for direct legislation. In 1989 and 1997, field polls asked respondents what they liked about ballot propositions: In both years, the most frequently mentioned reason (50% in 1989 and 40% in 1997) was that direct legislation gave people a chance to express their opinion about policy. The most frequently mentioned dislike reported in 1989 (12%) was that the propositions were too complicated and confusing (compared with 6% in 1997). The highest single reported dislike (13%) in 1997 was that initiatives were not enforced after they passed.

Californians are not naïve about the initiative process. For example, a 1997 field poll showed, by a large margin of 62 to 17 percent, that the public felt that the type of issues that appear on proposition elections generally reflect the concerns of "organized interest groups" rather than those of "the average voter." A September 2004 report summarizing a current field poll showed that today nearly half of the state's registered voters think that statewide ballot proposition elections come about because they are promoted by organized special interests; only one-third think that these elections usually reflect what most ordinary people want. Moreover, the percentage of registered voters saying that organized special interests most often win increased by 5 points between 1999 and 2004, while the percentage saying that the interests of the people generally prevailed decreased 9 percentage points over the same time period.

Despite concern about the role of special interests, Californians retain a strong belief in the value of direct legislation. In 1982, 1999, and 2004, field polls asked a variety of questions regarding the relative abilities of citizens and elected representatives to make good public policy. Table 5.2 summarizes these attitudes over the past two decades. A majority of California's voters now think that the public is more likely to consider the broad public interest in making decisions (56% to 35%), more likely to do what is right on important issues (63% to 22%), and better suited to decide on large government programs and projects (65% to 24%). It is striking that, despite the stream of books decrying the role of the influence process, the percentage of voters more confident in the judgment of the public as opposed to elected representatives actually increased substantially over the past five years.

There do remain issues for which voters recognize the superior capacity of elected officials—that is, highly technical or legal policies or circumstances that require a thorough review of each particular aspect of a proposed law—but, even here, Table 5.2 shows that the percentage trusting the voting public is higher today than in 1999. Specifically, when asked whether the voting public or elected representatives were more likely to enact "coherent and well thought-out policies," the 19 point margin in favor of elected officials dwindled to just 3 percent (43% to 40%) in 2004.

The concern about the lack of responsiveness of elected representatives explains the pervasive belief in the value of the initiative process, in spite of reservations about the quality of knowledge among ordinary voters. As Table 5.2 shows, substantial majorities believe that initiatives make the state government more responsive to the people and that the voting public is more likely than elected representatives to be trusted "to do what is right" and "to consider the broad public interest."

Despite realistic reservations about how the initiative process works, the widespread cynicism about elected officials sustains the public's support of

TABLE 5.2   Beliefs about popular control and citizen competence
in initiative elections.

"Do you think that proposition elections make the state government more responsive to the people, less responsive, or don't you think they make much difference?"

	1999
More responsive	58%
No difference	32
Less responsive	6

"Can elected representatives or the voting public be trusted more often to do what is right on important government issues?"

	1982	1999	2004
Elected representatives	22%	26%	26%
Voting public	63	58	63

"Do elected representatives or the voting public consider the broad public interest more in making decisions?"

	1982	1999	2004
Elected representatives	26%	26%	22%
Voting public	42	45	56

"In general, do you think statewide ballot proposition elections come out the way most people want or the way a few organized special interest groups want?"

	1999	2004
Most people want	42%	33%
Both/mixed/depends	9	10
Special interests	43	48

"Are elected representatives or the voting public more influenced by special interest groups?"

	1982	1999	2004
Elected representatives	64%	70%	67%
Voting public	29	19	24

"How much of the time do you think voters find out enough about the choices in a statewide ballot proposition election to make the best choice on that issue—nearly all the time, most of the time, some of the time, or hardly ever?"

	1999
Nearly all the time	6%
Most of the time	21
Some of the time	53

Table 5.2 - continued

	1999
Hardly ever	19
Don't know	2

"Do elected representatives or the voting public generally enact more coherent and well thought out government policies?"

	1982	1999	2004
Elected representatives	48%	50%	43%
Voting public	42	31	40

"Are elected representatives or the voting public better suited to decide upon highly technical or legal policy matters?"

	1982	1999	2004
Elected representatives	66%	66%	56%
Voting public	27	23	34

"Do elected representatives or the voting public give more thorough review to each particular aspect of a proposed law?"

	1982	1999	2004
Elected representatives	58%	60%	49%
Voting public	35	27	38

"Are elected representatives or the voting public better suited to decide upon large scale government programs or projects?"

	1999	2004
Elected representatives	28%	24%
Voting public	54	65

Note: Columns may not total to 100 percent because of rounding errors or because Don't Know responses are not included.

Source: Field Research Corporation, Field Polls in 1982, 1999, and 2004. Reported results are for California registered voters.

direct legislation as a safety valve that provides voice and the opportunity to overcome official recalcitrance toward action. Accordingly, the 1997 field poll found strong support for reforms that would limit campaign spending on initiatives (78%) and require sponsors to submit their proposal for prior review (73%); the poll also found that there is virtually no support for eliminating direct democracy. Indeed by a margin of two to one, Californians favored a plan to extend direct legislation to the national government.[22]

More recent polls conducted by the Public Policy Institute of California (PPIC) confirm the public's strong support for retaining the initiative process. The August 2004 PPIC Statewide Survey reports that three in four California adults think that it is a good thing that the state's voters can make and change public policies by passing initiatives. The percentages of Californians saying the initiative outlet is a good thing for the state are high and consistent across party lines: Seventy-nine percent of Republicans, 74 percent of independents, and 70 percent of Democrats think the initiative is a good thing for California. Californians' collective embrace of the initiative stems partly from a widely held belief that the public policy decisions made by the state's voters at the ballot box are probably better than those made by the governor and the legislature. Overall, about six in ten Californians think that policies decided at the ballot box are probably better than those made by the state's elected officials, only 23 percent think those policies are probably worse. Majorities of independents (64%), Republicans (61%), and Democrats (54%) alike think ballot box public policies are probably better than those that come out of the republican process.

For example, when it comes to reforming the state budget process, 65 percent of Californians thing the voters should decide policy at the ballot box and only 27 percent think the governor and legislature should pass new laws; this pattern is similar across specific and general policy domains. Moreover, this support for direct democracy extends to local government. A June 2004 PPIC survey found that only 15 percent of Californians expressed confidence in the ability of local officials to plan for the future and that 73 percent felt that local voters—as opposed to elected officials—should be making the important decisions regarding growth.[23]

In contrast to their long-documented and well-understood support for the initiative, Californians' support for the recall mechanism became apparent only when the possibility of the state's first gubernatorial recall election surfaced in the summer of 2003. Although recall campaigns have been waged at some level against every governor in modern California political history, before 2003, a "recall question" had not qualified for a statewide ballot. And although most Californians and worldwide observers only learned about this constitutional provision in the context of the partisan-fueled effort to recall a Democratic governor in an overwhelmingly "blue state," in theory, Californians expressed high levels of support for the recall. In practice, as used against Davis, who had won reelection less than a year before in November 2002, however, attitudes toward the recall showed a more partisan hue. Overall, on the eve of the October special election, only 48 percent of Californians thought that the recall effort against Governor Davis was an *appropriate use* of the recall provision; 45 percent thought it was not. More than three in four Republicans thought the recall provision was being used appropriately in 2003, an opinion shared by only a minority of independents (46%) and Democrats (30%). As we consider public reactions to arguments for and against the recall *process* in California, it must be stressed that these beliefs are strongly colored by attitudes toward a particular recall involving a Democratic governor and, as became increasingly clear as the recall campaign evolved, a certain famous likely Republican replacement.

A *Los Angeles Times* poll of registered voters conducted in July 2003 told respondents that "the California Constitution does not set a specific standard for what kind of conduct warrants the recall of a governor" and then probed beliefs about the appropriate conditions for such a recall. As Table 5.3 shows, quite unsurprisingly, 86 percent of registered voters surveyed felt that a governor should be recalled for "criminal wrongdoing" and there was a similar consensus (91%) that mere unpopularity was not a sufficient reason for a recall. Opinion was more divided and more partisan when people were asked about the more vague criteria of "unethical behavior" and poor performance in governing the state. In both cases, 60 percent of registered voters felt that these kinds of conduct warranted a recall, but there were significant gaps between Republicans and Democrats and conservatives and liberals. For example, 69 percent of Republicans compared with 52 percent of Democrats believed that a governor should be recalled for "doing a poor job governing the state."

This partisan divide also is evident in answers to questions about whether the state Constitution should outline specific standards for recalling a governor or whether it is satisfactory to leave the Constitution as it now reads. In 2003, 58 percent of registered Democrats favored reform that included specific standards for a recall, while 56 percent of Republicans said they were happy with things as they were.

At the same time, the registered voters surveyed in the July 2003 *Los Angeles Times* poll accepted some of the main criticisms of the recall process. By a margin of 61 to 36 percent, respondents agreed that California should require a larger percentage of voter signatures to qualify a recall measure for the ballot. By a smaller majority of 52 to 44 percent, respondents concurred that the success of Davis' opponents in qualifying the recall election was a dangerous precedent that would make "every elected governor from now on likely to face a recall attempt."

A field poll conducted in July 2003 found a similar pattern of opinion: 67 percent of likely voters agreed that a recall election was a legitimate way to express displeasure with the governor's poor performance; however, by a two to one margin, respondents in this survey agreed that because "the eventual winner will likely get only a small share of the vote, this is no way to elect a governor."

Many of the fears expressed about the 2003 recall were unrealized. The campaign stimulated political interest and turnout was significantly higher than in the November 2, 2002, gubernatorial election when Davis was reelected. Voters seemed to have little difficulty in confining their attention to just the few serious contenders among the 135 candidates on the ballot and making a reasoned choice. The fearful vision of a governor elected by a negligible proportion of the voters did not materialize: Schwarzenegger received 48 percent of the vote, as high a proportion as Davis had obtained one year earlier and with more votes.

One year after his election, the actor-governor was immensely popular. The October 2004 PPIC Statewide Survey found that 61 percent of respondents approved of the way he was handling his job. The seeming success of the 2003 recall undoubtedly has influenced feelings about the recall process itself. The 2004 PPIC survey also found that 71 percent of Californians, including solid majorities of both Democrats and Republicans, felt that it was a "good thing" that the state constitution included this provision, an unchanged response from the eve of the 2003 recall itself.

TABLE 5.3   Public opinion about the recall process.

"Do you think a governor should be recalled because of criminal wrongdoing, or is that not reason enough for a governor to be recalled?"

	RV	DEM	IND	REP
Should be recalled	86%	84	85	91
Not reason enough	7	8	4	6
Don't know	7	8	11	3

"Do you think a governor should be recalled because of unethical behavior, or is that not reason enough for a governor to be recalled?"

	RV	DEM	IND	REP
Should be recalled	60%	53	64	69
Not reason enough	24	28	24	18
Don't know	16	19	12	13

"Do you think a governor should be recalled because he or she is doing a poor job governing the state, or is that not reason enough for a governor to be recalled?"

	RV	DEM	IND	REP
Should be recalled	60%	52	62	69
Not reason enough	34	42	33	25
Don't know	6	6	5	6

"Do you think a governor should be recalled because he or she is an unpopular governor, or is that not reason enough for a governor to be recalled?"

	RV	DEM	IND	REP
Should be recalled	6%	4	3	8
Not reason enough	91	91	95	89
Don't know	3	5	2	3

"Do you think the state Constitution should have specific standards of conduct for recalling a governor, or are you satisfied with the way the Constitution reads now, not setting any specific standards for recalling a governor?"

	RV	DEM	IND	REP
Specific standards	52%	58	61	38
Satisfied with it	41	32	33	56
Don't know	7	10	6	6

"Which statement comes close to your view of the recall effort: 'The Republicans are attempting to reverse the outcome of the gubernatorial election they lost last November,' or 'The Republicans honestly believe that Gray Davis has mismanaged the state's finances'?"

TABLE 5.3 - continued

	RV	DEM	IND	REP
Reverse election	33%	51	24	14
Believed he mismanaged	53	33	55	80
Don't know	14	16	21	6

"Some people say that recall elections like this one interfere with an elected state official's ability to fulfill his or her duties and efficiently run state government. Do you agree or disagree?"*

	LV	DEM	IND	REP
Agree strongly	38%	60	33	17
Agree somewhat	16	15	25	14
Disagree somewhat	11	9	13	11
Disagree strongly	33	13	27	56
Don't know	2	3	2	2

"Some people say that this recall sets a dangerous precedent in California because after the success that Davis' opponents have had in calling this special recall election, every elected governor from now on is likely to have to face a recall attempt by his or her opponents. Do you agree or disagree?"*

	LV	DEM	IND	REP
Agree strongly	33%	48	36	18
Agree somewhat	19	26	20	12
Disagree somewhat	11	12	5	11
Disagree strongly	33	12	33	55
Don't know	4	2	6	4

"Some people say that California has made it too easy for a recall measure to qualify for the ballot and that the state should require a larger percentage of voters—more than the 12 percent it is now—to qualify a recall measure for the ballot. Do you agree or disagree?"*

	LV	DEM	IND	REP
Agree strongly	46%	68	48	23
Agree somewhat	15	13	16	17
Disagree somewhat	12	6	17	15
Disagree strongly	24	10	18	41
Don't know	3	3	1	4

Notes: RV, denotes registered voters, LV denotes registered voters deemed likely to vote, Dem denotes Democrats, Rep denotes Republicans, and Ind denotes independents.

*The final three questions listed in the table are from a *Los Angeles Times* poll conducted in August 2003 of 801 registered voters deemed likely to vote in the special recall election.

Sources: Survey results from a *Los Angeles Times* poll conducted in July 2003 of 1,127 registered voters.

While Californians are supportive of the recall process in general, and a majority of state residents are happy with the outcome of their first usage of the provision, they remain aware of the imperfections frequently highlighted in the media portrayals of the recall election. Even today, about half of those surveyed by PPIC in October 2004 said that the recall process needs major or minor changes, with Democrats far more interested than Republicans in advocating reform. What types of changes could Californians support?

First, the public does endorse several ways to raise California's uniquely low threshold for qualifying a recall. The 2004 PPIC survey showed that 57 percent of all adults and 56 percent of the state's likely voters would support increasing the required number of signatures from 12 percent of total votes cast in the previous election for that office to 25 percent, which would make the requirement approximately 1 million signatures higher for a gubernatorial recall. Six in ten Californians and likely voters also would like to change the recall provision so that an elected official could be recalled only for illegal or unethical activity, raising the bar for a recall even higher. In response to the fact that current low thresholds led to the wild list of 135 candidates in 2003, the public also would like to raise the number of signatures required but not the cost for entry into the replacement election.

Despite the potential confusion and strategic uncertainty caused by the present system, less than half of all California adults and fewer than four in ten likely voters support changing the recall process so that there are two separate elections instead of one single election. This means there would be one election about whether to recall the official and, if recalled, another election to replace the official. Californians are also committed to having recall elections when they deem necessary, not according to the state's predetermined elections schedule: Nearly seven in ten think that recalls should be decided in special elections, not in regularly scheduled elections. However, there is one change related to the electoral process itself that a majority of the public would like to see change: About two-thirds would support changing the law so that if no candidate on the second part of the ballot received more than 50 percent of the vote, there would be a runoff election between the top two candidates so that someone would get majority support. This reform, of course, would probably result in a separate election should the recall portion of the first vote pass.

Public opinion thus reveals both generalized support for the recall provision and reservations about how it can be misused. One possible interpretation of this ambivalence in public thinking is that institutional reform is feasible. To be sure, the *Washington Post's* proposal to "excise" the recall from the California institution is sheer fantasy. But more limited changes to make the recall harder to use could receive public approval. Any political impetus for initiating reform, however, seems to have been quenched by satisfaction with the new governor and his reliance on the threat of direct democracy to advance his policy agenda.

THE ROLE OF POLITICAL TRUST

Widespread cynicism about the trustworthiness and competence of elected officials among the general public is one reason for the gap between mass and elite assessments of direct democracy. Of course, suspicion of political power is deeply rooted in American political culture and history, and the past three decades have witnessed a steady decline in trust in government. The causes of this trend include major national failures such as the Vietnam War, Watergate, and periodic recessions as well as the rise of an oppositional bias in media coverage of politics that accentuates the negative. Trust in government does increase when times are good; even then, a bedrock cynicism about the motives of politicians remains pervasive.[24]

Between 2001 and 2003, in the wake of the state's electricity crisis and a deepening economic recession, Californians' trust in the government in Sacramento plummeted. In October 2003, just before the recall election, the PPIC survey found that only one-third of Californians trusted their state government to do what was right "just about always" or "most of the time"; nearly two-thirds said the government in Sacramento could be trusted to do the right things "only some of the time" or "never." Those who *distrusted* the state government were somewhat more likely than those who trusted it most or all of the time to think that the recall provision was a good thing for the state (75% to 67%). While this gap of only 8 percent is modest in size, a more complex analysis that takes account of other political and demographic variables shows that the connection between mistrust of state government and approval of the recall process remains statistically significant.

To demonstrate this, we estimated a logistical regression model predicting support for the recall process. As Table 5.4 shows, controlling for knowledge

TABLE 5.4   Predicting support for the recall provision as "good" for California.

	B	S.E.
Trust State Government	−0.439	0.116**
State Headed in Right Direction	0.376	0.088**
Approve of Governor	−0.580	0.115**
Knowledge of Recall	0.122	0.058*
Following Recall News	0.016	0.053
Education	0.029	0.043
Male	0.031	0.085
Age	−0.019	0.003**
Income	0.068	0.029*
Democrat	−0.089	0.097
Republican	0.987	0.136**
Latino	−0.668	0.104**
Ideology	0.016	0.040
Constant	1.304	0.293**

Notes: This table presents the results from a logistic regression on whether the recall provision is a good thing for the state of California (1 = good thing; 0 = otherwise). The data come from pooling PPIC Statewide Surveys in August 2003 (N = 2,001) and October 2003 (N = 2,002).

Trust in state government is coded as 1 = trust the state government to do what is right just about always or most of the time; 0 otherwise.

The model predicts 76 percent of cases correctly; log-likelihood 3546.384; Nagelkerke R-square 0.14.
**p < 0.001; *p < 0.05.

of the recall process, attentiveness to news about the recall, age, sex, education, household income, race, ethnicity, political ideology, approval of Governor Davis, beliefs about the direction in which the state is heading, partisanship, and trust in the state government has a *negative* effect on approval of the recall process. In other words, other things being equal, those who mistrust the state government to do what is right are significantly more likely say that it's good that the California Constitution includes a provision whereby state office-holders can be recalled. This finding is impressive, given the relationships among trust in government and other significant predictors of approval of the recall process, such as approval of Governor Davis, dissatisfaction with the state of the state, and party affiliation. Another noteworthy result is that knowl-edge about the recall process boosts support for it. Even among those who acknowledge the shortcomings of California's law, there is a sense that the process provides a useful corrective.

CONCLUSION

When weighing the costs and benefits of the initiative and recall, the public and the experts reach different conclusions. The public recognizes the defects spelled out by scholars and journalists—the role of special interests and consultants, the limited capacity of ordinary citizens to decide complicated issues, the pos-sibility of unintended consequences—but still votes in favor of the recall. To characterize the verdict in the people's court as naïve or, even worse, undemo-cratic, seems arrogant. The main empirical studies of direct legislation in California by Magleby and Gerber conclude that like juries in criminal trials, the outcomes sometimes reflect genuine majority opinion and sometimes not. Moneyed interests can ward off attacks more easily than they can change public policy to their advantage. Moreover, public officials have learned to form broad coalitions of stakeholders to win support for fiscal change through the ballot box, much as they have learned to do when dealing with legislators.

Direct democracy in California is fueled, in part, by gridlock in the state legislature, a state of affairs fostered by the virtual absence of competitive seats, ideological polarization among the parties, and the requirement that the state budget must pass by a two-thirds majority. The very opponents of direct democracy, however, often are defenders of partisan control of the reap-portionment process, which helps create a dysfunctional legislature.

California voters are not about to give up the voice provided by the ini-tiative or recall. But the summary of public opinion in this chapter suggests that they would be willing to accept "tweaking" the process along the lines suggested by Bruce Cain.[25] Specifically, raising the number of signatures to qualify a recall petition for the ballot and the number required to become a can-didate in the replacement election seem acceptable to the voters. It would be harder to implement a process that is even less user-friendly by establishing specific criteria for initiating a recall—such as giving the incumbent a certain length of time in office and designating the kinds of conduct that warrant a petition—partly because terms such as "unethical conduct" are hard to define and ultimately lead to litigation.

The 2003 California recall was opposed by some because of concerns that this kind of success by recent election losers inevitably would lead to copycat actions and thrust California into an unending cycle of elections. For the moment, the public's willingness to put this fear aside seems to have been vindicated by the new governor's effectiveness and popularity. In the end, the recall functioned as a partisan election in which the candidate arguably closest to the California median of fiscal conservatism and social liberalism triumphed. "As if" history is notoriously suspect, but it would be a sound wager to bet that Schwarzenegger would have defeated Davis in 2002. The recall provided an opportunity for a moderate Republican to run in a general election without winning the party primary, the kind of outcome Davis' attack on Richard Riordan was designed to prevent. In October 2003, it was clear that the perceived state of the state had laid the groundwork for throwing out the incumbent. Indeed, assuming that most Tom McClintock voters would have opted for Schwarzenegger had their first choice dropped out, it is fair to estimate that the new governor was preferred to his predecessor by about 60 percent of the electorate. In this context, appeals that a small "d" democrat should vote against the recall were unlikely to succeed, and it is clear that a majority of the public feels that the change they made has been beneficial.

Those seeking to reform California government face the dilemma of having to use direct democracy to limit direct democracy. We have argued that public mistrust of government makes a large-scale attack on either the initiative or recall futile. More limited reform in the name of "good government" or curbing the power of interest groups and professional consultants has a better chance. Yet any such proposal requires a champion, and the most likely Terminator of direct legislation is one of its biggest fans. It is less clear whether the present governor, party leaders, or organized interest groups would oppose a modest "tweaking" of the recall process. As always in California, the challenge for the small "d" democrats is to find the money to put their proposal on the ballot.

BIBLIOGRAPHY

Baldassare, Mark. "Californians and Their Government." *PPIC Statewide Surveys, 1998–2005*. Public Policy Institute of California, 2004.

Bowler, Shaun, and Bruce Cain. "Recalling the Recall: Reflection's on California's Recent Adventure." *Political Science and Politics* January (2004): 7.

Cain, Bruce. "The State's Recall laws could use a Little Tweaking." *Los Angeles Times*, August 17, 2003.

Citrin, Jack. "Who's the Boss? Direct Democracy and Popular Control of Government." In *Broken Contract*, edited by Stephen Craig. Boulder: Westview Press, 1996.

Ellwood, John. "Pulling the Plug on Davis won't Change Much." *Washington Post*, July 27, 2003.

Field Research Corporation. *California Field Polls 1979–2005*.

_____. "A Summary of the Findings of a Statewide Survey of California Voters about Proposition Elections," 2004.

Fuller, Bruce. "Media Coverage of the 2003 Governor's Recall Campaign." *Political Analysis for California Education Working Paper Series*, 2003.

Gerber, Elizabeth. *The Populist Paradox*. Princeton: Princeton University Press, 1999.

Glynn, Carroll, Susan Herbst, Garret O'Keefe, and Robert Shapiro. *Public Opinion*. 2nd ed. Boulder: Westview Press, 2004.

Hajnal, Zoltan, Elisabeth Gerber, and Hugh Louch. "Minorities and Direct Legislation: Evidence from California Ballot Proposition

Elections." *Journal of Politics* 64, no. 1 (2002): 154–77.

Hibbing, John, and Elizabeth Theiss-Morse, eds. *What is it about Government that Americans Dislike?* New York: Cambridge University Press, 2002.

Los Angeles Times. Los Angeles Times Poll. Los Angeles: *Los Angeles Times,* 2003.

Lupia, Arthur. "Shortcuts versus Encyclopedias: Information and Voting Behavior in California Insurance Reform Election." *American Political Science Review* 88 (1994): 63–76.

Lupia, Arthur, Matthew McCubbins, and Samuel Popkin, eds. *Elements of Reason.* New York: Cambridge University Press, 2000.

Magleby, David. "Opinion Formation and Opinion Change in Ballot Proposition Campaigns." In *Manipulating Public Opinion,* edited by Michael Margolis and Gary Mauser. Pacific Grove: Brooks/Cole, 1989.

Rasky, Susan. "Loyalty Test." *Los Angeles Times,* July 27, 2003.

Scheer, Robert. "Make the Recall Count." *Los Angeles Times,* August 12, 2003.

Schrag, Peter. *Paradise Lost* [updated edition]. Berkeley: University of California Press, 2004.

Will, George. "A Conservative Tragedy." *Washington Post,* October 9, 2003.

NOTES

1. P. Schrag, *Paradise Lost,* updated ed. (New York: Norton, 1998).
2. S. Bowler and B. Cain, "Recalling the Recall: Reflection's on California's Recent Adventure," *Political Science and Politics* (January 2004): 7.
3. P. Schrag, *Paradise Lost,* ix.
4. Bowler and Cain, "Recalling the Recall," 7.
5. Ibid., 8.
6. Schrag, *Paradise Lost,* viii.
7. For a review of this research, C. Glynn, S. Herbst, G. O'Keefe, and R. Shapiro, *Public Opinion,* 2nd ed. (Boulder, CO: Westview Press, 2004).
8. D. Magleby, "Opinion Formation and Opinion Change in Ballot Proposition Campaigns," in *Manipulating Public Opinion,* eds. M. Margolis and G. Mauser (Pacific Grove, CA: Brooks/Cole, 1989).
9. A. Lupia, M. McCubbins, and S. Popkin, eds., *Elements of Reason* (New York, Cambridge University Press, 2000) provide an excellent review of this issue.
10. J. Citrin, "Who's the Boss? Direct Democracy and Popular Control of Government," in *Broken Contract,* ed. S. Craig (Boulder, CO: Westview Press, 1996).
11. E. Gerber, *The Populist Paradox* (Princeton, NJ: Princeton University Press, 1999).
12. A. Lupia, "Shortcuts versus Encyclopedias: Information and Voting Behavior in California Insurance Reform Election," *American Political Science Review* 88 (1994): 63–76.
13. Z. Hajnal, E. Gerber, and H. Louch, "Minorities and Direct Legislation: Evidence from California Ballot Proposition Elections," *Journal of Politics* 64, no. 1 (2002): 154–77.
14. Bowler and Cain, "Recalling the Recall," 7.
15. Ibid.
16. Ibid.
17. J. Ellwood, "Pulling the Plug on Davis won't Change Much, *Washington Post,* B-3, July 27, 2003; R. Scheer," Make the Recall Count, *Los Angeles Times,* 2-15, August 12, 2003; S. Rasky, "Loyalty Test," *Los Angeles Times,* M-1, July 27, 2003.
18. G. Will, "A Conservative Tragedy," *Washington Post,* A-35, October 9, 2003.
19. B. Fuller, "Media Coverage of the 2003 Governor's Recall Campaign," Political Analysis for California Education Working Paper Series 03-4, 1. Berkeley: Policy Analysis for Public Education, 2003.
20. The term was included later in survey items about the recall. Another frequent plaint was that the recall was a political circus largely because of the media frenzy surrounding Schwarzenegger.
21. Field Research Corporation, "A Summary of the Findings of a Statewide Survey of California Voters about Proposition Elections," September 2004.
22. *California Field Poll,* August 1997, 7.
23. M. Baldassare, "Californians and Their Government," PPIC Statewide Survey, June 2004.
24. For a recent overview of political mistrust in America, see J. Hibbing and E. Theiss-Morse eds., *What is it about Government Americans Dislike?* (New York: Cambridge University Press, 2002).
25. B. Cain, "The State's Recall laws could use a Little Tweaking," *Los Angeles Times,* M-5, August 17, 2003.

6

Rational Voters and the Recall Election

R. Michael Alvarez

D. Roderick Kiewiet

Betsy Sinclair

California Institute of Technology

The 2003 California recall election presented voters with a pair of choices. First, voters had to decide whether to recall Gray Davis as governor of the state. Second, they were faced with a list of 135 potential replacement candidates, one of whom would be chosen in the event Davis lost on the initial recall question. The two ballot questions were formally separate questions, but they were interrelated and conditional in nature. If I vote in favor of recalling Davis as governor, which candidate should I support to replace him? Alternatively, voters who opposed recalling Davis as governor had to decide who to vote for as replacement candidate to try to ensure that, if Davis were recalled, an acceptable replacement candidate would be elected.

The task of choosing among 135 potential replacements for Davis posed some unique challenges of its own. As the campaign progressed, many of the once-prominent candidates, such as Bill Simon, Peter Ueberroth, and Arianna Huffington, dropped out of the race. Despite these departures, there remained a number of serious, well-known candidates—Arnold Schwarzenegger, Tom McClintock, and Cruz Bustamante—as well as some lesser-known political figures and celebrities, for example, Larry Flynt, Gary Coleman, and Peter Camejo, and hundreds of unknowns.

While the interaction of the two recall election decisions raises several potentially interesting research questions, in this chapter, we concentrate on some basic tenets of rational choice theory. Are voters able to order candidates in a rational way? If so, do voters then cast ballots consistent with their ordering? In seeking to answer these questions, we analyze data from a telephone survey conducted by the *Los Angeles Times* in the weeks before the October 7, 2003, election. We find, subject to the limitations of the data we use, that all but a small number of voters appear able to order their candidates rationally, and that they appear to have cast their ballots in a manner that was consistent with their preferences.

We view this as an important research question for reasons beyond the proximate question of the administration of the gubernatorial recall election.

In recent years, there has been considerable controversy in the political science research community over the role of rational choice theory generally (for example, Friedman 1996; Green and Shapiro 1994) and over its application to specific domains of political behavior, such as voter turnout (Aldrich 1993; Jackman 1993). This controversy echoes earlier debates concerning the behavioral assumptions of economic approaches to the study of individual behavior (for example, Kahneman and Tversky 1979).[1] Much of this debate has focused on whether individual decision makers make decisions in line with the basic assumptions of rational choice theory.

In elementary form, rational choice theory posits that individuals take actions to achieve a purpose, such as getting their most preferred candidate elected to office. This means that we must define a preference relation for voters, which typically requires assuming that a voter's preferences over outcomes is transitive (Ordeshook 1986). If we consider three outcomes, then transitivity exists "if the first outcome is no worse than the second and the second is no worse than the third, then the first is no worse than the third" (Ordeshook 1986, 12).

As applied to the context of voter choice in the gubernatorial recall election, this implies that voters should be able to determine whether they strictly prefer one candidate over another or whether they are indifferent between the two. Behaviorally, rational choice theory then posits that, if a voter prefers one candidate in a set of transitively ordered candidates, barring additional strategic considerations, he or she is expected to cast a vote for that preferred candidate.[2]

We are not the first to study the extent to which individual voters act consistently with rational choice assumptions. Brady and Ansolabehere (1989), using pair-wise comparison data over large numbers of candidates, find that "people's preferences satisfy the requirements of rational choice and that their preference can be represented in a convenient form" (148). Radcliff (1993) uses different data and a different methodology, but reaches largely the same conclusion: "the evidence presented here suggests that despite some slippage the bulk of the sample is quite capable of maintaining well-ordered preferences with as many as five alternatives" (716).

We seek to determine how California voters, when faced with the two-question recall and candidate replacement ballot with a list of 135 candidates—ordered the top candidates, and how their preference orderings were associated with the choices they made on the recall election ballot. In the next section of this paper, we discuss our methodology; we then present our results. The final section of this paper provides our concluding remarks.

METHODOLOGY

The telephone survey data we analyze is taken from the *Los Angeles Times* poll, distributed by The Roper Center for Public Opinion Research.[3] The survey was conducted September 25–29, 2003, and was based on a sample of adult California residents; 1,982 respondents were interviewed. Filter questions on citizenship and registration reduced the sample to 1,496 registered voters.

To develop an understanding of voter preference orderings across the primary candidates in the recall election, we require questions that ask respondents to evaluate the candidates. In an ideal world, we would adopt Brady and Ansolabahere's (1989) method of paired comparison questions, but unfortunately, the *Los Angeles Times* poll did not ask this type of question. This survey instead employed a battery that—for Davis, Bustamante, McClintock, and Schwarzenegger—asked voters, "What is your impression of [each candidate]? As of today, is it very favorable, somewhat favorable, somewhat unfavorable, very unfavorable—or haven't you heard enough about him to say?" The responses of those who hadn't heard of the candidate, who said they were unsure about their impression, or otherwise did not answer the question, are treated as missing data.

Previous studies in the area (Feld and Grofman 1988; Niemi and Wright 1987; Radcliff 1993) have generally employed the standard "feeling thermometer" measures of candidate evaluations. Such measures ask respondents to rate how favorably they feel about particular candidates on a zero to one hundred scale. Responses to the questions we are using here would thus appear to be equivalent to a coarse feeling thermometer. It turns out, however, that feeling thermometer ratings tend to cluster at a small number of points, especially 50, 60, 70, and 85 (Weisberg and Miller 1979). Using a method that allows respondents to assign candidates to only four categories of evaluation therefore may result in little loss of information concerning candidate evaluations. Not surprisingly, the measures we employ here do result in a large number of ties—for example, rating two or more candidates somewhat favorably—but so, too, do feeling thermometers. With these caveats in mind, we are hopeful that these measures will provide us with some ability to assess the extent to which voters are able to order the candidates and then vote consistently with these preference orderings.

We used these evaluations for each of the four major candidates—Davis, Bustamante, McClintock, and Schwarzenegger—to produce each voter's preference ranking of the four candidates. To provide some sense for the preference rankings held by voters at the end of September (one week before the recall election) we list the top fifteen preference orderings in the registered voter sample in Table 6.1.[4] This table lists each preference order, and the relative frequency in the sample. When registered voters had a clear preference between a pair of candidates (for example, if the voter prefers Davis to Bustamante), we use the notation "D p B." In situations where the data do not allow for clear ordering, in other words, when the evaluations provided by the voters lead to ties between pairs of candidates (for example, if the voter was indifferent between Davis and Bustamante), we use the notation "DB."

What we see in Table 6.1 is a predominance of preference orderings in which McClintock or Schwarzenegger were preferred to Bustamante or Davis. The top five preference orderings in our dataset, held by 333 of the 1,483 registered voters who provided an evaluation of at least one of the four candidates, were of this nature. The rest of the respondents reported dozens of different preference orderings and, in these, Davis and Bustamante tended to fare better. Still, that Davis lost the recall and Bustamante lost the replacement election are not surprising outcomes in light of these data. It should be noted

TABLE 6.1 **Most frequent preference orderings.**

ORDER	FREQUENCY	PERCENTAGE
MS p BD	98	6.6%
S p M p BD	87	5.9%
M p S p BD	70	4.7%
MS p BD	46	3.1%
S p M p B p D	32	2.2%
BD p MS	30	2.0%
MS p B p D	25	1.7%
MBD p S	24	1.6%
M p S p B p D	23	1.6%
BD p M p S	22	1.5%
MS p B p D	19	1.3%
BD p S	16	1.1%
BD p MS	16	1.1%
BD p S	15	1.0%
MB p SD	15	1.0%

Note: B, Bustamante; D, Davis; M, McClintock; S, Schwartzenegger.

that, as expected, the coarseness of the evaluation measure we used resulted in a large number of ties involving two or more candidates.

WERE VOTE CHOICES CONSISTENT WITH EVALUATIONS?

The next task was to examine what is probably the most modest expectation that one might derive from rational choice theory, that is, to determine whether voters' choices were consistent with their evaluations. This may seem like low criteria, but previous studies have found that candidate evaluations, as registered by ratings on feeling thermometer measures, do not always align well with vote choice. Respondents often do not vote for the candidate for whom they assigned the highest thermometer score. Others vote for the candidate for whom they assigned the lowest score, and yet others vote for candidates for whom they did not even rate. All told, in many cases, the mismatch between candidate evaluations measured by feeling thermometers and reported vote choice exceeds 20 percent (Alvarez and Kiewiet 2005). This slippage may arise because the feeling thermometer methodology is flawed, and not because respondents are inconsistent. This also means that our tests of the consistency between evaluations and vote choice are as much a test of the evaluation questions used as they are of respondent consistency.

We began by comparing evaluations of Davis to vote choice on the recall question. In these and in the analysis of other candidates' supporters, we confined our analysis initially to those voters who evaluated all four major candidates.

TABLE 6.2 Preference orderings and recall vote preference.

RECALL VOTE	DAVIS TOP-RANKED	DAVIS NOT TOP-RANKED
Against	94.5	13.9
For	5.2	85.2
No Opinion	0.3	0.9
Number of Cases	280	704

We considered Davis to be the top-ranked candidate in a voter's preference ordering if they evaluated Davis as better than, or at least as good as, all of the other candidates. Such voters should have voted against the recall. Every voter who evaluated Davis last, of course, should have voted for the recall.

The figures in Table 6.2 show that of the 280 registered voters who, according to our approach, ranked Davis as the top candidate, almost 95 percent voted against recalling him. On the other hand, 85 percent of those who did not rank Davis at the top of their preference ordering voted for the recall of Davis as governor. This degree of correspondence is remarkably high and, in fact, is a good deal higher than the typical level of correspondence found between vote choice and feeling thermometer ratings. As indicated earlier, Alvarez and Kiewiet (2005) argue that a number of features of the feeling thermometer measures make them suspect as a source of data from which to infer preference orderings. Thus, the findings here lend addition support to their critique of these commonly used measures.

But why would *any* Davis supporter favor the recall? We also found, conversely, that a similar number of voters who ranked Davis at the bottom of their preference ordering voted against the recall. Some amount of error in survey data is inevitable, but we suspect that some voters were confused as to whether "recalling" Davis meant that he would lose office or retain it. It is sometimes good to be recalled, after an audition, for example, because it means that you have survived a cut. Some voters may have believed incorrectly that recalling Davis would keep him in office.

Most likely, the recall question on the actual ballot was more helpful in this regard than the question on the poll. The *Los Angeles Times* poll asked, "... would you vote YES to recall Governor Davis or would you vote NO, not to recall Governor Davis?" The question that appeared on the California ballot was, "Should Gray Davis be recalled (removed) from the Office of Governor?" Including the word "removed" should have helped reduce confusion about what it meant to recall Davis.

For supporters of the other three candidates, we assessed the level of agreement between candidate evaluations and vote choice in the replacement election. As before, a voter who evaluated a candidate higher or at least as high as any other candidate was deemed to make that candidate a top choice. Table 6.3, which reports results for Bustamante supporters, shows that about 68 percent of the registered voters who evaluated Bustamante highest or at least as high as other candidates stated that they would vote for Bustamante

TABLE 6.3   Preference orderings and replacement vote: Bustamante.

REPLACEMENT VOTE	BUSTAMANTE TOP-RANKED	BUSTAMANTE NOT TOP-RANKED
Bustamante	67.9	2.4
Others	10.5	87.8
No Opinion	21.6	9.7
Number of Cases	316	523

in the replacement election. Eleven percent said they would cast a vote for some candidate other than Bustamante. This could include any one of several minor candidates, but Peter Camejo, candidate of the Green Party, and liberal commentator Arianna Huffington were the most common such alternatives. Only 2.4 percent of the voters who did not rank Bustamante at the top indicated an intention to vote for him, compared with 88 percent who said they would vote for someone else.

Table 6.4 repeats the analysis for Schwarzenegger's supporters. In this case, 76 percent of registered voters who rated Schwarzenegger higher or at a least as high as any other candidate said they were voting for him to replace Davis as governor, while 13 percent said they were voting for some other candidate—again, usually one of the many minor candidates on the replacement ballot. Of the registered voters who did not evaluate Schwarzenegger the highest, 78 percent said they would support another candidate, 20 percent had no opinion, and fewer than 2 percent indicated an intention to vote for Schwarzenegger.

In Table 6.5 we examine McClintock's evaluations and voter support. Here we find a much larger gap than previously experienced between evaluations and vote intentions. Less than half (39%) of the registered voters who rated McClintock the top candidate (or tied for top candidate) stated that they would cast a ballot for him to replace Davis as governor, while almost 50 percent said they were voting for another candidate—in almost all cases fellow Republican Schwarzenegger. Of those who did not rate McClintock at the top of their preference ordering, 70 percent said they were voting for other candidates, and a scant 0.5 percent said they were supporting McClintock. What we have here, then, is a large amount of strategic voting. Believing that McClintock

TABLE 6.4   Preference orderings and replacement vote: Schwarzenegger.

REPLACEMENT VOTE	SCHWARZENEGGER TOP-RANKED	SCHWARZENEGGER NOT TOP-RANKED
Schwarzenegger	76.0	1.8
Others	12.4	78.2
No Opinion	11.5	20.0
Number of Cases	515	393

TABLE 6.5   Preference orderings and replacement vote: McClintock.

REPLACEMENT PREFERENCE	McCLINTOCK TOP-RANKED	McCLINTOCK NOT TOP-RANKED
McClintock	38.5	0.5
Others	49.7	70.0
No Opinion	11.7	29.5
Number of Cases	575	247

had little or no chance of winning the election, many of his supporters had decided to support an acceptable alternative, Schwarzenegger, who had a far better chance of winning. Breaking down the vote of respondents who stated that their first preference was McClintock (575 respondents), of those who indicated a vote choice, 230 opted for Schwarzenegger and 222 remained loyal to McClintock.

We next repeated the cross-tabulations reported in Tables 6.2 through 6.5 after including respondents who were only capable of ordering their preferences over three candidates. We find an almost identical pattern of results, although this added 257 voters to the analysis.

CONSISTENCY IN CHOICE ACROSS THE RECALL QUESTION AND REPLACEMENT ELECTION

In the previous section, we found that most voters in the 2003 California recall satisfied the admittedly modest criterion of rationality, that of voting in a manner consistent with their preference orderings on both the recall question and the replacement election. It was common for voters who ranked one of the major candidates highest in the replacement election to announce a vote intention for one of the many minor candidates, and a large share of McClintock voters reported an intention to vote strategically for Schwarzenegger. Those who did not give a candidate the most favorable evaluation, however, rarely indicated that they would vote for that particular candidate.

The next question we investigated was the relationship between voters' choices on the recall question and in the replacement election. Those who preferred one of the three other major candidates to Davis presumably wanted that candidate to be governor. The primary interest here is whether such voters nonetheless voted against the recall of Davis, because they feared someone they liked even less than Davis might be elected.

Although such voters might be called strategic voters, we will instead call them "hedge" voters to highlight a difference between what they are doing and conventional strategic voting. Strategic voting, as it is commonly understood, occurs when voters believe the candidate they most prefer has no chance of winning and so they opt instead for a lesser-preferred candidate who does have a realistic chance of winning. In so doing, they are still choosing

TABLE 6.6   **Frequency of hedge voters.**

MOST PREFERRED CANDIDATE	HEDGE VOTERS (%)	NUMBER OF CASES
Schwarzenegger	9.0	524
Bustamante	84.2	260
McClintock	30.8	439

to vote for the candidate they want to win the election. In this case, voters are hedging their bets, supporting Davis by voting against the recall to prevent an even worse candidate from winning. The candidate they are voting for in the replacement election can thus win only if the outcome of the recall (Davis is recalled) runs counter to how they voted (against the recall). Those who are not hedge voters—that is, those who vote for their most preferred candidate except for the recall—we will call consistent voters.

Table 6.6 reports the frequency of hedge voters among the supporters of each of the major candidates. Those whose most preferred candidate was Davis, of course, could not be hedge voters. Not surprisingly, Bustamante supporters were much more likely than Schwarzenegger and McClintock supporters to hedge their bets and vote against the recall of Davis. For one thing, they were much more sanguine about the prospect of fellow Democrat Davis remaining in office, and considerably more negative in their perceptions of Schwarzenegger, the likely and eventual Republican winner.

This hedging strategy was, in fact, exactly what Democratic leaders during the recall campaign urged voters to do. Many worried, though, that Bustamante supporters would balk at voting against the recall, as the only way Bustamante could win was for Davis to lose. Davis supporters also perceived that Bustamante was soft-pedaling the "no on the recall" message. In either case, these data indicate that the vast majority of Bustamante backers followed the cues of party leaders and hedged on the recall.

To more comprehensively check for the incidence of hedge voting versus consistent voting, we conducted a logit analysis. Consistent voters, as indicated earlier, are those voters who voted for their most preferred candidate in the replacement election and for Davis' recall. Because so many of McClintock backers voted strategically for Schwarzenegger, we consider such voters to also be consistent. Those who are not consistent in this way are considered hedge voters, coded as 1; consistent voters are coded as 0. Only a limited set of independent variables could be derived from the survey, but we were able to specify the respondent's education level, income, gender, reported level of interest in the election, party registration (Republican or Democrat), and ethnicity. The ethnicity variable was converted into a dummy variable that takes on the value of 1 for Latinos, 0 otherwise. Our expectations were that Democrats were far more likely to be hedge voters than Republicans, but that Latinos, controlling for party registration, would be less likely to hedge because of greater support for Latino candidate Bustamante. We also expected that better-educated voters, higher-income voters, and those with a high degree of interest

TABLE 6.7   Logit analysis of hedge voting.

VARIABLE	COEFFICIENT (ERROR)
Constant	0.36
	(0.39)
Education	0.06
	(0.04)
Income	−0.02
	(0.02)
First-time voter	0.03
	(0.26)
Interest in election	−0.39*
	(0.07)
Female	−0.03
	(0.12)
Democrat	0.11
	(0.15)
Republican	−0.75*
	(0.17)
Latino	0.34*
	(0.14)

Note: * = $p < 0.05$; $n = 1,496$.

in the campaign might be politically more sophisticated and thus more likely to be hedge voters. The reverse expectation holds for first-time voters, who might be suspected of being less likely to adopt a hedging strategy because of political inexperience.

As the results reported in Table 6.7 indicate, registered Republicans were, as expected, far less likely than Democratic registrants to hedge their bets and vote against the recall. Latino voters, contrary to expectations, were more likely to hedge, giving greater support to Davis in his fight against the recall rather than less. Respondents' income, education, and gender was not predictive of what type of voter they were, and whether or not they were a first-time voter was also of no consequence.

The other significant effect evident from the results in Table 6.7 is the propensity of voters with a high interest in the campaign to vote consistently, which is also the opposite of what we had hypothesized. A further check of the data reveals that Republican voters, in general, and Schwarzenegger supporters, in particular, indicated having a particularly high level of interest in the campaign. Conversely, those whose highest-ranked candidate was Davis, on average, claimed to have considerably less interest in the campaign. To many of them, the recall might have seemed like a bad dream that they wished would just go away. As a consequence of these associations, higher interest in the campaign was linked to less, not more, hedge voting.

DISCUSSION

Our analysis of voting behavior in the recall election provides support for a number of arguments. First, despite the fact that the recall election was held on short notice, involved a long ballot with an unusual structure, and was subjected to a substantial amount of confusing preelection litigation, it appears that voters were able to rationally order the candidates and state voting intentions that were consistent with those orderings. Despite the problems associated with the recall election, administrative or otherwise, it appears that voters by and large got it right. While our data were limited to an analysis of only the top four candidates and also limited to what other measures were present on the *Los Angeles Times* survey, we did find that voters rarely stated vote intentions that were inconsistent with the way in which they evaluated the candidates.

This result simultaneously bolsters the validity of the candidate evaluation questions that were employed, which simply asked respondents to rate their impression of the major candidates as very favorable, somewhat favorable, somewhat unfavorable, or very unfavorable. Despite the coarseness of a measure allowing for only four response categories, the agreement between candidate evaluations and vote choice was consistent. From this we conclude that it is preferable to ask evaluative questions that repeatedly offer the same small number of response categories, rather than to ask for a zero to one hundred rating. When specific response categories are not offered, it appears that respondents have difficulty keeping a consistent calibration in their ratings and are more prone to make mistakes.

BIBLIOGRAPHY

Aldrich, John H. "Rational Choice and Turnout." *American Journal of Political Science* 37 (1993): 246–78.

Alvarez, R. Michael, and D. Roderick Kiewiet. "Rationality and the Recall." Manuscript, Pasadena, CA: California Institute of Technology, 2005.

Brady, Henry E., and Stephen Ansolabehere. "The Nature of Utility Functions in Mass Publics." *American Political Science Review* 83 (1989): 143–63.

Feld, Scott, and Bernard Grofman. "Ideological Consistency as a Collective Phenomenon." *American Political Science Review* 82 (1988): 773–88.

Friedman, Jeffrey. *The Rational Choice Controversy.* New Haven: Yale University Press, 1996.

Green, Donald, and Ian Shapiro. *Pathologies of Rational Choice Theory.* New Haven: Yale University Press, 1994.

Jackman, Robert W. "Response to Aldrich's 'Rational Choice and Turnout': Rationality and Political Participation." *American Journal of Political Science* 37 (1993): 279–90.

Kaheman, Daniel, and Amos Tversky. "Prospect Theory: An Analysis of Decisions Under Risk." *Econometrica* 47 (1979): 263–91.

Los Angeles Times Poll, September 25-29, #490.

Niemi, Richard, and Steven Wright. "Voting Cycles and the Structure of Individual Preferences." *Social Choice and Welfare* 4 (1987): 173–83.

Ordeshook, Peter C. *Game Theory and Political Theory.* New York: Cambridge University Press, 1986.

Radcliff, Benjamin. "The Structure of Voter Preferences." *Journal of Politics* 55 (1993): 714–19.

Weisberg, Herbert F., and Arthur H. Miller. "Evaluation of the Feeling Thermometer: A Report to the National Election Study Board Based on Data from the 1979 Pilot Study Survey," Ann Arbor, MI: National Election Studies Pilot Study Report, No. nes002241, 1979.

NOTES

1. An excellent summary of the early debates over rational choice theory is found in Ordeshook (1986, 485–86).

2. Strategic voting occurs when a voter, believing that their most preferred candidate has no chance of winning, opts for a lesser-preferred candidate. For an analysis of strategic voting in the 2003 California recall, see Alvarez and Kiewiet (2005).

3. We thank Susan Pinkus of the *Los Angeles Times* poll for her assistance in providing us with these data.

4. In the tables that follow, the data reported are weighted by the weight variable provided in the *Los Angeles Times* poll.

7

THE RACE CARD AND CALIFORNIA POLITICS:

MINORITY VOTERS AND RACIAL CUES IN THE
2003 RECALL ELECTION

MATT A. BARRETO

UNIVERSITY OF CALIFORNIA, IRVINE

RICARDO RAMÍREZ

UNIVERSITY OF SOUTHERN CALIFORNIA

As recently as 2002, pundits and scholars considered California out of reach for Republicans. Democrats controlled both houses of the state legislature; they were a majority of the congressional delegation, including both U.S. Senators; and they held all statewide offices from insurance commissioner to governor. It was suggested that this dominance by Democrats was largely caused by the political aftershocks of the race-targeting wedge issue politics employed by Republicans in the early and mid-1990s. Moderate whites and the growing minority vote were turned off by the divisive Republican agenda in the state and thus secured the state for the Democratic Party.

If California was truly a Democrat-dominated state, then how can we explain what happened during the 2003 recall election? In the October 2003 special election, neither the incumbent Democrat governor nor the Democrat replacement candidate were able to ward off the successful Republican surge for the highest statewide office. Although Democrats were perceived to enjoy dominance in state politics, their control, while broad, was tenuous. In sweeping the eight top statewide offices in 2002, the Democratic margin of victory was razor thin. Some contests, such as controller, were decided by less than 1 percent of the vote, which meant that even small changes in public opinion could result in a big difference in the election outcome. The answer to the recall question, we argue, has to do with the dual role of minority voters and racial cues in the recall election. More specifically, we contend that the political behavior of racial/ethnic voters and the use of racial cues were significant factors in determining the outcome of the two-stage process during the 2003 California recall election. The 2003 special election to recall Governor Gray Davis featured a renewed focus on racial issues and ethnic candidates. Opponents of Davis made campaign issues out of his support for driver's licenses for noncitizens and his association with Native American casino money. Meanwhile, four of the five top replacement candidates for governor were from first- or second-generation immigrant families leading many pundits to speculate on the role that minority voters would play in the recall election. Pollster Mark Baldassare noted, "Minority voters in California have proven the winning edge for Democratic candidates in the past ... and for the recall their vote will be a huge issue" (Sterngold 2003).

The remainder of this chapter is divided into four sections. First, we focus on the contemporary growth of minority voters in California politics. We then compare the role of racial cues during the recall campaign and during the 1990s. The third section draws on survey research to shed light on the difference in votes by race and ethnicity, which is followed by an examination of the racial/ethnic gap that emerged in voter preferences, evidenced by precinct-level analyses in Los Angeles County. Finally, we consider the implications of these differences for elite behavior and future election outcomes in California.

THE MINORITY VOTE IN CONTEXT

Over the past twelve years, minority voters have become a larger part of the California electorate, growing by almost 70 percent from 1990 to 2000, according to estimates from the U.S. Census Current Population Survey (CPS). In addition to population growth, this increase is in large part due to successful mobilization drives targeting Latino and Asian voters (Michelson 2003; Pachon 1998; Pantoja and Woods 2000; Ramírez 2002; Wong 2001). In 1990, whites accounted for 82.3 percent of all voters in statewide elections, compared with just 17.7 percent for Latino, black, and Asian voters combined. However, each year between 1990 and 2000 the minority share of the electorate grew and, by the 2000 presidential election, it stood at 29.8 percent. This growth primarily is the result of increases in Latino and Asian American voter registration and turnout, while black voting has remained roughly the same.

Minority participation reached a high in the 2000 presidential election and then fell in the 2002 gubernatorial election. Although turnout was low statewide, minorities were even less likely to vote in 2002, feeling alienated from their traditional Democratic base (Barabak 2002). Thus, in 2002, the minority share of the California electorate decreased for the first time in ten years, falling an estimated 4 percentage points from just two years earlier. With increased mobilization and the frenzy surrounding the 2003 recall, minority turnout was up in 2003 as compared with 2002 (Tomás Rivera Policy Institute 2002, 2003). Despite increased turnout in the recall election, levels of support for Democratic candidates were down among Latinos, blacks, and Asians.

Statewide victories by Democrats in the 1990s have been made possible by support from minority voters. In particular, Democrats have been successful in ten of eleven of the elections for governor, U.S. Senate, and president between 1992 and 2002 (Fraga and Ramírez 2003; Fraga, Ramírez, and Segura 2004). Six of those ten Democrat victories would have been defeats without the support of minority voters. In virtually every major election since 1992, minority voters were more likely to vote Democrat than were white voters.

A majority of African American and Latino voters consistently voted Democratic at rates of 15 to 30 percentage points higher than white voters. The average of the Democratic vote in ten elections among white voters is 45 percent, while the average among Latino, black, and Asian voters was 69 percent, 80 percent, and 54 percent, respectively. Latino voters grew consistently more Democratic during the early to mid-1990s and sustained high levels of Democratic support in 1996 (75% for Clinton), 1998 (71% for Davis), and 2000 (75% for Gore). This increase of about 10 percentage points coincides with the Republican-backed, race-targeting propositions discussed below that many viewed as anti-immigrant and anti-Latino (*California Journal* 1998; Fraga and Ramírez 2003).

While minority voters contributed to the success of most Democratic candidates who went on to win in California, it seems that white voters may hold the real key to victory. The only unsuccessful Democrat in that race (Brown, in 1994) saw her support dip to only 35 percent among white non-Hispanic voters, despite strong support from Latino and black voters. While less likely to vote Democrat than minorities, whites voted at least 40 percent Democrat in the nine elections that Democrats won. The reason white voters are so influential lies in their willingness to turn out and vote. Although California is a majority-minority state measured by total population (53% minority in the 2000 U.S. Census), whites are, and will likely continue to make up the majority of the electorate for some time (Citrin and Highton 2002).

RACE AS AN ELECTION ISSUE: THE GOOD, THE BAD, AND THE UGLY

With one of the most diverse state populations in the country, such issues as illegal immigration and bilingual education were important in shaping California's political landscape during the 1990s and have also shaped huge controversies in state politics. In the new century, the same pattern emerged as racial issues played an important role in the 2001 Los Angeles mayoral election. The promise of retaining the city's African American police chief helped secure the black vote for the Anglo candidate, while alleged support for a imprisoned Latino drug dealer badly hurt the Latino candidate in the eyes of moderate white voters. Over the past ten to fifteen years, California politics has become synonymous with racial and ethnic politics, even as white voters constitute a large majority of the electorate. Here, we highlight the racial overtones that were present during the 2003 recall election. While some references to race are seen as positive, others are clearly negative, and worse yet, border on racist campaigning.

THE GOOD

Candidates as Immigrants   Arnold Schwarzenegger, Cruz Bustamante, Ariana Huffington, and Peter Camejo (and to a lesser extent Van Vo; see HoSang and Masuoka, Chapter 9 in this volume). One of the most interesting elements about the recall election was that four of the top five candidates were immigrants or children of immigrants. Rather than seeing it as a negative, media accounts emphasized the positive aspects of the immigrant work ethic by these candidates, and their potential to mobilize immigrant voters in all communities. Candidates were portrayed as embodying the American dream, and immigrant voters were seen as an important swing vote, not as a threat.[1]

Proposition 54 as a Deracialized Initiative Proposition 54, the racial privacy initiative was not "racialized" in advertisements. While, in the past, race-based ballot initiatives have attracted heated debate in minority communities and on AM talk radio, Proposition 54 was portrayed as both a privacy issue and a health care issue by proponents and opponents, effectively deracializing its context. Although many observers expected it to have a similar impact as previous propositions (for example, Propositions 187, 209, and 227), in the end, a majority of Anglo and minority voters rejected the initiative as an attack on medical research instead of viewing it as a socalled wedge issue. This demonstrates the potential maturity of the California electorate to not fall victim to race baiting. However, other race issues did prevail.

THE BAD

History of Race as a Campaign Issue (Propositions 187, 209, and 227 The mid-1990s witnessed three racetargeting statewide initiatives that sought to deny undocumented immigrants access to social services, eliminate state-sponsored affirmative action programs, and end the use of bilingual education in the public school system. All three of these propositions were successful based on the election choice of white voters. It would have taken 100 percent minority voter opposition, and the exhibited white voting patterns, for these initiatives to narrowly defeat these voter initiatives (by 1% to 4%). The election outcomes using this majoritarian electoral device in California highlight the role that race can have on the election choice of white voters (Hajnal and Louch 2001; Ramírez 2002). Clearly, these race-targeting initiatives and issues do not occur in a vacuum. Not only did these initiatives qualify for the ballot, they were used by politicians as campaign issues, further dividing the state along racial and ethnic lines. During the 1990s, the voting patterns were structured by the racial and ethnic composition where white voters lived. Tolbert and Hero (1996) demonstrate that support for Proposition 187 was highest in counties with significant minority populations. Similarly, Ramírez (2002) finds that white public opinion regarding Proposition 209 (the anti–affirmative action statewide initiative) was structured by the demographic diversity in state assembly districts where whites lived and by the extent to which white assembly districts were adjacent to majority-minority districts.

THE UGLY

Native American Casinos as a Threat to California As the state found itself in the middle of a severe budget shortfall, the leading Republican candidates Schwarzenegger and McClintock turned to Indian gaming as a source of revenue. However, the issue was not simply portrayed in financial terms. Attack ads against Davis and Bustamante emphasized their close ties to Native American casino entrepreneurs and the large contributions made to their respective campaigns. By some accounts, the campaign commercials made it appear that Native Americans, who account for less than 1 percent of California's population, were running the top two offices in California. The message of the commercials was clear, that Native American casinos were not paying their fair share of taxes, and that they had undue influence over state politics because of their special treatment by Democratic leaders.[2] Although California voters approved the terms of Indian gaming (twice) via state ballot propositions, and despite the history of their massacre by early California settlers during the gold rush (the state has even passed a resolution apologizing for historic treatment of Native Americans), Native Americans were depicted as taking advantage of the state in 2003. Nevertheless, campaign commercials attacked Native Americans as greedy and even suggested they were to blame for the state's financial crisis by not paying their share of taxes to the state (which voters had previously agreed was to be none).

In particular, Schwarzenegger was able to effectively distance himself from Indian gaming while at the same time closely tie Bustamante to Native American interest groups and campaign donations. This was largely possible because of the attention drawn to the Indian tribes because of their prominent role in campaign contributions during the recall election. In fact, $1 in $5 spent on the recall came from these contributions. Following the release of the campaign commercials, a national, nonpartisan Native American association criticized the ads, "On behalf of the National Indian Gaming Association, I denounce the advertisements currently being played on California televisions stations, which are paid for by Californians for Schwarzenegger. While the National Indian Gaming Association is a nonpartisan organization that does not take a position in party politics, we are personally deeply offended by the tenor of Mr. Schwarzenegger's ad" (Nicholas 2003).

Lieutenant Governor Cruz Bustamante's Membership in a "Racist" Organization   In an effort to paint the moderate, Central Valley Democrat as a radical politician, opponents claimed Bustamante's association with his college MEChA (*Movimiento Estudiantil Chicano de Aztlán*) group signified that he was a racist, only concerned with Latino issues. The organization is a student-run group that promotes Mexican American awareness and is open to students of all backgrounds. Most notably, Tom McClintock, Republican candidate for governor, focused on a poor translation of the group's motto and insisted the lieutenant governor had a hidden Latino agenda that would exclude whites. Given that most non-Latinos in the state were unfamiliar with MEChA, they were prone to believe the attacks, especially when Bustamante defended the organization. Bustamante attempted to correct his opponents' depiction of MEChA and insisted he was not a racist. However, his refusal to apologize for his membership added to the discontent and suspicion among moderate and conservative white voters (for a richer account, see DeSipio and Masuoka, Chapter 8 in this volume).

Driver's Licenses for Undocumented Immigrants   A final blow to the Davis administration may have been his decision to sign the driver's license bill authored by Democratic State Senator Gil Cedillo, after previously vetoing it twice. The bill provided a mechanism for undocumented immigrants to obtain a California driver's license, as long as they had been in the United States for three years, had a steady job, and passed a background check. In 1992, former Governor Pete Wilson signed a bill that prevented undocumented immigrants from getting licenses, which they had previously been able to obtain. According to his supporters, Cedillo's bill reversed the 1992 law in the interest of public safety and welfare. Davis angered some in the Latino community when he twice vetoed a similar bill. When he signed the bill in 2003, many Latinos and non-Latinos questioned his sincerity and believed that he was pandering to Latinos solely as a last ditch effort to retain his post. Ultimately, this lead to a backlash among some non-Latino voters and simultaneously failed to garner additional support among Latino voters. Republican candidates Schwarzenegger and McClintock campaigned on the promise that they would immediately repeal the law, because undocumented (Latino) immigrants posed a security threat if they could get their hands on a valid state driver's license, and polls revealed there was great public opposition to the driver's license bill.

CALIFORNIA PUBLIC OPINION AND RACE

Leading up to the recall election, a majority of Californians were dissatisfied with Governor Davis' leadership and performance in office. Even following his successful reelection in 2002, polls suggested that voters were unhappy with both choices, Davis and his Republican opponent Bill Simon, leaving Davis' approval rating below 50 percent even after winning office (Barabak 2002). Therefore, it should not be viewed as a surprise that support for Davis was low among all racial and ethnic groups in 2003. A large survey of all four major ethnic groups in California was conducted just before the October 7 election to determine what differences of opinion existed among whites, Asian Americans, Latinos, and blacks (Table 7.1). To obtain a representative sample of minority voters, the 2003 Multilingual Survey of California Voters[3] was offered in English, Spanish, Mandarin, Cantonese, Vietnamese, and Korean.

The results presented in Table 7.2 suggest that white voters were the most disillusioned with Davis, but that all four ethnic groups were unhappy. While 60 percent of whites had a negative opinion of the governor, a substantial percentage of Asian Americans (48%) and Latinos (49%) had a negative opinion. Even among blacks, more than a quarter held a negative opinion of Davis. Furthermore, a majority of all groups felt that Davis' job performance as governor was mediocre or poor, with white voters being the most likely to rate him poorly. While there was dissatisfaction with Davis, there was also cynicism of the recall election itself. More than 50 percent of all racial groups in California viewed the recall as a political circus as opposed to a good example

TABLE 7.1 Public opinion of recall by race/ethnicity.

	WHITE	ASIAN	LATINO	BLACK
Opinion of Gray Davis				
Positive	31	40	45	63
Negative	60	48	49	27
Don't know	8	12	6	9
Performance of Davis as governor				
Excellent	1	4	4	4
Good	21	17	26	41
Mediocre	27	44	40	36
Poor	48	33	27	16
Opinion of the recall election				
Good example of democracy	39	33	28	12
Political circus	51	53	64	83
Don't know	10	14	8	5

of democracy. Latinos and blacks were the most likely to have a pessimistic view of the recall election. The opinion data presented in Table 7.2 show consistency among the four groups, but the data also show that some groups (such as Latinos and blacks) hold stronger opinions.

TABLE 7.2 Patterns of public opinion on race issues by race/ethnicity.

	WHITE	ASIAN	LATINO	BLACK
How important is the issue of racial discrimination?				
Very important	56	68	80	86
Somewhat	32	21	14	9
Not at all	8	7	4	4
Have you or family experienced racial discrimination?				
Yes	18	39	40	44
No	78	57	59	52
Race relations in California				
Improving	34	44	44	24
Worsening	16	4	10	27
Staying same	41	42	42	44
Don't know	9	10	4	4

In addition to assessing opinions about Davis and the recall election, the survey asked voters about racial discrimination and race relations in California. These questions provide an interesting insight into the significance of race as an issue in California politics. As demonstrated by Barreto, Segura, and Woods (2004), attitudes on racial issues are important predictors of behavior in California. They found that ten years after the Rodney King riots, race issues were still salient, and nearly half of all residents of Los Angeles were concerned that a race riot similar to the 1992 riot could occur between 2002–07. Thus, it is important to establish the prevailing attitudes on race-related issues and how they differed among the racial groups in California during the 2003 recall election.

As demonstrated in Table 7.2, racial discrimination is still considered a relevant issue in the twenty-first century by California voters, especially among minorities. While just over half of white voters said discrimination was a very important issue, the percentages of Asian, Latino, and black voters who viewed discrimination as very important was much higher. Almost 70 percent of Asian Americans, 80 percent of Latinos, and 86 percent of blacks felt discrimination was a significant issue. When asked whether they or their family had experienced discrimination, minorities were twice as likely to report that they had. Just 18 percent of whites experienced discrimination compared with 39 percent of Asians, 40 percent of Latinos, and 44 percent of blacks. Thus, for a large segment of California's electorate, racial discrimination is a real issue. Finally, when asked about the future of race relations, there was a sense of tempered optimism, with some differences by race. Latinos and Asians were the most likely to view relations as improving, while more blacks felt relations were worsening. Taken in full, these numbers suggest that race and ethnicity have the capacity to play a role in California politics. The only question is whether voters follow these race cues.

VOTE BREAKDOWN IN 2003 RECALL BY RACE/ETHNICITY

While minority voters have tended to soundly favor Democratic candidates and issues in California, the 2003 recall brought a small, but significant drop-off in support for the Democratic Party. Following the special election, had minority voter turnout been 2 to 4 percentage points higher and had minority voters voted no on the recall at the same rates they voted in favor of Davis in his 2002 election, we estimated that the recall would have failed (Barreto and Ramírez 2004). However, this was not the case. Table 7.3 reviews vote preference in the 2003 recall election and candidate replacement ballot as compared with the mean Democratic vote rates from 1992–2002 in California. In particular, Latino support for Davis in 2003 was down 10 points from their levels of support in 2002 and 14 points lower than their average support for Democrats over the ten-year period. Similarly, although Bustamante was the only major Democrat replacement candidate on the ballot, black and Asian support for Bustamante fell off by 14 and 19 percentage points to 65 percent and 34 percent, respectively. White support for Davis and Bustamante also fell off significantly in the recall election.

TABLE 7.3   Average democratic vote 1992–2002 and recall preference 2003.

GROUP	1992–2002		95% CONFIDENCE		RECALL	CRUZ
	AVERAGE	S.D.	LOWER	UPPER	No	BUSTAMANTE
White	44.8	4.7	41.7	47.9	40	26*
Latino	68.6	4.4	65.7	71.5	55	56*
Black	80.3	6.7	75.9	84.7	79	65*
Asian	53.7	7.3	48.9	58.5	53	34*

Note: S.D., standard deviation.
*More than two standard deviations away from the mean.

Two points are notable about the levels of Democratic support in the recall election. First, only Latinos maintained equal support for Democrats on both parts of the ballot, voting to retain Davis and elect Bustamante at virtually the same rate. Every other ethnic group witnessed a sharp drop in support for Bustamante as the replacement candidate for governor, as compared to their no vote on the recall. Although blacks were more likely to vote for Bustamante than Latinos were, there was a large inconsistency between their vote for Davis and Bustamante, the two top Democrats in the election. Second, the difference between the average Democratic vote, and the vote for Bustamante is considerably outside the expected vote range. None of the support levels for Bustamante are in the predicted 95 percent confidence range that the ten-year history of previous voting projects. What's more, for all ethnic groups, the vote for Bustamante was more than two standard deviations away from their mean levels of support for Democrats in state elections, including four standard deviations away for white voters. While most of the negative attention was on the state's top Democrat, Davis—so negative, in fact, that he was facing a recall petition—it was Bustamante who received significantly lower than expected levels of support.

Although the exit poll results presented above provide a nice overview of voting patterns by race and ethnicity in California, some have called into question the reliability of the numbers for each subgroup (DiCamillo and Field 2003; Pachon and Barreto 2003). While the overall statewide percentages are very accurate (a margin of error of 2 points), the sample size for each ethnic group is smaller, making the margin of error larger (Latino ±4.3; black ±6.2; Asian ±6.2) and creating the potential for uncertainty. In addition to the margin of error issue, the sampling objective is to get a random and representative sample of the entire state, not one particular ethnic group. To alleviate these concerns, we offer a second strategy for assessing minority voting patterns in the California recall election: precinct level analysis.

Of all the fifty-eight counties in California, none is larger or more diverse than Los Angeles County, making it the ideal point of departure for studies of ethnic voting (for example, Barreto, Segura, and Woods 2004; Ramírez 2002). For each of the 1,781 precincts in Los Angeles, we compare the vote results for the recall to the adult population by race. This establishes a statistical and graphic presentation of voting trends by race in California, which makes it clear that racial voting differences do exist.

For the two main questions on the ballot—the recall of Davis and the replacement governor—we have created an XY scatterplot where the X axis is percent population (for each ethnic group) and the Y axis is vote preference. In addition, we have overlaid the regression line for each group indicating the slope. While the main scatterplot data is for the recall vote, for ease of comparability, we include the Bustamante vote regression line (dashed) in the same graph.[4]

Overall, the scatterplots confirm the trends in the exit poll data, that is, black and Latino voters were more supportive of Davis and Bustamante than were white and Asian American voters. In addition, as precincts become more heavily black and Latino, the vote results also become more consistent, suggesting that these groups are more likely to block vote as compared with whites and Asians. For example, Figure 7.1 does not show a clear upward or downward vote trend in relation to the white population. While the regression lines do show a downward slope, there are some heavily white precincts that voted 80 percent against the recall and some that voted 80 percent in favor of the recall. For replacement governor, there appears to be somewhat more block voting among whites in opposition to Bustamante. Among precincts that have no white voters, the lowest marks Bustamante received were 40 percent, while in heavily white precincts, he received as low as only 5 percent of the vote. Furthermore, the regression slope for Bustamante is much lower than for the recall (Davis), suggesting that Bustamante received even less support than Davis did among white voters.

While there are only a handful of heavily Asian American precincts, as demonstrated in Figure 7.2, the picture that emerges is similar to that for whites.

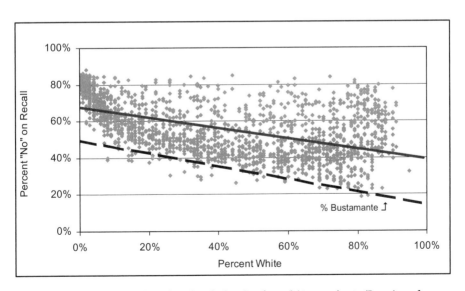

FIGURE 7.1   **Scatterplot of voting behavior for white precincts (Los Angeles county, 2003 recall election).**

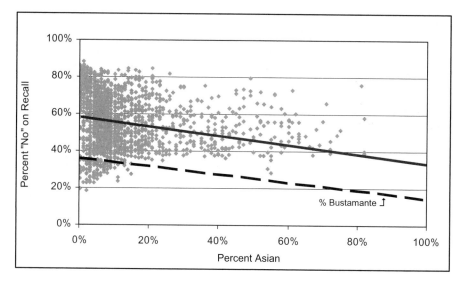

FIGURE 7.2   Scatterplot of voting behavior for Asian American precincts
(Los Angeles county, 2003 recall election).

As precincts become more heavily Asian, support levels for Davis hover around the middle of the chart, with some voting to recall and some voting to retain the governor. With respect to the Bustamante vote, Asian precincts demonstrate the same trend, but support levels are somewhat lower than for Davis. Overall, white and Asian American precincts were somewhat more likely to vote in favor of the recall and somewhat less likely to vote for Bustamante, although many outliers exist.

The scatterplots depict a clearer relationship between race and vote in the recall election with respect to Latinos and African Americans. First, the Latino population chart (Figure 7.3) clearly resembles a triangle, with a wide base that come to a point where precincts approach 90 to 100 percent Latino, and, second, both trend lines are noticeably upward. In both the recall and the replacement governor election, heavily Latino precincts were much more likely to side with the Democrats, Davis and Bustamante. Further, while non-Latino precincts displayed a wide range in support levels, predominantly Latino precincts were consistent in their vote preferences. On the recall question, Latino precincts ranged only from 70 to 80 percent against, compared with white precincts who varied widely in both support and opposition (Figure 7.1). Similarly, Latino precincts all came out in strong support for Bustamante at rates of 65 to 75 percent.[5]

African American precincts demonstrated the highest rates of opposition to the recall initiative at 75 to 85 percent, with every precinct that was greater than 80 percent black voting 80 percent No on the recall. However, there appears to have been considerably less support for Bustamante in black precincts than for Davis. According to Figure 7.4, heavily black precincts supported Bustamante at a rate between 40 and 50 percent, over 30 percentage

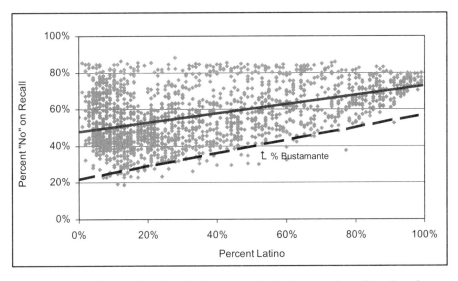

FIGURE 7.3　Scatterplot of voting behavior for Latino precincts (Los Angeles county, 2003 recall election).

points lower than their opposition to the recall. While the exit poll shows strong support for the lieutenant governor among African American voters (65%), Bustamante never received more than 52 percent of the vote in any of the predominantly African American precincts in the county, even as these same precincts voted 80 percent or more against the recall of Davis.

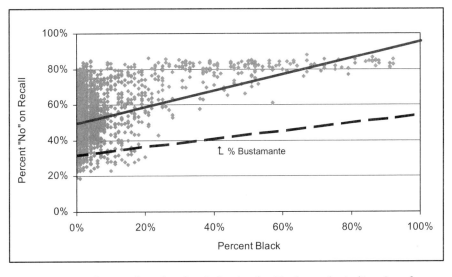

FIGURE 7.4　Scatterplot of voting behavior for black precincts (Los Angeles county, 2003 recall election).

CONCLUSION—LOOKING TO THE FUTURE

Leading up to the recall election, observers of California politics argued that "the minority vote will be more critical in this election than in any election in the past 25 or 30 years" (Sterngold 2003). While the minority vote did not impact the outcome, racial and ethnic politics did play a significant role in the election, as we have outlined in this chapter. Focusing on the voting trends of Latino, black, and Asian voters is only half of the puzzle of California politics. The other half, we argue, is the role of racial issues and campaign appeals by candidates during the election, which may mobilize or demobilize minority and, perhaps more importantly, white voters. Because they continue to represent a majority of the voting pool, the reaction of white voters to racial issues is a crucial factor in any California election. In the case of Proposition 54, the racial privacy initiative, race-based claims failed to resonate with Anglo or minority voters, and the ballot measure was soundly defeated. In the recall election, however, racial issues seemed to play a prominent role among all Californians.

More importantly, the recall election provided another indication that race will likely continue to play a significant and increasing role in California politics. The office-holding gains by minorities in labor organizations and elected office, as well as the involvement of Native American casinos through campaign contributions, will keep issues of race and ethnic minorities in the public eye for years to come. As the face of the electorate continues to change, and their partisan preferences evolve, both parties are likely to make race/ethnicity/immigration one of the key considerations as they seek to consolidate their electoral coalition. Depending on the political outcomes, California's handling of race in state politics may then be emulated by states facing similar demographic trends in years to come.

BIBLIOGRAPHY

Barabak, Mark Z. "Tepid Voters Favor Davis." *Los Angeles Times*, October 29, 2002.

Barreto, Matt A., and Ricardo Ramírez. "Minority Participation and the California Recall: Latino, Black, and Asian Voting Trends, 1990–2003." *PS: Political Science & Politics* 37 (January 2004): 11–14.

Barreto, Matt A., Gary Segura, and Nathan Woods. "The Effects of Overlapping Majority-Minority Districts on Latino Turnout." *American Political Science Review* 98 (February 2004): 65–75.

California Journal. "Race, Ethnicity and California Politics." November 1998.

Citrin, Jack, and Benjamin Highton. *How Race, Ethnicity and Immigration Shape the California Electorate*. San Francisco: Public Policy Institute of California, 2002.

DiCamillo, Mark, and Marvin Field. "A Different Take on 'Why Polls Matter.'" September 16. San Francisco: Field Institute, 2003.

Fraga, Luis, and Ricardo Ramírez. "Latino Political Incorporation in California, 1990-2000." In *Latinos and Public Policy in California: An Agenda for Opportunity*, edited by David López and Andrés Jiménez. Berkeley: Institute for Governmental Studies, University of California, 2003.

Fraga, Luis, Ricardo Ramírez, and Gary Segura. "Unquestioned Influence" Latinos and the 2000 Elections in California." In *Muted Voices: Latinos and the 2000 Elections*, edited by Rodolfo O. de la Garza and Louis DeSipio. Oxford: Rowman & Littlefield Publishers, Inc, 2004.

Hajnal, Zoltan, and Hugh Louch. *Are There Winners and Losers? Race, Ethnicity, and California's Initiative Vote.* San Francisco: Public Policy Institute of California, 2001.

Michelson, Melissa. "Getting Out the Latino Vote: How Door-to-Door Canvassing Influences Voter Turnout in Rural Central California." *Political Behavior* 25, no. 3 (2003): 247–63.

Nicholas, Carla. "Statement from the National Indian Gaming Association: Schwarzenegger Fundamentally Misunderstands Indian Tribes." September 24, 2003. http://www.indiangaming.org (accessed).

Pachon, Harry. "Latino Politics in the Golden State: Ready for the 21st Century?" In *Racial and Ethnic Politics in California*, edited by Byran O. Jackson and Michael B. Preston. Berkeley: Institute for Governmental Studies, University of California, 1998.

Pachon, Harry, and Matt A. Barreto. "Latino Impact on the California Recall Election." *Latino Journal* (November 2003).

Pantoja, Adrian D., and Nathan D. Woods. "Turning Out the Latino Vote in Los Angeles County: Did Interest Group Efforts Matter?" *American Review of Politics* 20 (2000): 141–62.

Ramírez, Ricardo. *The Changing Landscape of California Politics, 1990-2000.* Unpublished Doctoral Dissertation. Palo Alto: Stanford University, 2002.

Sterngold, James. "Poll Finds Minority Voters Dubious of Recall." *San Francisco Chronicle,* October 2, 2003.

Tolbert, Caroline, and Rodney Hero. "Race/Ethnicity and Direct Democracy: An Analysis of California's Illegal Immigration Initiative." *Journal of Politics* 58 (1996): 806–18.

Tomás Rivera Policy Institute. "Assessing the Latino Vote in the California Recall Election" Press Release. November 21. Claremont, CA: Tomás Rivera Policy Institute, 2003.

_____. "Was the California Latino Vote Key to Governor Davis' Re-Election?" Press Release. November 21. Claremont, CA: Tomás Rivera Policy Institute, 2002.

Wong, Janelle S. "The Effects of Age and Political Exposure on the Development of Party Identification Among Asian American and Latino Immigrants in the United States." *Political Behavior* 22 (2000): 341–71.

NOTES

1. In contrast, in 1996, Republican Congressman Robert Dornan argued that hundreds of immigrant voters in Santa Ana were illegal aliens and broke election laws in going to the polls and voting against him. Although an independent study after the election found no basis for his claim, he continued to campaign against immigrant issues in his 1998 effort to regain the seat he lost in 1996 to Loretta Sanchez.

2. Proponents of Proposition 68 (Card Clubs and Race Tracks) in the 2004 general election have capitalized on this message by reiterating the message that Native American tribes do not pay a fair share on their Web site: "We agree with Governor Schwarzenegger. We agree that it makes zero sense for an $8 billion industry to operate in California while paying virtually nothing to support the common good. It's time for these immensely profitable Indian casinos to give something back to the state that's given them the most lucrative gaming monopoly in the nation. *It's time for the people of California to get their fair share!*" (emphasis in original text).

3. The survey was designed and implemented by a partnership of four organizations: the Institute for Justice and Journalism, Pew Hispanic Center, New California Media, and Tomás Rivera Policy Institute. The survey contacted 1,608 registered voters between September 6–16, 2003.

4. For Figures 7.1–7.4, each dot represents a precinct in Los Angeles. The horizontal axis (x) indicates the racial composition of the precinct and the vertical axis (y) indicates the percent of the precinct that voted no on the recall referendum. The regression lines represent the predicted vote value for each point along the racial spectrum, given the distribution of the existing data.

5. While the regression line for Latinos and Bustamante vote predicts just below 60 percent support for the lieutenant governor among Latinos, the actual precinct data show that these heavily Latino precincts exceeded the regression predictions (similar to the recall vote, note that most of the data points for heavily Latino precincts are actually above the regression line).

8

OPPORTUNITIES LOST?

LATINOS, CRUZ BUSTAMANTE, AND CALIFORNIA'S RECALL

LOUIS DESIPIO
NATALIE MASUOKA

UNIVERSITY OF CALIFORNIA, IRVINE

As California's gubernatorial recall formally began in August 2003, the state's Latinos were poised to play an influential role in the race's outcome. Lieutenant Governor Cruz Bustamante entered the race at the last minute and stood as the only major Democrat competing to replace Governor Gray Davis if the recall passed. Were the recall to succeed—a position Bustamante publicly opposed throughout the campaign—and he were to win, a Latino would occupy the governor's office for the first time since 1875. For the recall to fail, Latinos and other Democrats would have to vote in large numbers to keep Davis in office.

When the race ended two months later, Latinos had seized neither of these opportunities. They divided their votes on recall and, although providing majority support for Bustamante, voted at surprisingly high numbers for Arnold Schwarzenegger and conservative Republican State Senator Tom McClintock. Bustamante not only lost the replacement race by a sizeable margin, but also tarnished his credentials for a 2006 race for the office.[1]

In this chapter, we examine the recall race to assess the Latino role in its outcomes and, more importantly, to evaluate the symbolism and the substance of California Latino politics. We assess Latino preferences and ask whether Latinos could have influenced the outcomes of the race if they had been more unified or had turned out in larger numbers. Finally, we assess the implications of the recall for the broader study of Latino politics in California and nationally.

LATINO AND THE RECALL/REPLACEMENT CAMPAIGNS

Although the recall of Governor Davis was initially framed around partisan politics and citizen disapproval, Latino loyalties and interests quickly took center stage over the course of the election. Issues such as immigration, driver's licenses for undocumented immigrants, the *Movimiento Estudiantil de Chicano de Aztlán* (MEChA), the legacy of Republican-Latino relations in the 1990s, and Latino ethnic attachment were topics driving the political discourse of the election. Interestingly, most of the major issues in the recall election included Latino themes. Moreover, not only were Latino issues central to the debate, but also Latino electoral mobilization was critical to calculations of who would win, particularly early in the race. Candidates, the media, and political analysts all looked to the Latino vote as the bloc to be captured and one that could be decisive. Despite this potential importance, most Latino outreach was symbolic. Candidates spoke to Latino communities by asserting similarities—often without much evidence—with each focusing on different aspects of the Latino experience. We review the course of the election to show how central Latinos and Latino issues were to candidate strategies and how these efforts often missed their targets.

RECALL

Throughout his tenure as governor, Davis had an erratic history addressing Latino concerns. Like other constituency groups, many Latinos felt Davis did not pay attention to the needs of their community. Latino leaders complained that Davis failed to advocate on behalf of Latino needs in his legislative agenda, particularly in such areas as health care, labor, and education. Latinos were, nevertheless, central to Davis' hopes of retaining the governorship.

Davis had received strong support from Latino electorates in both of his gubernatorial races. In his 1998 race, *Los Angeles Times* exit polls found that Davis won 71 percent of the Latino vote, much higher that the 51 percent support that he received from whites. By 2002, Davis' support from Latinos had declined to 65 percent, but this support proved more critical because Davis lost the white vote to his Republican opponent by a margin of 43 to 46 percent (*Los Angeles Times* 2002). This support in 2002 came despite the fact that the legislative Latino Caucus refused to endorse Davis.[2] Assuming that the experience of 2002 would guide voters in the recall, Davis and his advisors recognized that they would need big antirecall majorities from Latino and black voters to balance more tepid support or opposition from white voters.

Going into the recall, Latinos, like the majority of other California voters, rated Davis' job performance poorly (Field Institute 2003; Pinkus 2003). The fact that the Latino vote could not be taken for granted was immediately acknowledged by Davis who, as talk of a recall intensified in the spring and summer, began to court Latino voters. He made personal appearances at many Latino events and spoke publicly of his long record of supporting Latino needs. The antirecall campaign was advertised on Spanish language media and Davis granted repeated interviews to Spanish language news stations.

Understanding the potential strength of the Latino vote, Latino leaders capitalized on Davis' vulnerability in the polls. Pressing the electoral power of the Latino community, they demanded recognition and response from the endangered governor. At a Latino banquet dinner in late July, the *Los Angeles Times* reported,

> [Davis'] vulnerability was palpable at a Latino civil rights group's recent dinner in a Los Angeles hotel ballroom. The banquet host, Antonio Gonzalez, president of the Southwest Voter Registration Education Project, was blunt. "The governor is in a bit of a pickle, and he needs the Latino vote," Gonzales told the crowd of several hundred Latinos. "So I thought I'd take the opportunity to tell the governor to help us help him." As Davis chatted with Mayor James K. Hahn at a front-row table, Gonzalez whipped up cheers by cranking up pressure on the governor. Shouting with a preacher's cadence, he called on Davis to sign the driver's license bill. "You all know the *Jerry Maguire* movie? 'Help me help you,'" Gonzalez said. "Well, governor, we want you to help us help you" (Finnegan 2003).

Davis' most obvious attempt to connect with Latino voters and establish a favorable record on the needs of the community was his approval and signature of SB 60, which would grant undocumented immigrants driver's licenses. As the recall election transitioned into full swing, Davis had begun to openly voice his support for such legislation. With his open endorsement, a fifth version of the bill—relatively unchanged since the version that he had vetoed in 2002—quickly passed the legislature. At the height of the recall campaign, Davis held a large public event with the author of the bill, Senator Gil Cedillo, and other members of the Latino Caucus, celebrating his signature and approval of the bill. Critics, of course, were quick to attack Davis for pandering to Latino voters, noting the fact that Davis repeatedly rejected similar versions of the bill when his job was not on the line.

Laws regarding state treatment of immigrants, particularly undocumented immigrants, have had a volatile history in California. Most notable was Proposition 187, which denied state education and health benefits to undocumented immigrants (Ono and Sloop 2002). In 1994, California voters passed Proposition 187 by a significant majority. Republican Governor Pete Wilson invigorated his reelection campaign by supporting the proposition and linking his reelection themes to the proposition's anti-immigrant message. Arguably, though, this was a Pyrrhic victory for Wilson and the state's Republican Party. Wilson damaged his formerly moderate political legacy, for which he paid a price in his brief 1996 presidential campaign, and Republicans saw a steady decline in Latino support the state, just as the Latino vote grew dramatically (Field Institute 2000, Table 12; Fraga, Ramírez, and Segura 2004).

State politics had not changed by 2003. Immigration-related legislation was still highly politically charged, although strategic calculations were somewhat different than in 1994. SB 60 could be specifically considered a "Latino" issue given its attention to undocumented immigrants, framed primarily as Latino immigrants. Like Proposition 187, the idea behind SB 60 was fairly unpopular among other—primarily white—voters, so a position on either side of the issue could be politically dangerous, alienating large constituencies. Davis' choice to support the unpopular legislation demonstrated the risk he was willing to take to court Latinos. Analysts speculated that to win the election, Davis would have to galvanize key Democrat constituencies: liberals, unions, and minority groups.

TABLE 8.1 Support and opposition to recall.

	June 28–July 2 (%)	Sept. 6–10 (%)	Sept. 25–29 (%)	Oct. 7 (%)
Latinos				
Support	56	53	49	45
Oppose	39	41	48	55
State Electorate				
Support	51	50	56	55
Oppose	42	47	42	45

Sources: Los Angeles Times 2003a, b, c, d.

Latinos, being the largest racial minority group in the state, were understood to be one of the primary groups that needed to be secured on Election Day and worth the political risk for Davis. His signature on SB 60 ensured that a Latino issue would be debated for the duration of the election.

As the recall campaign progressed, Davis and the "no on recall" campaign played a diminishing role. Polls showed that among the electorate as a whole, recall advocates were in the majority (see Table 8.1). Although there were moments when this pro-recall consensus diminished—particularly in the day or two after the *Los Angeles Times* printed charges of Schwarzenegger's serial groping of women in the entertainment industry (Cohn, Hall, and Welkos 2003), as the campaign progressed, popular attention increasingly focused on the replacement race. One unknown factor in this equation was whether Latinos supporting Bustamante would also bring enough Latino support to the recall race to salvage the antirecall effort.

"No on Recall, Yes on Bustamante": The Replacement Race

Davis' support of SB 60 did much to bring Latinos into the recall election, but, most likely, it was Bustamante's entrance into the race that cemented the potential importance of Latinos to recall outcomes. Bustamante staked his potential for victory on being able to win the Latino vote decisively in a crowded race. If the recall passed, the replacement candidate with the most votes—regardless of how small a share of the total votes cast—would win the race. Bustamante and his advisors saw this structure as a distinct advantage for Bustamante, particularly relative to the 2006 gubernatorial race: In 2003, there was a single race without a party primary and with a large number of candidates, so any candidate with a cohesive constituency had a strategic advantage.

Politically speaking, Bustamante, regardless of his position as lieutenant governor and history as the first Latino assembly speaker in the twentieth century, was a relatively unknown elected official. In fact, initially, Democrats urged U.S. Senator Dianne Feinstein to enter the race to replace Davis as a protection if Davis were to be recalled. Feinstein had wide name recognition and was highly regarded among most California voters. Bustamante, on the other hand, was known to few outside Sacramento and had little name recognition among voters; he appeared not to be "ready for prime time" by many. He was a poor public speaker who was not particularly photogenic, particularly in a race against a body-building movie star. He was unable to shape the issue debate and spent much of the campaign on the defensive. Perhaps most importantly, Bustamante was the consummate insider in a "throw-the-bums" out election.

While many people felt that he should not have entered the race at the last minute, particularly after indicating that he would not run, many Democrats breathed a sign of relief. Democrats assumed his name on the ticket would assuredly galvanize the Latino vote, which could protect Davis from recall and, if that failed, elect Bustamante to office. Indeed, regardless of his recognition among other Californians, Bustamante's Latino appeal was understood as his greatest asset in the campaign.

Given these expectations, Bustamante highlighted his Mexican and immigrant roots to demonstrate to Latino voters that he understood how it was to be like them. He openly discussed his love for his culture, his dedication to his community and family, and his personal history as a migrant farmworker. His candidacy was consistently described as the "chance to elect California's first Latino governor in 128 years." Thus, his symbolic value was a central theme of his campaign. Many in the Latino community responded. In a *Los Angeles Times* article, Latino voters discussed the importance of having a Latino governor in the state:

> Though Ysiano is a Republican, he said he planned to vote for Bustamante. Many of those who oppose the recall also said they would vote for Bustamante. "I think if we have a Latino governor, it'll make it better for us," said Julissa Cabrera, who said she was still undecided on whether to oust Davis, but favored Bustamante as his potential replacement. "Just being Latino, he would have more passion to do more for our community" … [Bonavita] Quinto, who said she hosted then-Assemblyman Bustamante at a gathering with Latino college students years ago in Fresno, acknowledged that she had an affection for the lieutenant governor. "He does come from an immigrant family," she said, "and for that reason alone he must understand the issues we face" (Bustillo and Gorman 2003).

Latino activists contended that a Latino governor would fight for the needs of Latinos in the state and understand the challenges their community faced in terms of immigration, education, health care, and other issues. Interestingly, Bustamante's positions on issues and his public service career were less publicized than his personal life history, once again, demonstrating his appeal as a Latino rather than an experienced political player.

Bustamante presented himself not simply as a Latino, but more importantly as an immigrant success story. His official biography states the following:

> Cruz's rise from the fields of California's Central Valley to his elections as an Assemblyman, Speaker of the Assembly and then California's Lieutenant Governor was, " … the direct result of the lessons I learned about work, honesty and loyalty from my family and my community. I worked hard. I took advantage of opportunity when it came my way. And I benefited immensely from all of those who preceded me in the constant struggle for fairness,

equality and opportunity that has allowed working-class kids like me to pursue the American dream" (Bustamante 2004).

Latino activists strongly supported Bustamante's candidacy and garnered support to place a Latino in the governor's seat. Almost immediately after Bustamante announced his candidacy, the Latino Legislative Caucus endorsed his campaign. Although it was strongly speculated that Bustamante would win the Latino vote, Latino leaders and groups dedicated themselves to mobilizing voters to guarantee that the final results would include not just a high share of the Latino electorate voting for Bustamante, but also many new Latino voters going to the polls. Latino activists fought legal battles to extend the election into March so that they had more time to mobilize Latino voters to support Bustamante at the polls. Claiming potential vote dilution that would violate provisions of the Voting Rights Act, Latino activists identified six counties where polling machines were allegedly grossly inadequate and had not been updated to meet state standards. Ultimately, the courts rejected these challenges.

Although his Latino identity and connection with Latino issues was potentially an asset to his campaign, Bustamante's so-called Latinoness was also used by his opponents to attack him. As the election increasingly became competitive, Bustamante was criticized by opponents for two major things: his membership in MEChA when he was an undergraduate at California State University, Fresno, in the early 1970s and his acceptance of large donations from Native American tribes. Attacks on Bustamante's membership in MEChA hit the news stories nationwide, when conservative groups described the student organization as a racist and anti-American group that advocated ceding the southwest back to Mexico. McClintock compared MEChA to the Ku Klux Klan, saying that the nationalistic bent of the organization is radical and racist (anti-white). Bustamante never successfully undermined these charges.

Bustamante was also widely criticized for his campaign financing strategies. Initially, Bustamante used an account from his 1998 campaign for lieutenant governor that was not covered by newer campaign finance limits.[3] His campaign financing, however, became even more suspicious in the eyes of the public when candidate Schwarzenegger observed that Bustamante had received large contributions from Native American tribal groups and labeled these "special interests," because of the interest of many of these tribal groups in opening and expanding casinos. This introduced another racial group into the election's issue focus. All of the major candidates charged that Bustamante was being "bought" by special interests because he had accepted upwards of $3 million from Native American tribes. The attacks on Bustamante, whatever their merit on substantive grounds, were reminiscent of recent California campaigns in which race and the taint of illegality was used to reduce white liberal support for Latino Democrats. While California's diverse population makes race an asset to a campaign by identifying and mobilizing a group of minority voters using ethnic cues, race also is used as an issue to mobilize primarily conservative white voters to act against a minority group's cause.

The other candidates in the replacement race did not cede Latino votes to Bustamante. Schwarzenegger, Peter Camejo, Arianna Huffington, and McClintock each spoke of symbolic ties to Latinos and policy connections to the Latino agenda. Many made use of Spanish media to articulate their platforms to the Latinos. Camejo, also a Latino, stressed his connections with the community and spoke of the Green Party agenda as a Latino agenda. Schwarzenegger and Huffington were both immigrants and highlighted their immigrant experiences in the United States. Schwarzenegger made symbolic attempts to demonstrate his openness to the needs of Latinos. He celebrated the tenth anniversary of his naturalization in Los Angeles with a group of Latino and Asian immigrants to show his experience with adjusting to life in the United States. His team of advisors included Jaime Escalante, the famous Latino public school teacher profiled in the movie *Stand and Deliver*, who was asked to consult him on education policy. Schwarzenegger's advisors also identified another connection between the candidate and Latinos: A significant audience for the candidate's action films was young Latino males. They hoped that this audience would also become Schwarzenegger voters. Finally, McClintock spoke to the moral conservatism of Latinos by highlighting his opposition to abortion and support for Latino small-business owners.

Latino interests dictated a candidate's disadvantages as well. Schwarzenegger had a self-inflicted barrier to winning support in Latino communities, specifically his campaign's connection to former Governor Pete Wilson who headed his team of political advisors. Many Latinos, and particularly Latino leaders, were suspicious of Schwarzenegger simply because of his connection to Wilson. Because Wilson was one of Schwarzenegger's closest political confidants, Latinos worried about the degree to which Wilson would have influence in the governor's office if Schwarzenegger were to be elected to office. Schwarzenegger also committed to repealing the newly signed bill granting driver's licenses to undocumented immigrants (although saying that he would approve a new driver's license bill if it included new security protections).

Midway through the recall, Schwarzenegger charged that Bustamante was participating in and promoting race-based politics through his attempts to identify with Latino voters. His comment underlines the salience of racial issues in California elections. Schwarzenegger's comment alleged that it was bad for candidates to use racial or ethnic cues to mobilize voters and that doing so should be seen as pandering to certain ethnic groups for political support. Racial cues, however, were used by all sides of the political spectrum to galvanize voters: from Bustamante's positive appeal as a Latino and the opportunity his candidacy offered to elect California's first Latino governor in more than a century to the negative appeal by his opponents initiating such concepts as racial hatred and suspicion to mobilize conservative white voters. Given the growing Latino population, it is reasonable to expect that this debate over how to use the Latino identity in campaigns will grow in future years.

Ultimately, these debates declined in importance as Schwarzenegger cemented his lead. Schwarzenegger's Hollywood appeal, which gained increasing national attention as the recall progressed, overshadowed all of the other candidates. Bustamante consistently placed second in statewide polls, well behind the leader. Polls of Latinos demonstrated that some of the early expectations for Latino support of Bustamante were overstated. While this reflects an arguably healthy diversity among Latino voters (a theme that we return to later), it also was an indication of Bustamante's poorly run campaign. His travel schedule was unpredictable and there seemed to be little planning. At times, Bustamante would disappear from the campaign trail. As the Bustamante campaign faltered, his organizational supporters—particularly Latino civic organizations and trade unions—reduced their mobilization efforts and withdrew money they had committed to get-out-the-vote efforts.

Proposition 54

In another political move to represent the Latino community, Bustamante also spearheaded a "no on 54" campaign to defeat the ballot proposition that would ban racial information in government document information. Many Latino leaders felt that the passage of Proposition 54 would slow Latino progress in education and hiring. Proposition 54 would have prevented the state from collecting data on race and ethnicity. Such data provided a resource to challenge inequities in the delivery of public services and ensure that the number of Latinos in schools and jobs were representative of the number of Latinos in the state's population. Along with other racial groups, Latino activists mobilized against this proposition by educating Latinos about the law's true implications and its effects on the Latino community. Remarkably, these efforts were not particularly successful; many Latinos (and state residents generally) were unaware of Proposition 54 (Institute for Justice and Journalism et al. 2003).

With Bustamante bringing attention to the proposition, public opinion about it turned negative as the campaign progressed. The proposition's backer, Ward Connerly, unhappily protested the strength of the opposition campaigns, which his own could not compete with.[4] Weeks before the election, Connerly announced what he believed was the inevitable defeat of the proposition. Some speculated that the placement of Proposition 54 and Bustamante on the ticket would galvanize Latino voters and increase Latino turnout substantially, perhaps saving Davis in the process. Near the campaign's end, Latino organizations shifted some of the resources they had committed to supporting the Bustamante candidacy to opposing Proposition 54.

Latino Attitudes and Vote Choice on the Recall

Given their central place in candidate and campaign strategies, how did Latinos perceive the recall election and the candidates vying to be Davis' replacement? Table 8.1 presents the change in Latino perceptions of the recall question compared with general California voters and demonstrates that Latinos followed a pattern opposite of the general voting population. The first opinion poll found Latinos to generally support the recall, along with the general population. As the recall election progressed, however, mobilization efforts by the Democratic Party and Davis supporters convinced Latinos to oppose the recall. By Election Day, the majority of Latino voters chose to vote no on the recall question, while the general population took the opposite position. The ability to change Latino perceptions on the recall question demonstrates the influence that mobilization had on this set of voters, as well as their strong Democratic partisanship. Within three months, albeit in heavy doses, campaign cues were able to turn the tide of Latino opinion on the recall.

TABLE 8.2   Latino support for the replacement candidates.

	SEPT. 6–10 (%)	SEPT. 25–29 (%)	OCT. 7 (%)
Candidate			
Bustamante	47	54	55
Schwarzenegger	29	24	31
McClintock	13	13	10

Sources: Los Angeles Times 2003b, c, d.

Bustamante seemed to enjoy a majority of Latino support throughout the duration of the election. Ethnic attachment and Democratic partisanship most likely played a key role in determining Latino support for Bustamante. The lieutenant governor received consistently high degrees of support from his ethnic community within the last month of the election cycle. Table 8.2 presents the percentage of Latinos who claimed they would vote for either Bustamante or Schwarzenegger in polls conducted between September and Election Day in October. Generally speaking, Latino support for Bustamante increased over the course of the month. Schwarzenegger, although receiving a higher-than-expected percentage of Latino support, saw his Latino support slightly fluctuate through September. Regardless of name recognition and catering to the Latino community, Latino support for Schwarzenegger never came close to overtaking the support given to Bustamante.

ELECTION RESULTS

On Election Day, Latinos opposed the recall and supported Bustamante in the replacement election. Latinos strongly opposed Proposition 54. Conversely, non-Latino voters supported the recall and Schwarzenegger. Latino turnout was comparable to recent elections but not as high as many had predicted (or perhaps hoped).

Exit polling of Latinos is not an exact art, so specific figures sometimes vary slightly, but overall CNN (2003) found that Latinos opposed the recall by a margin of 55 to 45. This opposition was much weaker than that of African Americans (79 to 21) and quite comparable to Asian Americans (53 to 47). Whites supported the recall by a margin of 59 to 41.

In the replacement race, the *Los Angeles Times* and CNN exit polls showed majority Latino support for Bustamante, although by slightly different margins. According to the *Los Angeles Times* (2003), Bustamante earned 55 percent of the Latino vote to Schwarzenegger's 31 and McClintock's 10. CNN saw a weaker Latino majority for Bustamante—52 percent—with Schwarzenegger and McClintock winning 31 and 9 percents, respectively. Overall, blacks were much more supportive of Bustamante (and less so of the two leading Republican candidates) than were Latinos, with Bustamante earning 64 percent of the black vote. Whites gave a majority of their votes and Asian Americans a plurality to Schwarzenegger.

All racial/ethnic groups opposed Proposition 54. Blacks were the strongest opponents, with 88 percent voting no. Latinos and Asian Americans opposed the proposition by three-to-one margins as did six in ten whites.

DID LATINO VOTES COUNT?

In contrast to early predictions, Latino turnout did not grow dramatically in this election. Although there are no exact figures, we offer two indicators to substantiate this assertion. First, turnout in high-concentration Latino cities in Los Angeles county indicated that turnout among registered voters in these cities was lower than that for the county as a whole and roughly comparable to turnout in recent gubernatorial elections (which was considerably lower than turnout in presidential election years) (Tomás Rivera Policy Institute 2003). It is possible that Latinos in other parts of the state—particularly the Central Valley where Bustamante grew up—could have reacted more positively to his campaign and been better mobilized. Aggregate turnout data from other parts of the state, however, do not suggest dramatic Latino mobilization for the recall election. Second, the two exit polls show that Latinos made up between 11 (the *Los Angeles Times*) and 18 (CNN) percent of the respondents to these polls. Exit polls are not designed to measure the share any subpopulation makes up of the electorate, although they are often used for this purpose. They do, however, offer an indication of the change in a subpopulation's share of the electorate in two exit polls using similar methodologies. In 2002, following the November gubernatorial race, the *Los Angeles Times* exit poll reported that 10 percent of its exit poll respondents were Latino. Because of problems with the Voter News Service consortium, CNN did not report California exit poll results in 2002. In sum, there is no evidence that the Latino vote increased dramatically in 2003 and there is modest, but convincing, evidence that Latinos voted at roughly the same levels that they had in recent state races, a turnout level lower than for non-Hispanic whites.

These results raise two questions that are important not just for understanding the outcome of the recall races, but also for the broader study of Latino politics. First, we analyze the lower-than-expected Latino support for Bustamante and consider whether the recall race is a harbinger of increasing Latino support for Republican candidates as some analysts have suggested. Second, we assess whether Latinos could have made a difference had they united behind Bustamante or the antirecall position that many Latino leaders advocated.

In the days after the recall election, the symbolic importance of the Latino electorate shifted. From the monolithic and mobizable force pundits saw in August, it became a "swing" vote in October to these same pundits based largely on the combined exit poll results, which showed that roughly 40 percent of Latinos supported the two leading Republicans in the race, Schwarzenegger and McClintock.

We see these results as unsurprising (and not as a harbinger) for two reasons. First, although this share of votes for Republicans is high, it is not unprecedented, particularly in a race such as this in which the leading Republican had high name recognition, an identity outside politics, and, most importantly, tried to position himself as above the partisan fray. In past elections, Republicans routinely earn between 25 and 30 percent of the Latino vote, even in California. When combined with a lackluster campaign by Bustamante, in this race, Republicans earned on the high end of what they traditionally earn in national, if not state, races. More importantly, we believe that the exit polls inflated the Republican share of the Latino vote, as they have in past elections (de la Garza, Shaw, and Lu 1999). Exit polls are not designed to be representative of racial/ethnic subpopulations. Instead, their purpose is to cue news organizations about who won in the hours after the polls close and what issues or groups drove that vote. State-level exit polls have samples that are representative at the state level, but not necessarily for any specific population. With Latinos, exit polls tend to oversample Latinos who live in non-Latino concentration areas. As a result, they include somewhat more Republican and Republican-leaning Latinos than does the electorate. As evidence for the recall race, we look to the analysis of high-concentration Latino cities mentioned earlier (Tomás Rivera Policy Institute 2003). While this analysis is an imperfect mirror of the Latino vote,[5] cities such as these provide an overwhelming share of the total Latino votes in the state. In these high-concentration cities, Bustamante's share of the vote was generally 10 percentage points higher than the statewide exit polls (in the low to mid-60s) and Schwarzenegger was generally in the high teens.

Should California Democrats rest easy based on these findings? Absolutely not. Latinos showed that they need more than symbolism to vote for any candidate. Bustamante ran a lackluster campaign and paid the price in very weak Latino support. Latinos demonstrated, as they have repeatedly in the past, that they respond to substantive outreach. Candidates and parties seeking their votes need to speak to their policy needs and invest in voter mobilization to ensure that their potential is turned into active voting on Election Day.

If the Democrats should not rest easy, should Schwarzenegger be confident about support from a high, although not majority, share of Latinos as he looks to reelection in 2006? Probably not, although there is little evidence from the recall election to evaluate Governor Schwarzenegger's future with Latino voters. Schwarzenegger's first liability is that he is a Republican and Latinos routinely offer Democrats at least 60 percent of their votes in California statewide elections. He could overcome this liability with active outreach on policy issues of concern to Latinos. His 2003 campaign, however, does not suggest a willingness to reach out for their votes. Aside from efforts to make symbolic connections to Latinos around shared experiences with immigration and adaptation to U.S. society, candidate Schwarzenegger did little to win Latino votes. On one of the major issues of the campaign—the driver's license bill—Schwarzenegger took a position opposed by most Latino leaders in the state and, from limited polling evidence, by the Latino electorate as well (acknowledging that he made the promise to find a compromise that would grant driver's licenses to some undocumented immigrants). Yet he did well among Latinos, earning somewhere between 20 and 30 percent of the vote in a multicandidate race that included a prominent statewide Latino officeholder.

Had there been greater unity or mobilization that ensured high Latino turnout, could Latinos have made a difference in the recall or replacement

TABLE 8.3   Scenarios for Latino influence, 2003 recall race.

	LATINOS SHARE OF STATEWIDE VOTE	
	11% (LAT)	*18% (CNN)*
Recall		
Latino opposition to recall		
Reported – 54/55% opposition	Recall Won	Recall Won
Scenario 1 – 70% opposition	Recall Wins	Recall Wins
Scenario 2 – 100% opposition	Recall Wins	**Recall Defeated**
Replacement		
Latino support for Bustamante		
Reported – 52/55% Bustamante support	Schwarzenegger	Schwarzenegger
Scenario 1 – 70% Bustamante support	Schwarzenegger	Schwarzenegger
Scenario 2 – 100% Bustamante support	Schwarzenegger	Schwarzenegger

Note: CNN, Cable News Network; LAT, *Los Angeles Times*; bold reflects change in outcome based on scenario.

Sources: CNN 2003; *Los Angeles Times* 2003d.

races? Yes, but only under the most optimistic of scenarios. Table 8.3 examines the potential impact of California's Latino electorate under various scenarios. The two exit polls offer a boundary for the Latino share of California's electorate at present levels.[6] The *Los Angeles Times'* reported 11 percent is on the low side of the current Latino share of the statewide electorate and CNN's 18 percent is on the high side, with the actual percentage of the Latino vote in the 2003 race likely somewhere in between. We examine what would have happened at each of these percentages of the statewide vote if Latinos had opposed the recall and supported Bustamante at 70 percent levels (scenario 1) and at 100 percent levels (scenario 2). The 70 percent level is a realistic benchmark. In two-person races, Democrats in most states (and Republicans in Florida) can, with successful candidates and campaigns, earn 70 percent of the Latino vote. The 100 percent scenario is unrealistic, but instead it is meant to show the difficulty in achieving Latino influence in California statewide races when Latinos oppose the position or candidate taken by the white majority.

Only one of the scenarios tested shows a change in the Latino vote changing the outcome of the election. If the CNN exit poll did accurately reflect the 2003 electorate and Latinos made up 18 percent of voters, and if all Latinos had opposed recall, Governor Davis would be serving out his second term. Latinos could not have changed the recall outcome regardless of their unity, if the *Los Angeles Times* estimate was correct and Latinos made up just 11 percent of California voters. Similarly, Schwarzenegger's margin of victory was sufficiently large (1,308,333) that, even if all Latinos had supported Bustamante, they could not have made a difference at either tested level of the electorate.

LATINOS AND CALIFORNIA'S GUBERNATORIAL RECALL: LESSONS FOR THE STUDY OF LATINO POLITICS

The relative lack of influence of Latinos in determining the outcome of the recall and replacement elections is not an isolated event in California statewide races (Fraga, Ramírez, and Segura 2004). Expectations for Latino influence have frequently preceded its ability to deliver in both national and state elections (DeSipio and de la Garza 2004). California's recall offers several important insights into the broader process of Latino politics in the United States. Specifically, the recall emphasizes the price that California Latinos pay for institutions of direct democracy. California is home to more of these institutions and they are used more frequently than in other state. Second, Bustamante's campaign during the recall demonstrates that the role of shared ethnicity is not an overriding factor, but one among many, that influences Latino vote choice. Given the diversity of Latino preferences shown during this election, other factors (primarily partisanship) played additional roles in shaping Latino voting behavior. Finally, the election demonstrates that expectations for the influence of the Latino electorate are still well ahead of the ability of Latinos to deliver on Election Day, although the resounding defeat of Proposition 54 hints of the electorate's continued political potential. For Latino influence to be felt, there needs to be more than symbolic outreach and potential electoral "firsts"; instead, mobilization is required for Latinos to live up to popular expectations.

Recall is just one form of direct democracy; the reforms instituted in many states in the early twentieth century limited the power of entrenched interests and in principle gave free voice to the ordinary citizen (Schrag 1998). Although the use of recall at the state level is new in California, the state has long been a user of statewide ballot initiatives, such as Proposition 54 in this election and Proposition 187 in the 1994 election, to transfer legislative power to statewide voter majorities. Like the vote on recall, the electoral majority on statewide ballot propositions is overwhelmingly white (much more so than the state population as a whole) and will remain so for many years to come. Thus, Latinos—even when much more unified than they were in the recall and replacement races—will not be able to determine election outcomes when their position opposes that of a unified non-Hispanic white vote (Guerra and Fraga 1996). To the extent that voting in California is racially polarized, these institutions of direct democracy will not serve their original goal of cracking concentrated power. On the contrary, they will entrench white power even as the state becomes increasingly non-white. One risk, that cannot be evaluated at this writing, is that repeated electoral defeats in statewide elections (including propositions and future recalls) might dampen the trust of California Latinos in efficacy of electoral politics. Overall, these institutions of direct democracy will dampen the policy benefits of the gains Latinos are making in electing co-ethnics to office at the local and legislative levels.

Although the questions we raise about the accuracy of Latino exit polls cannot be resolved here, we acknowledge that preelection polls confirm that many Latinos did not support Bustamante. This should not come as a surprise as the Latino electorate—like all electorates—has cleavages. In most national elections, for example, the Democratic candidate earns between

63 and 70 percent of the Latino vote (DeSipio, de la Garza, and Setzler 1999, Table 1.1). Latinos, then, are much more united than non-Hispanic whites, but are less unified than African Americans, who often provide Democratic candidates with eight-to-one margins.

These national elections, however, have not placed Latino candidates at the top of the ticket. Many assumed that the presence of Bustamante would unify the Latino electorate and drive nonvoting Latinos to the polls like no election before. But Election Day proved to be a disappointment. This offers the second lesson for the broader study of Latino politics: Shared ethnicity is not the only salient factor that drives Latino preferences. In several recent elections, Latinos (in areas of Latino Democratic dominance) have had the choice of an Anglo Democrat and a Latino Republican. Even when the Latino Republican has been well funded and had a serious chance of victory, the Democrat has won the Latino votes (*Houston Chronicle* 2003; Michelson and Leon 2001). Clearly, the Bustamante case is somewhat different; a majority of Latinos supported him. But the relatively high and unexpected Latino vote for, in particular, Schwarzenegger shows that Latino candidates must mobilize and solidify a Latino electoral base and not just assume co-ethnic loyalty. Bustamante's campaign counted on an overwhelming Latino vote that would carry the lieutenant governor to victory, but a poorly run campaign built on this assumption failed to attract Latino voters. Bustamante's poor showing on Election Day speaks to a sophistication of the Latino electorate. Latinos vote with Latino interests in mind and will support the candidate that can best represent them. Symbolic connections may well serve as a starting point to get their attention, but given the choice, Latinos, like all electorates, look to the candidate who best speaks to Latino needs. In 2003, Bustamante failed to transcend symbolic connections. As Latino votes become more critical to electoral outcomes, Latino (and non-Latino) candidates must heed this call for substantive, rather than simply symbolic, outreach to Latinos.

This finding has implications for the role of Latinos in the 2006 gubernatorial election. Schwarzenegger's appeal in 2003 cut across party and ideology in the electorate as a whole (*Los Angeles Times* 2003d) and extended to some traditionally Democratic Latinos as well. This higher-than-expected support from Latinos provided an opportunity for Governor Schwarzenegger and, possibly, for other California Republican leaders to build bridges to Latinos and marginally increase Latino support for Republican candidates. At this writing (fall 2004), however, Governor Schwarzenegger does not appear to have seized this opportunity. His Latino outreach has remained symbolic, he has not fulfilled his campaign commitment to find a compromise on the driver's license bill (vetoing the latest version in September 2004), and he has cut state spending in areas that Latinos identify as most important in opinion polls, such as education, social service spending, and health care. So, while Schwarzenegger had the opportunity to build on a personal popularity to make political inroads among Latinos for himself and Republicans, he has not seized this opportunity. A September 2004 poll found that just 42 percent of Latinos approved of his performance as governor (compared with 71% of whites). Just 27 percent of Latinos in the same poll rated Schwarzenegger highly in terms of working for their best interests (Public Policy Institute of California 2004). In a reelection race against a strong opponent who clearly articulates a Democratic agenda, he will probably earn the same 20 to 30 percent of the Latino vote, a less notable accomplishment in a two-person race.

A final lesson offers a conclusion to our study of Latinos and California's 2003 gubernatorial recall. Despite the rapid growth of the Latino electorate nationally and, in California over the past decade, the emergence of an elected leadership cadre who can represent Latino interests at all levels of government (of which Bustamante is an example), Latinos in California are not yet at the stage where Latino unity alone is sufficient to determine statewide electoral outcomes. Until this point is reached, coalitions will be necessary for Latinos to be elected statewide. The anti-54 campaign, a coalition among the various racial groups, demonstrates the important role Latinos could play in coalitional politics. However, California's laws for the replacement of a recalled candidate are unusual; the effect of these rules was to preclude coalitional politics. California merges the recall with the replacement election. In other states with recalls, the replacement election is conducted separately after the decision to remove the officeholder has been made. Had California followed this more common model, there would have been fewer strategic choices for voters, and Bustamante would have not been able to claim that his presence in the race would increase the antirecall vote. He would have been somewhat less likely, in this scenario, to jump into the race at the last minute without a clear campaign strategy. In this more customary model (for what is admittedly an unusual practice), the electoral system would increase the likelihood of coalitional strategies. Perhaps in recall replacement races, individual ambition will always win out. In planned elections, however, both parties would be well advised to ensure that their statewide tickets are ethnically diverse and responsive to Latino policy needs to ensure Latino support.

BIBLIOGRAPHY

Bustamante, Cruz M. "Biography." Lieutenant Governor Cruz M. Bustamante Web Site. http://www.ltg.ca.gov/about/biography.asp (accessed August 29, 2004).

Bustillo, Miguel, and Anna Gorman. "Davis Tries to Strengthen Support Among Latino Voters." *Los Angeles Times*, August 23, 2003, A-26.

CNN. 2003. "California Recall. Exit Polls: Governor." http://www.cnn.com/2003/recall/pages/epolls/governor.html (accessed October 8, 2003).

Cohn, Gary, Carla Hall, and Robert Welkos. "Women Say Schwarzenegger Groped, Humiliated Them." *Los Angeles Times*, October 2, 2003, A-1.

de la Garza, Rodolfo O., Daron Shaw, and Fujia Lu. "Where Have all the Democrats Gone? Latino Turnout and Partisanship in Texas." Paper presented at the annual meetings of the American Political Science Association, Atlanta, September 1999.

DeSipio, Louis, and Rodolfo O. de la Garza. "Between Symbolism and Influence: Latinos and the 2000 Elections." In *Muted Voices: Latinos and the 2000 Elections*, edited by Rodolfo O. de la Garza and Louis DeSipio, 13–60. Lanham, MD: Rowman and Littlefield, 2004.

DeSipio, Louis, Rodolfo O. de la Garza, and Mark Setzler. "Awash in the Mainstream: Latinos and the 1996 Elections." In *Awash in the Mainstream: Latino Politics in the 1996 Elections*, edited by Rodolfo O. de la Garza and Louis DeSipio, 3–47. Boulder, CO: Westview Press, 1999.

Field Institute. "California's Expanding Latino Electorate." *California Opinion Index*. San Francisco: The Field Institute, May 2000.

_____. "Voter Opinions of Davis Hit a Record Low. Most Term Recall Effort a Bad Idea. But, If a Recall Election Were Held, It's Outcome Would Be a Toss-Up." *The Field Poll.* #2067. San Francisco: The Field Institute, April 2003.

Finnegan, Michael. "Davis Seeks to Rally His Base." *Los Angeles Times,* July 20, 2003, A-1.

Fraga, Luis, Ricardo Ramírez, and Gary Segura. "Unquestioned Influence: Latinos and the 2000 Elections in California." In *Muted Voices: Latinos and the 2000 Elections,* edited by Rodolfo O. de la Garza and Louis DeSipio, 173–94. Lanham, MD: Rowman and Littlefield, 2004.

Guerra, Fernando, and Luis Fraga. "Theory, Reality, and Perpetual Potential: Latinos and the 1992 California Elections." In *Ethnic Ironies: Latino Politics in the 1992 Elections,* edited by Rodolfo O. de la Garza and Louis DeSipio, 131–45. Boulder, CO; Westview Press, 1996. Institute for Justice and Journalism, Pew Hispanic Center, New California Media, and Tomás Rivera Policy Institute. *2003 Multilingual Survey of California Voters.* Los Angeles, CA: Institute for Justice and Journalism, USC Annenberg School for Communication, September 25, 2003.

Los Angeles Times. Los Angeles Times Poll. Study #486: Recall of Gov. Davis, California: August 2003. Los Angeles: *Los Angeles Times,* 2003a.

_____. Los Angeles Times Poll. Study #487: Recall of Gov. Davis, California: September 2003. Los Angeles: *Los Angeles Times,* 2003b.

_____. Los Angeles Times Poll. Study #488: Recall of Gov. Davis, California: September 2003. Los Angeles: *Los Angeles Times,* 2003c.

_____. Los Angeles Times Poll, Study #490: Exit Poll California Special Recall Election October 7, 2003. Los Angeles: *Los Angeles Times,* 2003d.

_____. Los Angeles Times Poll. Study #478: Exit Poll California General Election, November 5, 2002. http://www.latimes.com/media/acrobat/2003-03/6236873.pdf (accessed August 20, 2004).

Michelson, Melissa, and Enia Leon. "Does Ethnicity Trump Party? Latino Voting Behavior in California's 20th District." Paper prepared for presentation at the Western Political Science Association Meetings, Las Vegas, March 21-24, 2003.

Ono, Kent, and John M. Sloop. *Shifting Boundaries: Rhetoric, Immigration, and California's Proposition 187.* Philadelphia: Temple University Press, 2002.

Pinkus, Susan. "Poll Analysis: Davis Begins Second Term as a Very Unpopular Governor." *Los Angeles Times,* March 8, 2003.

Public Policy Institute of California. *Californians and Their Government.* San Francisco: Public Policy Institute of California, September 2004.

Houston Chronicle. "Runoff Results By Geography, Economics." http://www.chron.com/cs/ CDA/ssistory.mpl/ec/runoff/2278122 (accessed December 7, 2003).

Schrag, Peter. *Paradise Lost: California's Experience, America's Future.* New York: The New Press, 1998.

Tomás Rivera Policy Institute. "2003 California Recall Election Results by City in L.A. County Sorted by Percent Latino (Among Registered)." Los Angeles: Tomás Rivera Policy Institute, 2003.

NOTES

1. Bustamante would have been a leading candidate in the 2006 race had there been no recall campaign.
2. The legislative Latino caucus refused to endorse Davis because of his failure to sign a bill granting driver's licenses to undocumented immigrants.
3. In the face of criticism, Bustamante reversed himself, leaving his campaign underfinanced late in the campaign.
4. Ward Connerly and the proposition's backers were also ill-prepared for the recall election; they anticipated that the proposition would be on the March 2004 primary ballot.
5. Some of the registered voters analyzed are not Latino, and these cities, by definition, exclude most Latinos who live around non-Latinos.
6. We do not examine a scenario of heightened and unprecedented Latino mobilization in part because we have never observed such mobilization and in part because it would most likely result in a strong non-Latino countermobilization.

9

POLITICAL POTENTIAL: ASIAN AMERICANS, CALIFORNIA POLITICS, AND THE RECALL ELECTION

NATALIE MASUOKA

UNIVERSITY OF CALIFORNIA, IRVINE

DANIEL HOSANG

UNIVERSITY OF SOUTHERN CALIFORNIA

Although California's Asian American population has grown rapidly in the last thirty years, opportunities to consider the nature and trajectory of the Asian American electorate and its influence on state politics have been limited. But the growth in the size and influence of the Asian American community has gradually attracted recognition by scholars and elected officials. Today, Asian American political power is challenged by two major obstacles that discourage political mobilization: (a) they are a numerically small group, accounting for only 12 percent of the state population; and (b) they make up a culturally, economically, and linguistically diverse group, which makes it difficult to reach a general consensus on political issues. Taken together, this means that Asian American political mobilization and behavior will require close and careful examination of the myriad social factors that shape Asian American political behavior. The recall experience provides an important look into the dynamics of Asian American political participation, influence, and affiliation. As an exercise in direct democracy, the recall election provided small groups, such as Asian Americans, an opportunity to play a role in the governing of the state. Given this, the recall provides an opportunity to examine the diversity, mobilization, and public opinion of the Asian American community. In this chapter, we first review the composition and characteristics of California's polyglot Asian American population. Then we consider the role Asian Americans played in the recall contest as voters, opinion leaders, and political organizers. We pay special attention to the role of Asian Americans in the campaign around Proposition 54, an initiative that appeared on the recall ballot, which sought to end state and local government collection of some types of race and ethnicity data. We ultimately conclude that while clear-cut or unambiguous assertions about the California Asian Pacific Americans electorate are difficult to make based on the recall experience, some preliminary trends do emerge.

CALIFORNIA'S ASIAN AMERICAN POPULATION

Figure 9.1 presents the ethnic or national origin makeup of the Asian American community in California according to the 2000 Census.[1] Although there are more than forty different Asian ethnic groups in California, the graph represents only those populations above 1 percent.[2] Underscoring the cultural and linguistic diversity, two out of every three Asian Americans in California were born outside the United States, although this figure again varies among different ethnic groups. The large proportion of immigrants alone explains many of the obstacles that challenge Asian American empowerment. However, these Asian American immigrants do not remain altogether detached from public life in the United States. Of those who claim they speak a language other than English, 77 percent claimed they spoke English either "very well" or "well," meaning the majority of California's Asian Americans are comfortable communicating in English. Additionally, Asian Americans nationally have become naturalized at high rates; in California, slightly less than half of foreign-born Asian Americans are U.S. citizens. This proportion is slightly lower than that found among foreign-born non-Hispanic whites and double that found among foreign-born Latinos.

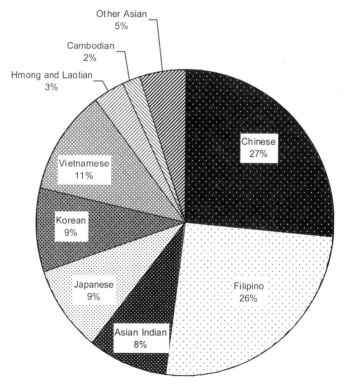

FIGURE 9.1   California's Asian Americans by national origin.

SOURCE: 2000 Census.

In terms of socioeconomics, Asian Americans as a group generally tend to be older, wealthier, and better educated then the state's population at large. The median income for Asian American families was $61,383 in 1999, which was higher than the state's median family income of $53,025. But disaggregating by ethnic group reveals startling and important variations. For example, in Los Angeles, 51 percent of Hmong families, 38 percent of Cambodian families, and 23 percent of Laotian families lived below the poverty level, a higher proportion than for both black and Latino families in the county (Asian Pacific American Legal Center [APALC] 2003). On the opposite end, only 7 percent of Filipino families in Los Angeles and 9 percent of Japanese families live below the poverty level. The overall numbers for the Asian American community as a whole conceal the many differences among Asian national origin groups. The extent of the diversity found among these various measures reveals how difficult it is to find common experiences and attitudes about politics. While their racial category in many ways forces dissimilar groups into one "Asian" category, it is difficult to locate one voice of consensus.

PATTERNS OF PARTICIPATION

Asian American voting patterns have not been found to follow the same patterns established for other racial groups (Lien 2001; Lien, Conway, and Wong 2004, Tam 1995, Wong 2000). Although on aggregate, Asian Americans are comparatively better educated and have higher incomes than the general population, they also have one of the lowest voter turnout rates. This has confounded political scientists as it is well documented that education and income are positively correlated with turnout rates (Verba, Schlozman, and Brady 1995). As we have discussed, the primary reason Asian Americans do not vote is because of the large number who are noncitizens. But even when taking this factor into account, Asian Americans still turn out at low rates. When comparing the voting-age population with registration and voting rates among Asian Americans in California and those nationwide, only 63 percent of the total Asian American population were citizens eligible to vote and, out of those who were eligible, only one-third were registered. An even lower percentage of those eligible, 28 percent, actually voted.

While this turnout puzzle remains unsolved, studies of Asian American political behavior and attitudes have recently begun to emerge (Chang 2001; Nakanishi and Lai 2003b). More surveys are including adequate samples of Asian American respondents, increasing our understanding about Asian American political behavior and attitudes. The Pilot National Asian American Political Survey (PNAAPS) polled more than 600 Asian Americans in both San Francisco and Los Angeles (see also Lien, Conway, and Wong 2004) and found Asian Americans generally lean toward the Democratic Party. Thirty-five percent of respondents claimed they were Democrats while 14.3 percent declared they were Republicans. The largest proportion of Asian Americans said they were independent or did not think in terms of traditional partisan affiliations. Exit polls conducted by the Asian American Pacific American Legal Center (APALC) in Los Angeles found a similar pattern among Asian

American voters in the 2002 election (Ichinose 2003). Alternatively, when the PNAAPS asked its California respondents about their ideology, 36 percent declared they were liberal, 21 percent declared they were conservative, and a fairly significant 33 percent felt they were somewhere in the middle. As these results demonstrate, it is difficult to assume that Asian Americans will act as a political bloc, because they seem to lack an overall unanimity in terms of partisanship and ideology (see Lien 2001; Tam 1995). The lack of a clear and cohesive ideology or party affiliation is a product of the inherent diversity of the Asian American population. However, a possible pattern arising out of these surveys is that Asian Americans are less likely to define themselves by classic partisanship or ideological labels, gesturing toward their potential status as swing voters.

Other than voting, Asian Americans are running for and being elected to political office in increasing numbers. Only Hawaii exceeds California in the number of Asian Americans in political office. In 2003, two members of Congress, six state representatives, eighteen mayors, and thirty-eight city council members in California were Asian Americans (Nakanishi and Lai 2003c). Interestingly, many of the districts these elected officials represent are *not* traditional "ethnic enclaves" (Lai et al. 2001). Because Asian Americans are not a significant voting majority in most districts in California, Asian American elected officials cannot rely exclusively on the Asian American vote to propel them to office and must have a large degree of crossover appeal. In this sense, Asian American political players have stressed building multiracial coalitions with others as well as practicing consensus politics to achieve political success. While Asian American elected officials do pay special attention to their Asian American constituents, their politics tend to be less ethnic focused given the composition of their electorates. The numbers of elected officials also demonstrate that much of Asian American politics in California takes place at the local levels (Nakanishi and Lai 2003a), where political and community organizations tend to be strongest.

Given the focus on local-level politics, the majority of Asian American political participation has been focused outside the electoral arena. Community-level mobilization and change is where Asian Americans have made the strongest impact. Primarily, Asian Americans influence the changing nature of California politics by raising issues specific to their communities. Some of these Asian American issues have integrated transnational concerns into local politics. In the Orange County community of Westminster, in an area known as Little Saigon, the largest Vietnamese enclave in the United States has given rise to many new forms of political activity. Although most Vietnamese Americans have immigrated within the past three decades, they have quickly incorporated themselves into American political life by integrating the politics of their homeland. In 1999, Vietnamese community members organized a protest against the display of a Ho Chi Minh poster in a Westminster video store.[3] In 2004, residents proposed and passed a city ordinance banning Communist Party members from visiting the city as a symbolic act against the Communist regime in Vietnam. In the Los Angeles suburb Monterey Park, Asian American residents in the late 1980s built a coalition with Latino and white residents to fight the implementation of an English-only policy and an effort to require English translations to accompany Chinese language business signs (Fong 1994; Saito 1998). This Monterey Park example demonstrates how diverse groups of Asian Americans can mobilize, across ethnic and racial divisions, groups facing similar obstacles. As these and other instances of local organization confirm, Asian Americans have a wide array of political interests and issues, both transnational and domestic. Indeed, the majority of scholarly attention on Asian American politics are those focused on local-level mobilization efforts.

ASIAN AMERICANS AND THE RECALL

Although, in the past, candidates for California statewide offices tended to put little effort into wooing Asian American voters as a bloc, most of the leading contenders in the recall contest deliberately reached out to this emerging electorate. As a diverse group with relatively weak political preferences and party affinities, the Asian American electorate plausibly seemed up for grabs. The recall election was an opportunity for Asian Americans to bring their issues into focus. As the recall election's short history demonstrates, Asian American issues were given a degree of recognition as the recall candidates sought to attract Asian American votes.

Because Asian American voters have leaned toward the Democratic Party in previous elections, Gray Davis spent time on the campaign trail in Asian American community meetings and events, hoping to retain a similar level of support as he received in the November election. The Southern California Voter Survey conducted by the APALC found that 57 percent of Asian Americans voted for Davis in the 2002 general election (Ichinose 2003). At an Alhambra rally to mobilize Asian American support against the recall, Davis contrasted his record of support for Asian Americans, claiming Arnold Schwarzenegger had only fought in movies. "I've worked hard to advance the interests of Asian Pacific Californians," Davis told the crowd, citing some of the 280 Asian Americans he said he appointed to leading government positions, more than any other governor in California (Smith and Bluth 2003). Additionally Davis staked a clear position opposing Proposition 54, the race data collection initiative, which was a focus of many Asian American community organizations and political activists. By aligning with Asian American activists on this issue, Davis demonstrated support for what was considered an important Asian American issue.

Two of the major replacement candidates, Schwarzenegger and Lieutenant Governor Cruz Bustamante, also portrayed themselves as advocates of Asian American issues. Schwarzenegger emphasized his immigrant roots in his appeals to Asian American voters. He publicly celebrated the anniversary of obtaining his citizenship with a group of Asian and Latino immigrants in Los Angeles. Bustamante similarly promoted his own immigrant experience to connect with Asian American voters. A sizable number of South Asian Indians, who felt connected to Bustamante by a shared immigrant experience, donated large sums to the Bustamante campaign (Joseph 2003). Conversely, Schwarzenegger, while winning the support of some Asian American voters, also received some negative press from the Asian American media after choosing to decline an invitation to an Asian American event. An *Asian Week* editorial asserted the following:

> Voters should ask, "Where's the beef?" now that the brawny actor has snubbed two major recall debates. Last week, Schwarzenegger skipped the Walnut Creek debate broadcasted in the San Francisco Bay Area, which is home to 1.5 million Asian Americans. Tuesday, he snubbed the Los Angeles debate sponsored by New California Media's 600 ethnic media outlets, some of which reach 4.5 million Californians of APA descent (2003).

Asian American elected officials did not unanimously champion one candidate (Lin 2003a). Generally speaking, Asian American elected officials tended to tow their party's line: Democrats denounced the recall, while Republicans supported it. However, because most Asian Americans in state-level offices are Democrats, those politicians urged Asian American voters to oppose the recall. Assembly member Judy Chu (D-Monterey Park) wrote,

> The recall of [Gray Davis] threatens to turn back the clock on these notable accomplishments for the APA community. No other candidate for governor, past or present, has shown the same sincere and substantive level of empathy and support that Davis has for the APA community … Furthermore, more APAs have been appointed to high-level cabinet positions and the state courts than at any other time in the history of California under the leadership of Davis … (2003).

Others did not evoke party rhetoric and voiced concern over the extent to which the recall hurt California's image and the ideal of democracy. John Tateishi, executive director of the Japanese American Citizens League (JACL), one of the oldest Asian American organizations in the nation contended, "If I were living in Florida, I would write to the newspapers in California and say, 'Thank you so much. We're no longer the laughingstock of the nation'" (Lin 2003b). Overall, Asian American elites seemed to voice the same types of concerns and arguments that are heard within the broader Californian electorate.

Regardless of the attention paid to Asian American voters, Asian American turnout did not appear to increase for the recall election. The *Los Angeles Times* exit poll estimated Asian American voters made up approximately 6 percent of the recall electorate. This is roughly equal to the turnout in the 2002 statewide election (6%) and the 2000 presidential election (5%) (*Los Angeles Times* 2000, 2002). Given the constantly changing nature of this special election, we will examine Asian American attitudes and vote choice both before and after the election to best understand the direction of Asian American preferences throughout the recall election period. The two surveys employed here are the 2003 Multilingual Survey of California Voters, which polled a significant sample of 250 Asian American registered and likely voters approximately one month before the election, and the *Los Angeles Times* California Recall Election Exit Poll, which surveyed voters exiting the voting booths on Election Day.[4]

TABLE 9.1   Recall question.

	ASIAN AMERICAN	WHITE	LATINO	AFRICAN AMERICAN
Before Election[*]				
Yes	44%	56%	45%	23%
No	46%	35%	47%	65%
Don't know	10%	9%	8%	11%
Election Results[†]				
Yes	47.2%	59%	44.6%	21.4%
No	52.4%	40.1%	54.6%	78.6%

Sources: [*]USC Annenberg's Institute for Justice and Journalism, Pew Hispanic Center, New California Media, and Tomás Rivera Policy Institute 2003.
[†]*Los Angeles Times* 2003.

Before the election, Asian Americans were evenly split on the decision to recall Davis from office (see Table 9.1). Forty-four percent of the Asian American respondents claimed they would vote yes on the recall while 46 percent said they would vote against the recall. While 76 percent of yes respondents and 80 percent of no respondents claimed they would definitely vote their stated position at the time of the election, there was significant room for change. Ten percent of Asian American respondents in the survey had not made a definite choice on the recall. Like Latino voters, Asian American voters, in general, were more likely than black voters but less likely than white voters to support the recall. This pattern was also evident within Asian American attitudes toward the Davis administration. Only 21 percent of respondents rated Davis' job performance as "good" or "excellent."

A general ambivalence among Asian Americans was also demonstrated in their choice for Davis' replacement. When asked their opinion on each of the candidates running to replace the governor, compared with white and Latino voters, a greater proportion of Asian American respondents claimed they had "no opinion." Given their choice of candidates, 30 percent of Asian American respondents did not know who they would vote for on Election Day (Table 9.2). Of those who did have a preference, the top two choices for governor were Bustamante and Schwarzenegger, although each was predicted to receive only slightly more than 20 percent of Asian Americans votes.

Interestingly, 10 percent of Asian American respondents claimed they had a preference for a lesser-known candidate. Perhaps the inclusion of numerous Asian American candidates on the replacement ballot guided Asian Americans to vote for other Asian Americans. Asian Americans from numerous ethnic groups placed their names on the ballot. These candidates were supported to various degrees by their fellow Asian Americans and were given particular attention within their respective national origin communities (Nash 2003). South Asian communities promoted the three South Asian Americans on the ballot, while a Filipino newspaper article on the Filipino candidate,

TABLE 9.2   Replacement candidate for Governor.

	Asian American	White	Latino	African American
Before Election*				
Bustamante	25%	22%	57%	17%
Camejo	2%	0%	1%	5%
McClintock	4%	15%	6%	2%
Schwarzenegger	22%	20%	13%	7%
Other candidate	10%	14%	4%	29%
Don't know	30%	28%	16%	34%
Election Results†				
Bustamante	31%	25.1%	52.9%	57.8%
Camejo	2.4%	3.1%	1.5%	2.1%
McClintock	14.6%	13%	9%	7.2%
Schwarzenegger	43.1%	51%	30%	15.6%
Other candidate	2.4%	2.8%	1.3%	3.8%

Sources: *USC Annenberg's Institute for Justice and Journalism, Pew Hispanic Center, New California Media, and Tomás Rivera Policy Institute 2003.
†*Los Angeles Times* 2003.

Monty Manibog, humorously quoted, "Manibog very likely won't make it to Sacramento. But this will not stop this space from rooting for him against all odds" (Pelayo 2003). One Asian American candidate, a Vietnamese American radio host named Van Vo, received special attention from not only ethnic but also mainstream media (Pasco 2003). Vo, who campaigned on a pan-Asian platform, traveled across the state to garner the Asian American vote. Vo's candidacy was focused on the desire to bring attention to the Vietnamese American community in the state and the issues it faces.

On Election Day, the split on the recall question became more pronounced, with a slightly greater percentage of Asian Americans voting against the recall, 47 percent to 55 percent. By examining maximum likelihood estimates of California voters, we found that Asian American voters were more likely to vote for the recall than blacks or Latinos but less likely to do so as compared with whites.[5] Among Asian Americans, specifically, older voters and those voting for the first time were more likely to vote for the recall.[6] Asian American Democrats, those who voted for Davis in 2002, and those who felt the economy was going well were more likely to vote against the recall. These findings are interesting given the contention made by those who study Asian American political behavior that Asian Americans tend to be influenced more by the issues than classic ideology proxies, such as political party. Preferences for the replacement candidate also became more distinctive, as Asian Americans appeared to vote for well-known candidates. Although the split between Bustamante and Schwarzenegger was less polarized compared with voters from other racial groups, Asian Americans were slightly more likely to choose Schwarzenegger over the other candidates. Party identification did not seem to play a role in the choice of the replacement candidate. While a slightly greater proportion of Asian Americans voted against the recall, they gave a greater proportion of their votes to the moderate Republican candidate as opposed to the Democrat. Scholars have also found that Asian Americans are more hesitant to declare a party preference than other groups. So, perhaps, they felt comfortable voting for Schwarzenegger, who, although running as a Republican, promoted himself as an independent candidate.

ASIAN AMERICAN MOBILIZING POTENTIAL: PROPOSITION 54

While the lion's share of media and voter attention focused on the recall in general and Schwarzenegger's candidacy in particular, many Asian American advocacy groups and activists directed their energies toward a ballot initiative that unfolded in the shadows of the gubernatorial contest (Chow 2003). Proposition 54 sought to ban state and local government agencies, including public schools, hospitals, and law enforcement bodies, from collecting data on race or ethnicity. The chief proponent of the proposed constitutional amendment, University of California Regent Ward Connerly, claimed his "racial privacy initiative" was necessary to "work towards a "colorblind society" and to "de-emphasize the racial distinctions that divide us" (American Civil Rights Institute [ACRI] 2002).

Asian American organizations, elected officials, and activists joined the broad-based coalition organized to defeat Proposition 54 and launched their own efforts to specifically target Asian American voters (Table 9.3). The strongest example of the latter was Asian Pacific Americans for an Informed California (APAIC), which formed in mid-2002 when the Connerly initiative qualified for the ballot. Convened under the auspices of the Sacramento-based

TABLE 9.3 Proposition 54.

	ASIAN AMERICAN	WHITE	LATINO	AFRICAN AMERICAN
Before Election[*]				
Yes	40%	34%	48%	43%
No	34%	25%	30%	32%
Don't Know	26%	41%	22%	25%
Election Results[†]				
Yes	28%	38%	25%	13%
No	72%	62%	75%	87%

SOURCES: [*]USC Annenberg's Institute for Justice and Journalism, Pew Hispanic Center, New California Media, and Tomás Rivera Policy Institute 2003.
[†]Los Angeles Times 2003.

Asian Americans for Civil Rights and Equality, APAIC brought together community-based groups, including the Asian Law Caucus, the APALC, Chinese for Affirmative Action, and the Asian Pacific Islander American Health Forum, with individual activists and elected officials. More than 100 organizations and individuals joined the coalition by Election Day. While many APAIC members participated in the statewide efforts of the Coalition for an Informed California (CIC) and other groups, the coalition launched a fundraising and voter education project around Proposition 54 focused on the Asian American electorate.[7]

By the summer of 2003, when Proposition 54 was placed on the October 7 ballot as a result of the successful recall petition, APAIC had begun a series of house meetings to explain the initiative to voters and raise money for the campaign. In a few short months, individual donors contributed more than $30,000 to APAIC's efforts. In four Bay Area counties, more than 50,000 bilingual mailers in Chinese, Korean, Tagalog, and Vietnamese were sent to Asian American voters to bring attention to the issue. Regular phone banking generated nearly 40,000 calls to the same group. APAIC also held five press conferences, focusing primarily on the ethnic and Asian language media, conducted weekly briefings for ethnic press reporters, and authored several opinion-editorials. On Election Day in San Francisco, APAIC coordinated a major "get out the vote" mobilization within specific precincts.[8]

In the Bay Area, smaller formations—including Concerned Desis Against Proposition 54 (highlighting the initiative's effect on South Asian Americans), Filipinos Against Proposition 54, and the Oakland-based Power in Asians Organizing—also led grassroots field operations to educate the Asian American electorate. The statewide Hapa Issues Forum, an advocacy and education group for Asian Americans of multiracial descent, also took a strong stand against Proposition 54, blunting Connerly's claim that mixed-race individuals unequivocally supported the end of racial data collection. Finally, all six members of the APALC who serve in the state assembly opposed the measure and joined APAIC to work for its defeat.[9]

Asian American advocacy groups mobilizing against Proposition 54 cited three main concerns. First, they feared that the measure could prevent public health agencies and the University of California from tracking diseases and health issues by race or ethnicity. For example, existing data reveals that Asian Americans account for approximately 60 percent of all hepatitis B cases nationwide, although Asian Americans constitute only 4 percent of the national population.[10] Proposition 54 threatened to ban the collection and use of such information, essentially forcing health care providers and administrators to forge a one-size-fits-all strategy for disease prevention and treatment. Dr. Alexander Li of the San Francisco Department of Public Health and Chinatown Public Health Center explained that the diverse health care needs and interests of California's polyglot Asian American population would not be served well through such an approach. "Race and ethnicity data helps doctors and health care professionals address chronic diseases, formulate effective prevention programs, and save lives." Dr. Li explained that successful, targeted programs—for example, to address high rates of smoking among Asian American youth—could be declared illegal.[11]

Second, Asian American leaders warned that Proposition 54 would eviscerate the state's ability to enforce antidiscrimination legislation in housing and employment. For example, in the three years following Proposition 209's implementation, the state reported an 8 percent decline in the promotion of Asian American women in the state government workforce.[12] Discriminatory "glass ceilings," which limit the mobility of Asian Americans in the workplace are an ongoing concern for Asian American civil rights leaders. Edward Lee, a Korean-American organizer who coordinated the umbrella Coalition for an Informed California (CIC) to defeat Proposition 54 explained that the measure would "make it impossible to prove known patterns and practices of racial discrimination faced by Asian Americans. Without this data, employers and landlords would face few repercussions for the obvious acts of discrimination."[13]

Third, Proposition 54 threatened to end law enforcement monitoring of hate crimes and other public safety issues by race. Asian American leaders warned that in the wake of September 11, with an upsurge in incidents of harassment reported by many South Asian Americans, ending hate crime monitoring and awareness would be reckless. Recent legislation requiring police officers to record the data of motorists they stopped to monitor "racial profiling" practices by the police would also be ended. Data collection targeted by Proposition 54 also serves crime victims. For example, in some locales, Asian American women account for a large number of domestic violence victims, requiring some linguistic and culturally specific responses.

Although polls of likely voters conducted for the Connerly initiative in early 2002 and 2003 found voters favoring the measure by a three-to-two margin, its support plummeted after the October 7 special election date was announced in mid-July. APAIC's efforts unfolded alongside a well-funded statewide television and radio campaign against Proposition 54—Connerly's opponents outspent him substantially—and most newspaper editorials and many elected officials, including candidate Schwarzenegger, declared their opposition to the measure. In addition, the recall controversy itself captured much of the media and public attention as the election neared, which hurt Connerly's efforts to raise awareness about the initiative.[14] While it may be difficult to conclude that the efforts of APAIC decisively influenced the Asian American electorate—too many mitigating circumstances limit any singular causal determinations—the campaigns were still important because they represented one of the first statewide electoral efforts specifically targeting Asian American voters. In a short time span, APAIC developed voter outreach materials, recruited and deployed volunteers, won the endorsements of many Asian American elected officials, and sustained an effective statewide organization.

Indeed the initiative's most enduring impact may lie in the organization and mobilization it spurred among Asian American political organizations and activists. In comparison with controversial ballot initiatives surrounding undocumented immigration in 1994, affirmative action in 1996, and bilingual education in 1998, Asian American organization fell almost exclusively on one side of the issue (Table 9.3). APAIC determined its collaborative work around Proposition 54 was so effective that it would remain intact as a community education and empowerment coalition. Given the limited emphasis historically placed on grassroots electoral organization among Asian American community-based organizations, the collaboration and organizing witnessed during the anti-54 campaign could prove to be a watershed moment. Perhaps as importantly, it publicly voiced the support of Asian American political actors for the continued enforcement of civil rights legislation, and racial justice principles.

CONCLUSION

Three primary ideas describing Asian American politics were explored in this chapter: Diversity, mobilization, and political potential. How do they all come together as a result of the recall election? The inherently diverse nature of the Asian American population in California, and its varied interests, suggests that the Asian American electorate is unlikely to act as a cohesive or unified voting bloc in statewide elections in the near future. Asian Americans voters were almost evenly divided on the recall question itself, and did not rally behind a single gubernatorial candidate. The split in vote preference occurred even without controlling for national origin, which probably would make the differences within the community even more apparent. The recall results, in addition to the general diverse makeup of the Asian American community, suggest that singular characterizations of the Asian American electorate will continue to be difficult to make.

The fact that, regardless of the political environment, Asian Americans have demonstrated a diversity of political preferences places continued importance on the study and understanding of the inherent socioeconomic, cultural, and political diversity that exists within the community. Diversity is a characteristic that will dictate the ways in which Asian Americans can address political issues, mobilize around a political cause, and wield their political power. The recall experience confirms that Asian Americans most likely will not mirror the patterns of voting preferences and behavior demonstrated by Latinos, African Americans, or whites and that efforts to define them within an existing racial paradigm will conceal as much as they reveal.

Hence, effective efforts to mobilize Asian American voters must focus on these issues. Attempts that presume a unified racial group bloc will likely fail. The strategies used by recall candidates that assumed a uniform Asian American experience did not attract a cohesive Asian American vote: Davis attempted to appeal to Asian American voters as part of a broader Democratic coalition by emphasizing his support for civil rights issues (such as opposing Proposition 54) and his appointments of Asian Americans to state offices. Schwarzenegger and Bustamante stressed to Asian American voters their shared roots as immigrants, hoping to build support around a common political and social identity as well as around a series of policy positions. Neither strategy appeared to be influential with the Asian American electorate, which is highly differentiated by language, immigration status, geography, income, and issue preferences. As the recall experience suggests, Asian American political behavior must be studied on its own terms through an approach that is sensitive to the particular experiences and sensibilities of this diverse group.

But while the recall did not reveal a cohesive Asian American voting bloc, it did illustrate the ways that Asian Americans continue to participate in and shape electoral politics in California. The attempts by nearly all the leading candidates to woo Asian American voters as might represent a new stage of potential incorporation and influence in statewide politics: Proactive Asian American candidates and advocacy groups might make use of such interest in future elections to advance their particular agendas. The mobilization efforts and the coalition building around Proposition 54 could mark a significant milestone in Asian American electoral activism. Asian Americans formed an umbrella anti-54 coalition, garnered the support of leading elected officials and other opinion leaders, raised funds from individual Asian American donors, and contacted tens of thousands of voters in several languages. The networks and organization built through this effort alone increases the opportunity for Asian American activists to influence future elections.

So while it may be premature to describe the Asian American electorate as the next "sleeping giant" in California politics, Asian Americans are increasingly participating in all levels of the political process: As grassroots activists, elected officials, individual donors, issue advocates, and voters. In spite of the diversity that marks this electorate, future candidates seeking statewide office are likely to make efforts to appeal specifically to Asian American voters. Most importantly, Asian Americans, individually and collectively, will continue to influence and shape California elections and political discourse, even if they do not consolidate as a singular and distinctive electoral bloc.

BIBLIOGRAPHY

American Civil Rights Institute (ACRI). "Racial Privacy Initiative Submits Almost 1 Million Signatures." Press Release, April 19, 2002.

Asian Pacific American Legal Center (APALC). "The Diverse Face of Asians and Pacific Islanders in Los Angeles County." Los Angeles: Asian American Pacific Legal Center, 2003.

AsianWeek editorial. "Where's the Beef?" *AsianWeek* 25, no. 3 (2003): 4.

Chang, Gordon, ed. *Asian Americans and Politics: Perspectives, Experiences, Prospects.* Stanford: Stanford University Press, 2001.

Chow, May. "APA Leaders Condemn Prop. 54; But Connerly Says Health Argument is Bogus." *AsianWeek* 24, no. 50 (2003): 11.

Chu, Judy. "APAs Lose Most From California Recall." *AsianWeek* 25, no. 3 (2003): 9.

Fong, Timothy. *The First Suburban Chinatown: The Remaking of Monterey Park, California.* Philadelphia: Temple University Press, 1994.

Haldane, David. "Vietnam Officials Should Stay Away, Westminster Council Says City Joins Garden Grove in Formally Opposing Visits by Representatives of Communist Regime. Ex-video Store Owner Criticizes Move." *Los Angeles Times*, May 20, 2004, B-3.

Ichinose, Daniel. "Asian Americans and California's 2002 General Election: Findings from the November 2002 Southern California Survey." Los Angeles: Asian Pacific American Legal Center, 2003.

Joseph, George. "Community Raises $100,000 for Bustamante Campaign." *India Abroad* 33, no. 52 (2003): C6.

Lai, Eric, and Dennis Arguelles. *The New Face of Asian Pacific America Numbers, Diversity and Change in the 21st Century.* San Francisco: AsianWeek, 2003.

Lai, James, Wendy Tam-Cho, Thomas Kim, and Okiyoshi Takeda. "Campaigns, Elections and Elected Officials." *PS: Political Science and Politics* 34, no. 3 (2001): 611–17.

Lee, Don. "Protests in Little Saigon: Fresh Start or Last Grip? Immigrants: Some See Renewed South Vietnamese Spirit. Others See Final Grip of Homeland Politics." *Los Angeles Times* February 28, 1999, A-1.

Lien, Pei-te. *The Making of Asian Pacific America through Political Participation.* Philadelphia: Temple University Press, 2001.

Lien, Pei-te, M. Margaret Conway, and Janelle Wong. *The Politics of Asian Americans Diversity and Community.* New York: Routeledge, 2004.

Lin, Sam Chu. "Mixed APA Feelings about Davis Recall." *AsianWeek* 24, no. 49 (2003a): 8.

_____. "Californians Having Butterflies Over Ballot; APAs React to Schwarzenegger Entry in Recall Election." *AsianWeek* 24, no. 51 (2003b): 9.

Los Angeles Times. Los Angeles Times Poll Study #490: Exit Poll California Special Recall Election, October 7, 2003. Los Angeles: *Los Angeles Times*, 2003.

_____. Los Angeles Times Poll Study #478: Exit Poll California General Election, November 5, 2002. Los Angeles: *Los Angeles Times*, 2002.

_____. Los Angeles Times Poll Study #449: General Election: Nation and California, November 7, 2000. Los Angeles: *Los Angeles Times*, 2000.

Nakanishi, Don, and James Lai. "Introduction: Understanding Asian American Politics." In *Asian American Politics Law, Participation, and Policy*, edited by Don Nakanishi and James Lai. Lanham, MD: Rowman and Littlefield Publishers, Inc., 2003a.

_____, eds. *Asian American Politics Law, Participation, and Policy*. Lanham, MD: Rowman and Littlefield Publishers, Inc., 2003b.

_____, eds. *National Asian Pacific American Political Almanac 2003–2004*. Los Angeles: UCLA Asian American Studies Center Press, 2003c.

Nash, Phil Tajitsu. "Terminating Democracy." *AsianWeek* 24, no. 51 (2003): 10.

Pasco, Jean. "Little Saigon Radio Host Seeks to Be Heard." *Los Angeles Times,* September 28, 2003, A-30.

Pelayo, Libertito. "Filipino Throws Hat in Wacky CA Recall Election." *Filipino Reporter.* 31, no. 41 (2003): 34.

Saito, Leland. *Race and Politics: Asian Americans, Latinos and Whites in a Los Angeles Suburb.* Chicago: University of Illinois Press, 1998.

Smith, Dan, and Alexa Bluth. "Governor Takes Dig at Accent: Remark about Schwarzenegger is Made to a Rally Participant." *Sacramento Bee,* September 7, 2003.

Tam, Wendy. "Asians-A Monolithic Voting Bloc?" *Political Behavior* 17 (1995): 223–49.

USC Annenberg's Institute for Justice and Journalism, Pew Hispanic Center, New California Media, and Tomás Rivera Policy Institute. *The 2003 Multilingual Survey of California Voters.* Los Angeles, CA: Institute for Justice and Journalism, USC Annenberg School for Communication, September 25, 2003.

Verba, Sidney, Kay Schlozman, and Henry Brady. *Voice and Equality: Civic Volunteerism in American Politics.* Cambridge, MA: Harvard University Press, 1995.

Wong, Janelle. "The Effects of Age and Political Exposure on the Development of Party Identification among Asian American and Latino immigrants in the United States." *Political Behavior* 22 (2000): 341–71.

NOTES

1. Although we personally examined data from the 2000 Census, we also reference and compare our numbers with Lai and Arguelles (2003) for many of these figures throughout the rest of the section.

2. Proportions used in this graph were calculated with population numbers, including multiracial populations, for a more accurate picture of Asian Americans in the state.

3. See Haldane (2004) and Lee (1999) for newspaper accounts on these two events.

4. The 2003 Multilingual Survey of California Voters was sponsored by the USC Annenberg Institute of Justice and Journalism, Pew Hispanic Center, New California Media, and the Tomás Rivera Policy Institute. This telephone survey was conducted between September 6–16 and sampled registered voters of all four racial groups. Two hundred and fifty Asian Americans were randomly located but were collected to be representative of the Asian American makeup in California, with a sampling error of +/−6 percent. Asian American respondents were given the option of taking the survey in English, Cantonese, Mandarin, Vietnamese, or Korean. The *Los Angeles Times* California Recall Election Exit Poll randomly selected 5,205 voters exiting 74 different voting booths across California on the day of the recall election. Respondents were given the option to take the survey in English or in Spanish only. The survey composition was collected to represent voters in California and had a sampling error of approximately +/−2 percent for the entire sample. The total number of Asian Americans surveyed was 247. As with all survey data, possible inaccuracies and biases may be found in the surveys employed here. However, given that most surveys do not include

large enough Asian American samples, these two represent our best indicators of Asian American opinion and voting.

5. Logistic estimates were run on the entire sample (n = 4598), with the dependent variable being vote choice on the recall and the independent variables being the race dummies. By comparing the direction of the coefficients of the race dummies with the excluded category, we were able to make comparisons among the different racial groups. Because of sampling, the Asian coefficient is not always statistically significant.

6. Logistic estimates were run on just the Asian American sample, with the dependent variable being vote choice on the recall, and included various independent variables that measured different socioeconomic status (SES) factors and other political behavior proxies. The relationships reported in the text are only those that came out statistically significant at p < 0.10. We warn against generalizing these results, however, because the sample size is small, n = 135. We present these results to hopefully provide slightly more context to Asian American voting patterns.

7. APAIC organizational files in authors' possession.

8. Ibid.

9. Ibid.

10. Letter to Senator Martha Escutia and Assemblymember Ellen Corbett from sixteen Asian Pacific American organizations in opposition to Proposition 54, August 22, 2004.

11. Comments made at Proposition 54 APA community forum, September 18, 2003, San Francisco, CA.

12. Letter to Senator Martha Escutia and Assemblymember Ellen Corbett, from sixteen Asian Pacific American organizations in opposition to Proposition 54, August 22, 2004.

13. Interview with Daniel HoSang, August 10, 2004.

14. For example, the *Los Angeles Times* exit poll found that only 2 percent of voters cited Proposition 54 as the reason they decided to vote—the vast majority cited the recall—a much lower percentage than for Proposition 187 in 1994.

RACE, GENDER, AND THE RECALL VOTE

BECKI SCOLA

LISA GARCÍA BEDOLLA

UNIVERSITY OF CALIFORNIA, IRVINE

According the political commentators, the California recall election was unique because it had little to do with partisanship. Both Gray Davis' inadequacies and Arnold Schwarzenegger's candidacy as Davis' replacement were cast as being more about the characteristics of the individuals themselves, rather than their party affiliations. Because party identification is highly correlated with race in California (as it is across the United States), one could extrapolate that race would be less salient in this election than it was in the past. In addition, because of the allegations of Schwarzenegger's sexual misconduct that were published in the *Los Angeles Times* shortly before Election Day, many expected gender to play a role in the election, with men and women reacting differently to Schwarzenegger's candidacy and to those allegations. Given these general perceptions surrounding the recall, we thought it would be useful to examine how race *and* gender interacted to affect voting for the recall itself.[1]

Previous studies have shown important racial and gender differences in American political behavior. In terms of race, significant racial polarization has been found in black and white voting patterns (Collet 2004; Grofman, Handley, and Niemi 1992; Shaw 1997) and in public opinion (Dawson 2000). In California, specifically, research has shown that the California electorate is consistently divided along racial lines in terms of voting for candidates and propositions, as well as political party registration (Cain 1991; García Bedolla 2005; Hajnal and Louch 2001; Jackson 1991; Regalado and Martínez 1991; Tolbert and Hero 1996). In terms of gender, studies have shown differences between men and women in public opinion (Shapiro and Mahajan 1986; Wilcox, Ferrara, and Allsop 1993), partisanship (Box-Steffensmeier, De Boef, and Lin 2004; Kaufmann and Petrocik 1999), and presidential voting patterns (Kennedy Chaney, Alvarez, and Nagler 1998). Yet, largely because of small sample sizes, few studies have examined gender differences within racial groups. Dawson (1994), Tate (1993), and Mangum (2004) have had conflicting results in terms of how gender affects African American party identification. Studies using the Latino National Political Survey showed no significant

differences between Latino men and women in terms of their party identification, and a recent study using 1999 survey data had similar results (Alvarez
and García Bedolla 2003).

So, we know about racial differences and gender differences in political
behavior, but little about how race and gender interact. Crenshaw (1991) was
first to define this interaction between race and gender as "intersection."
According to intersection theorists, race and gender are socially constructed
characteristics that differentially shape peoples experiences, which in turn
color their political attitudes, opinions, and behavior (Cohen 1999; Crenshaw
1991; Hill Collins 2000; hooks 2000). In other words, women's experiences as
women result in political responses that are different from men's experiences.
Likewise, racial and ethnic experiences result in political responses that vary
among races. As a result, the intersection of these ascriptive identities also
should yield varied responses. As race and gender interact, we can expect to
witness behavior that cannot be accounted for simply by locating only one or
the other of these characteristics, either race *or* gender. Instead, we must consider the combination of gendered racial experiences. Within the American
context, because of our nation's particular historic experiences, it is understood that in many cases racial identity trumps gender identity (Gay and Tate
1998; Mansbridge and Tate 1992). But we must keep in mind that this is not
because of any particular characteristic inherent in gender or race, per se, but
rather in how these characterizations have been constructed historically within
the American political context.

The California recall election thus provides an excellent opportunity to
explore how race and gender interact to affect voting patterns. The uniqueness
of the political context, along with the diversity of the California electorate,
make the recall election especially appropriate for this type of study. The findings from previous research, along with the particular characteristics of the
political context of the recall, led us to two competing hypotheses. The first is
that, because of the allegations of sexual misconduct, gender identity was
more salient in this election than racial identity, making women look more
similar across groups than would normally be the case. This hypothesis is
supported by the idea that the recall election was less partisan than "regular"
California elections. Because partisanship and race are highly correlated in
California, the absence of partisanship should make race less salient in voting
patterns. The second hypothesis is that the recall election was not all that different from other elections, and therefore racially polarized voting was present
despite the supposed lack of partisanship and traditional coalitions surrounding the election. The expected result here is that differences would be
greatest among the racial groups, and that women's voting would not necessarily be similar across those groups.

DATA AND METHODS

To test these hypotheses, we employ a simple statistical analysis using data from
the *Los Angeles Times* Recall Election Exit Poll conducted on October 7, 2003. The
total sample size consists of 5,205 registered voters from 74 polling locations

across California, weighted using demographic data and actual returns to reflect absentee approximations. The sample included 3,367 white respondents (1,724 male, 1,643 female), 245 black respondents (130 male, 115 female), 509 Latino respondents (260 male, 249 male), and 244 Asian respondents (131 male, 113 female). The main strength of this data set is that it has a large enough sample to break California voters down by race and gender, something that is often not possible with smaller surveys. While exit polls have important methodological problems, particularly when used to look at racial groups, we believe the size of the survey and its geographic scope across California mitigate these problems and make it appropriate for use in this analysis (Levy 1983).

Because we are interested in testing whether gender and/or race had a significant effect on vote choice, we chose to conduct cross-tabulations among race, gender, and vote choice. Our independent variables include "Gender of Respondent" and "Ethnicity of Voter." Racial categories include white, black, Latino, and Asian. The response variable is "Yes or No on Recall."[2] While partisanship is certainly an important part of the story, as Greene (2002) points out, partisanship is best conceptualized as an affective group attachment. Given that we know that attachment is highly correlated to race in California, a finding that partisanship affected vote choice is not necessarily substantively different, from an attachment standpoint, than a finding that race affected vote choice (Alvarez and Brehm 2002, 19–22). Our interest here is in examining whether gender and/or race affected the vote choice of various groups differently, rather than using multivariate analysis to discern all the possible factors that influenced vote choice.

We examine four models.[3] Within each of these models, chi-square tests of independence are performed and compared for each group, gender, and/or race.[4] In other words, we examine the variation in vote patterns among the selected groups by comparing chi-squares. Model 1 looks at the voting patterns for men and women of the same race. For example, it compares the yes and no votes among men and women within each racial category. Model 2 investigates patterns among racial groups in contrast to all other races combined. For example, black voting is compared with voting from the aggregate of all other racial categories (white, Latino, and Asian). Model 3 compares yes and no votes across gender and race categories. This allows us to examine distinctions among women of dissimilar racial groups and the distinctions among men in different racial groups. Model 4 attempts to assess specific racial group variations. This model analyzes reported yes or no votes among six pairs of groupings: whites and blacks, whites and Latinos, whites and Asians, blacks and Latinos, blacks and Asians, and Latinos and Asians. Aligning vote choice in this manner assists us in detecting racial or gender polarization in voting among the different groups.

RESULTS: VOTE ON THE RECALL

As seen in Figure 10.1, there was significant variation in the extent to which different racial groups and women supported the recall. In terms of gender overall, there was a significant gap between men and women's vote on the

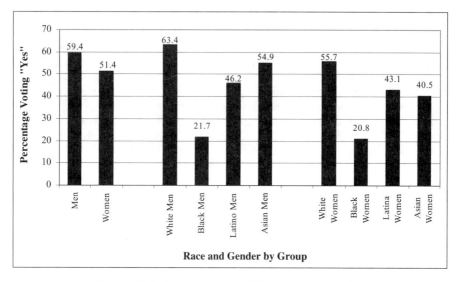

FIGURE 10.1   Yes vote on recall by race and gender.

recall, with 59.4 percent of men supporting the recall compared with 51.4 percent of women. Once those numbers are broken down by the different racial groups, however, we see quite a bit of heterogeneity among women and men. The question, then, becomes whether or not these differences are significant.

Figure 10.2 provides a visual representation of the gender gap in the recall vote by racial group. Again, we see important differences among the different groups. We measure the statistical significance of those differences in Model 1. Model 1 compares yes or no votes between men and women of the same race, and shows that the gender differences seen in Figure 10.1 are significant and that they vary among racial groups. We only see a statistical association between gender and vote choice among white men and women and a slight association among Asian men and women, with women in both categories opposing the recall more so than men. Conversely, black and Latino men and women voted in a similar manner, although men favored the recall slightly more than women. So, gender is associated with vote choice for white and Asian women, but not for black women or Latinas. This result is consistent with other research and offers partial support for our first hypothesis. We can detect a gender gap in vote choice, but it varies among racial groups. This suggests that the experience of gender varies among women and is informed by race in important ways.

Table 10.1 summarizes the results for the first three models. Model 2 compares yes or no votes across racial groups. In general, we find that whites supported the recall at a much higher rate than any other racial group, 59.5 percent. Blacks were the least likely to support the recall, with only 21.5 percent voting in favor. Latinos and Asians fell in between these two extremes, favoring the recall at 44.8 percent and 47 percent, respectively. In Model 2, these differences

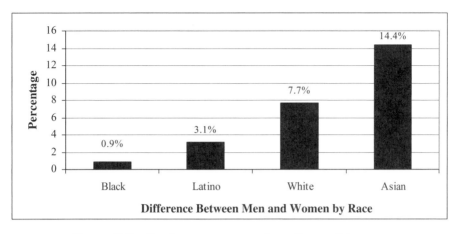

FIGURE 10.2   Gender gaps on yes vote on the recall by race.

represent a statistically significant association between race and voting for or against the recall when compared with the aggregate vote of all other racial groups combined. In other words, compared with all of the other racial categories included in this analysis, the pattern of white, black, Latino, and Asian

TABLE 10.1   Vote on the recall by gender and race.

	YES (%)	NO (%)	MODEL 1 χ^2	MODEL 2 χ^2	MODEL 3 χ^2
Men	59.4	40.6	30.872***		
Women	51.4	48.6			
White Men	63.4	36.6	20.887***		68.370***
White Women	55.7	44.3			56.797***
Black Men	21.7	78.3	0.034		68.315***
Black Women	20.8	79.2			51.533***
Latino Men	46.2	53.8	0.497		18.165***
Latino Women	43.1	56.9			8.031**
Asian Men	54.9	45.1	5.055*		0.0715
Asian Women	40.5	59.5			6.589**
White	59.5	40.5		123.638***	
Black	21.5	78.5		118.385***	
Latino	44.8	55.2		24.439***	
Asian	47.0	53.0		6.699**	

Notes: *$p < 0.05$, **$p < 0.01$, ***$p < 0.001$. Model 1 compares yes or no votes between men and women of the same race. Model 2 compares yes or no votes among different racial groups. Model 3 compares yes or no votes across gender categories (men or women) to yes or no votes of the same gender category for all other races.

voting is distinct. This result is uniform with previous studies and suggests support for our second hypothesis in that we do indeed observe racially polarized voting on the recall. Race appears to have been relevant in this election, just as it has been found in previous California elections.

Model 3 compares yes or no votes by race and gender, that is, it examines the intersection between gender and race across all groups. When we breakdown the vote results in Model 3, we find that race matters for women. White women supported the recall by 55.7 percent, black women by 20.8 percent, Latinas by 43.1 percent, and Asian women by 40.5 percent. Additionally and similar to the Model 2, these observed results constitute a significant association when comparing one racial group of women with all other racial groups of women combined. White and black women exhibit the most prevalent relationship among gender, race, and vote on the recall, while Latinas and Asian women demonstrate a more moderate association.

White men voted for the recall at a higher percentage than any other racial group at 63.4 percent. At the other extreme, black men favored the recall by only 21.7 percent. Forty-six percent of Latino men supported the recall, compared with 54.9 percent of Asian men. For white, black, and Latino men, gender, race, and vote on the recall showed a statistically significant association in reference to all other racial groups of men collectively. Voting among Asian men did not result in a significant relationship. For Asian men, gender, race, and vote on the recall appear to be independent. Model 3 provides evidence in support of our second hypothesis and in opposition to our first; women do not look similar across racial categories. Similarly, Model 3 provides an indication that the idea of intersections between race and gender holds merit. We detect differences across racial groups, both in terms of voting patterns and in terms of the effect of gender on those patterns.

While Models 2 and 3 are helpful in determining patterns among racial and gender groups, in general, it would be more illustrative to investigate specific pairings of racial categories to detect particular associations. Model 4 consists of six such groupings with separate calculations conducted for (a) men and women together, (b) women separately, and (c) men separately for the following pairs: white/black, white/Latino, white/Asian, black/Latino, black/Asian, and Latino/Asian. Accounting for both genders, we find that there is a significant association for vote on the recall for all pairings except for Latinos and Asians; there does not appear to be a significant difference for Asians and Latinos on the recall vote in reference to each other. This holds for women separately as well: All other pairs of racial categories produce a statistically significant association for recall voting except for comparisons among Asian women and Latinas. Asian men, on the other hand, do not demonstrate a statistically significant association for two pairings, white/Asian men and Latino/Asian men.

By and large, a majority of the dichotomous pairings exhibit statistically significant associations between race and vote on the recall for both genders as a whole and for women and men considered separately. Notably, Asians and Latinos are the only group for which there is no statistically significant difference in the association between race and vote on the recall for any of the three calculations. In addition, for whites and Asians, the calculation for men is the only result that displays statistical independence within the group. Thus, we see racially polarized voting patterns among all racial groups except for the variation between Latinos and Asians, as a whole, and white and Asian men considered separately from women. Hence, we not only witness an aggregate racial difference in vote on the recall, as evidenced in Model 2, but also we see variations among most racial groups in relation to one another. Considering the evidence from all four models, we find greater endorsement for the second hypothesis and conflicting evidence for the first. While there are statistically significant racial inconsistencies, the gender gap is only apparent for whites and, to a lesser extent, Asians. Overall, the greatest disparities on voting for the recall occur among racial groups and not between gender categories.

DISCUSSION

The previous analysis shows that race and gender do interact, in that both affected vote choice in this election. In addition, their effects vary among women and among racial groups. So why does this matter? First, this provides important empirical support for the idea of intersection. Intersection theorists have long argued that the experiences of women of color are qualitatively different from those of white women. Historically, these women have had very different experiences in the United States, so it is intuitively logical that they would also have different attitudes toward politics. Yet, this claim has been subjected to few empirical tests (Dawson 2000; Gay and Tate 1998; Tate 1993). To our knowledge, no one has ever looked at its effects across multiple groups simultaneously, as we have done here. The fact that we find important differences across racial groups and across women provides rare empirical support for the contention of intersection and other racial theories that multiple marginalizations vary across groups, time, and circumstance.

Second, this analysis should push scholars to consider more deeply why we believe group membership and identities matter in politics. Feminists of color and critical theorists have emphasized the need to look at the intersections of race, class, and gender to fully understand the social, political, and economic experiences of U.S. communities of color (Cohen 1999; Crenshaw 1991; Dawson 2001; hooks 2000). Yet, the attempt to incorporate this kind of analysis into empirical work raises important theoretical problems. We must consider why exactly we believe that race, class, and gender affect an individual's group consciousness and political ideology. As Michael Dawson points out, a racially stratified society creates "systematically different patterns of outcomes ... [that] shape individual life chances as well as the perceptions of society, thereby providing the basis for the huge racial gulf in public opinion" (2001, 4). But, what exactly do those patterns look like? How do they vary both within and among racial groups, especially in terms of class and gender? As political scientists, we have just begun to examine and address these questions.[5]

Looking at the effects of race and class in particular, Leighley and Vedlitz (1999, 1095–97) delineate five models of minority political participation: socioeconomic status (SES), psychological resources, social connectedness, group consciousness, and group conflict. The SES model has been the dominant paradigm in studies of political behavior (Campbell et al. 1960; Rosenstone and Hansen 1993; Verba and Nie 1972; Verba, Schlozman, and Brady 1995). These studies have found that a person's SES—their education, income, and occupation—is the best predictor of their likelihood to vote. Recent work by Verba, Schlozman, and Brady (1995) has moved beyond SES to examine what resources SES actually provide people to facilitate their political participation. The authors found that the factors driving different kinds of participation are different and that,

> unique configurations of participatory factors—and, therefore, unique participatory publics and sets of issue concerns—are relevant for voting, for forms of participation that require inputs of time, and for forms of participation that require inputs of money (1995, 5).

But, despite the robustness of the SES model in studies of Anglos, the results in studies of the political behavior of other racial groups has been mixed. Katherine Tate (1993) found that education and income only occasionally are related to African American participation, and studies of Latinos have found that SES can only explain part of the gap between Latino and Anglo electoral and nonelectoral participation (García, Falcón, and de la Garza 1996). The SES model does not seem to explain why, despite the fact that education and SES have increased overall in the United States over the past few decades, political participation levels have decreased (Leighley and Vedlitz 1999, 1094). Scholars searching for other explanations have turned to psychological resources—feelings of efficacy, trust in government, and civic duty—as the explanatory factors. Studies using this approach have found that political interest and efficacy have a significant affect on participation (Rosenstone and Hansen 1993). Leighley and Vedlitz (1999) treat the emphasis on psychological factors as analytically distinct from social connectedness and group consciousness explanations. But, in fact, all these explanations center around the idea that feelings of "linked fate," (Dawson 1994) "political alienation," (Olsen 1969) "group identity," (Hardy-Fanta 1993; Tate 1993), and "group conflict" (Tajfel and Turner 1979) have an impact on political attitudes and behavior. In other words, individuals feel connections to particular groups (or not), and their political attitudes and participation are affected by those feelings.

All of these models assume that groups will behave in a monolithic fashion, driven by either class or race. The SES model presumes that all people of a particular class, regardless of race or gender, will engage in political activity at the same rate, even if they are not necessarily expressing a class-conscious identity. Group consciousness/identity models assume that members of a particular racial group, regardless of their gender or class, will behave in similar ways. The fact that these models have not been successfully applied to multiple groups across multiple situations suggests that they are missing important aspects of how participation patterns vary within groups and among different contexts—namely, how the same racial identification can coincide with varied feelings of efficacy and political engagement, and how that may vary by gender.

The same may be true in terms of our understanding of the effect gender has on political participation. Burns, Schlozman, and Verba (2001) argue that there are roughly six competing hypotheses that attempt to explain the relationship between gender and political activity. Two emphasize how differential demands on women's time, especially in terms of the responsibilities of childrearing and other household duties, keep women from participating in organizations that provide political information and access to political networks. Another focuses on how patriarchal family structures relegate women to the "private" sphere rather than the "public" sphere of politics (Schlozman et al. 1995; Sunstein 1990). Similarly, another argues that male and female socialization patterns in childhood create unique environments for women and men that influence how they make political decisions. The final two emphasize socioeconomic issues, arguing that women's generally lower levels of income, education, and occupational status, in addition to the discrimination they experience in economics and the law, are what decreases their participation (MacKinnon 1987). Burns, Schlozman, and Verba (2001) test these hypotheses and find that, because of differences in overall political engagement and access to politically relevant resources, men are more interested, informed, and efficacious about politics than women.

As was the case with theories of group consciousness, this analysis tends to treat women as a monolithic group. An important factor that is missing in the study of race and gender is how marginalization along any of these dimensions affects the way individuals see themselves in relation to their community(ies) and the political system in general (Cohen 1999; Crenshaw 1991; Hill Collins 2000). The key question is what exactly we believe causes gender, race, or class differences in behavior and/or attitudes. Is it group identity, marginalization, socialization, or some combination? Does one trump the other in particular contexts (Gay and Tate 1998; Mansbridge and Tate 1992)? This highlights the need to better understand the effects of what Vigil (2002) and Cohen (1999) call "multiple marginality," that is, the marginalization of particular populations across multiple dimensions. Intersections scholars argue that we must remember that racial, gender, and class oppressions are not separate, but rather are mutually constitutive (Cohen 1999; Crenshaw 1991; Hill Collins 2000; hooks 2000). As such, analyses need to look at the "whole person," as we attempt to do here, rather than break up individuals into their component parts (that is, race, separate from gender, separate from class, and so on). Race and gender are important in politics because they shape our view of the world and our understanding of our relative place within that world. Getting a better handle on the relational effects of that experience could be the first step toward operationalizing intersectionality in our empirical work (Emirbayer 1997).

CONCLUSION

The recall election in California was unique in that it was framed as a "time out" from regular, partisan politics. It was understood that both Democrats and Republicans were unhappy with the governorship of Davis, and that

Schwarzenegger successfully avoided strong identification with any party. In addition, the allegations of Schwarzenegger's sexual misconduct initially suggested that gender could play an important role in the outcome of the race. In fact, this analysis suggests that this was not the case. While white and Asian women were slightly less likely to support the recall, the differences were not overwhelming.

The greatest differences among the groups fell along racial lines. This finding reflects the continued salience of race in California politics, even in a so-called nonpartisan and ostensibly nonracialized election. Race is so powerful that it clearly affects how black and Latina women experience their gender, making them more likely to vote in line with members of their racial group than with other women, particularly white women. We must always keep in mind that this result is not "natural," but rather a product of the turbulent history of race relations in California and the United States (Almaguer 1994; Smith 1997; Takaki 1993). It also reminds us that an accurate analysis of the California electorate requires inclusion of multiple measures—race, class, gender, sexuality—to understand fully how marginalization affects groups' political attitudes and behavior.

BIBLIOGRAPHY

Almaguer, Tomás. *Racial Fault Lines: the Historical Origins of White Supremacy in California.* Berkeley: University of California Press, 1994.

Alvarez, R. Michael, and John Brehm. *Hard Choices, Easy Answers.* Princeton: Princeton University Press, 2002.

Alvarez, R. Michael, and Lisa García Bedolla. "The Foundations of Latino Voter Partisanship: Evidence from the 2000 Elections." *Journal of Politics* 65 (2003): 31–49.

Box-Steffensmeier, Janet M., Suzanna De Boef, and Tse-Min Lin. "The Dynamics of the Partisan Gender Gap." *American Political Science Review* 98 (2004): 515–28.

Burns, Nancy, Kay Lehman Schlozman, and Sidney Verba. *The Private Roots of Public Action: Gender, Equality and Political Participation.* Cambridge: Harvard University Press, 2001.

Cain, Bruce. "The Contemporary Context of Ethnic and Racial Politics in California." In *Racial and Ethnic Politics in California*, edited by Byran O. Jackson and Michael B. Preston. Berkeley, CA: Institute of Governmental Studies, 1991.

Campbell, Angus, Phillip E. Converse, Warren E. Miller, and Donald E. Stokes. *The American Voter.* New York: John Wiley and Sons, 1960.

Collet, Christian. "Bloc Voting, Polarization and the Panethnic Hypothesis: The Case of Little Saigon." Paper presented at the Western Political Science Association Annual Meeting, Portland, Oregon, March 12–15, 2004.

Cohen, Cathy J. *The Boundaries of Blackness: AIDS and the Breakdown of Black Politics.* Chicago: University of Chicago Press, 1999.

Crenshaw, Kimberlé. "Mapping the Margins: Intersectionality, Identity, Politics and Violence Against Women of Color." *Stanford Law Review* 43 (1991): 1241–99.

Dawson, Michael C. *Behind the Mule: Race and Class in African-American Politics.* Princeton: Princeton University Press, 1994.

_____. *Black Visions: the Roots of Contemporary African-American Political Ideologies.* Chicago: University of Chicago Press, 2001.

_____. "Slowly Coming to Grips with the Effects of the American Racial Order on American Policy Preferences." In Lawrence Bobo, eds. *Racialized Politics: the Debate about Racism in America*, edited by David O. Sears and Jim Sidanius. Chicago: University of Chicago Press, 2000.

Emirbayer, Mustafa. "Manifesto for a Relational Sociology." *American Journal of Sociology* 103 (1997): 281–17.

García, F. Chris, Angelo Falcón, and Rodolfo de la Garza. "Ethnicity and Politics: Evidence from the Latino National Political Survey." *Hispanic Journal of Behavioral Sciences* 18 (1996): 91–103.

García Bedolla, Lisa. *Fluid Borders: Latino Power, Identity and Politics in Los Angeles*. Berkeley: University of California Press, 2005.

Gay, Claudine, and Katherine Tate. "Doubly Bound: The Impact of Gender and Race on the Politics of Black Women." *Political Psychology* 19 (1998): 169–84.

Greene, Steven. "The Social-Psychological Measurement of Partisanship." *Political Behavior* 24 (2002): 171–97.

Grofman, Bernard, Lisa Handley, and Richard Niemi. *Minority Representation and the Quest for Voting Equality*. Cambridge: Cambridge University Press, 1992.

Hajnal, Zoltan, and Hugh Louch. *Are There Winners and Losers? Race, Ethnicity, and California's Initiative Process*. San Francisco, CA: Public Policy Institute of California, 2001.

Hardy-Fanta, Carol. *Latina Politics, Latino Politics: Gender, Culture and Political Participation in Boston*. Philadelphia: Temple University Press, 1993.

Hill Collins, Patricia. *Black Feminist Thought: Knowledge, Consciousness and the Politics of Empowerment*. 2nd ed. New York: Routledge, 2000.

Hochschild, Jennifer. *Facing Up to the American Dream: Race, Class, and the Soul of the Nation*. Princeton: Princeton University Press, 1995.

hooks, bell. *Feminist Theory: From Margin to Center*. Boston: South End Press, 1984.

Jackson, Byran O. "Racial and Ethnic Voting Cleavages in Los Angels Politics." In *Racial and Ethnic Politics in California*, edited by Byran O. Jackson and Michael B. Preston. Berkeley, CA: Institute of Governmental Studies, 1991.

Jones-Correa, Michael. *Between Two Nations: the Political Predicament of Latinos in New York City*. Ithaca: Cornell University Press, 1998.

Kaufmann Karen M., and John R. Petrocik. "The Changing Politics of American Men." *American Journal of Political Science* 43 (1999): 864–87.

Kennedy Chaney, Carole, R. Michael Alvarez, and Jonathan Nagler. "Explaining the Gender Gap in U.S. Presidential Elections." *Political Research Quarterly* 51 (1998): 311–39.

Leighley, Jan E. *Strength in Numbers? The Political Mobilization of Racial and Ethnic Minorities*. Princeton: Princeton University Press, 2001.

Leighley, Jan E., and Arnold Vedlitz. "Race, Ethnicity and Political Participation: Competing Models and Contrasting Explanations." *Journal of Politics* 61 (1999): 1092–14.

Levy, Mark R. "The Methodology and Performance of Election Day Polls." *Public Opinion Quarterly* 47 (1983): 54–67.

MacKinnon, Catharine. *Feminism Unmodified: Discourses on Life and Law*. Cambridge: Harvard University Press, 1987.

Mangum, Maurice. "Exploring the Social Network Effects of Church on Black Party Identification." Paper presented at the Midwest Political Science Association Annual Meeting, Chicago, Illinois, March 25–28, 2004.

Mansbridge, Jane, and Katherine Tate. "Race Trumps Gender: Black Opinion on the Thomas Nomination." *PS: Political Science and Politics* 25 (1992): 488–92.

Olsen, Marvin E. "Two Categories of Political Alienation." *Social Forces* 47 (1969): 288–99.

Regalado, Jaime A., and Gloria Martínez. "Reapportionment and Coalition Building: A Case Study of Informal Barriers to Latino Empowerment in Los Angeles County." In *Latinos and Political Coalitions: Political Empowerment for the 1990s*, edited by Roberto E. Villarreal and Norma G. Hernandez. New York: Praeger, 1991.

Rosenstone, Steven J., and John Mark Hansen. *Mobilization, Participation and Democracy in America*. New York: Macmillan, 1993.

Schlozman, Kay Lehman, Nancy Burns, Sidney Verba, and Jesse Donahue. "Gender and Citizen Participation: Is There a Different Voice?" *American Journal of Political Science* 39 (1995): 267–93.

Shapiro, Robert Y., and Harpreet Mahajan. "Gender Differences in Policy Preferences: A Summary of Trends from the 1960s to the 1980s." *Public Opinion Quarterly* 50 (1986): 42–61.

Shaw, Daron. "Estimating Racially Polarized Voting: A View from the States." *Political Research Quarterly* 50 (1997): 49–74.

Smith, Rogers M. *Civic Ideals: Conflicting Visions of Citizenship in U.S. History*. New Haven: Yale University Press, 1997.

Sunstein, Cass, ed. *Feminism and Political Theory*. Chicago: University of Chicago Press, 1990.

Tajfel, Henri, and J. C. Turner. "An Integrative Theory of Intergroup Conflict." In *The Social Psychology of Intergroup Relations*, edited by William G. Austin and Stephen Worchel. Monterey, CA: Brooks/Cole Books, 1979.

Takaki, Ronald. *A Different Mirror: A History of Multicultural America*. Boston: Back Bay Books, 1993.

Tate, Katherine. *From Protest to Politics: the New Black Voters in American Elections*. Cambridge: Harvard University Press, 1993.

Tolbert, Caroline J., and Rodney E. Hero. "Race/Ethnicity and Direct Democracy: An Analysis of California's Illegal Immigration Initiative." *Journal of Politics* 58 (1996): 806–18.

Verba, Sidney, and Norman H. Nie. *Participation in America: Political Democracy and Social Equality*. Chicago: University of Chicago Press, 1972.

Verba, Sidney, Kay Lehman Schlozman, and Henry E. Brady. *Voice and Equality: Civic Voluntarism in American Politics*. Cambridge: Harvard University Press, 1995.

Vigil, James Diego. *A Rainbow of Gangs: Street Cultures in the Mega City*. Austin: University of Texas Press, 2002.

Wilcox, Clyde, Joseph Ferrara, and Dee Allsop. "Group Differences in Early Support for Military Action in the Gulf: The Effects of Gender, Generation and Ethnicity." *American Politics Quarterly* 21 (1993): 343–59.

NOTES

1. To avoid some methodological problems, we looked only at the vote for the recall itself, rather than candidate choice. We believe support for the recall can be treated as a freestanding vote, whereas candidate choice must be considered in relation to recall vote.

2. In terms of the variables of interest, each respondent was asked the following questions: (a) Gender: "Are you: Male or Female?" (b) Ethnicity: "What is your racial or ethnic background?" (c) Yes or No on the Recall: "In the election to recall Governor Davis, did you just vote: Yes, to recall Gov. Davis or No, not to recall Gov. Davis?"

3. Gender and vote on the recall were recoded as dummy variables for all models. Race was recoded to include only white, black, Latino, and Asian respondents. Dummy variables for race were constructed and used in the second and third models. Separate variables for each race were created for Model 4, which included respondents from only one racial category.

4. While chi-square can tell us whether or not the observed results are independent or dependent, it does not allow us to say anything about the strength or direction of the relationship. In addition, chi-squares are directly related to the size of the data set, with large samples yielding large chi-squares. Caution should be used when evaluating the chi squares in Table 10.1.

5. Some examples of political scientists that do address these questions are Michael Dawson, *Behind the Mule: Race and Class in African-American Politics* (Princeton: Princeton University Press, 1994) and *Black Visions: the Roots of Contemporary African-American Political Ideologies* (Chicago: University of Chicago Press, 2001); Jennifer Hochschild, *Facing Up to the American Dream: Race, Class, and the Soul of the Nation* (Princeton: Princeton University Press, 1995), Michael Jones-Correa, *Between Two Nations: the Political Predicament of Latinos in New York City* (Ithaca: Cornell University Press, 1998); Katherine Tate, *From Protest to Politics: the New Black Voters in American Elections* (Cambridge: Harvard University Press, 1993); and Jan E. Leighley, *Strength in Numbers? The Political Mobilization of Racial and Ethnic Minorities* (Princeton: Princeton University Press, 2001).

CIRQUE DU SACRAMENTO AND WEARY CALIFORNIA:

STATE AND NATIONAL COVERAGE OF THE RECALL CAMPAIGN

MARTIN JOHNSON

UNIVERSITY OF CALIFORNIA, RIVERSIDE

CHRIS STOUT

UNIVERSITY OF CALIFORNIA, IRVINE

SHAUN BOWLER

MAX NEIMAN

UNIVERSITY OF CALIFORNIA, RIVERSIDE

> The word most commonly used to characterize this political event is "circus." Everyone from Eureka to San Diego, from PBS to HBO, has characterized the campaign as a three-ring or, to be more accurate, a 135-ring circus. I'm not surprised that the recall race has been named the Cirque du Sacramento.
>
> *–Boston Globe* columnist Ellen Goodman

> To daily read about California being a circus and the laughingstock of the nation is getting to be a little weary. I have talked to friends from California to New York and none feel we are a laughingstock. Only rednecks who wish they were in California make these silly remarks.
>
> *–San Marcos North County Times* reader Bernie Schroer

Observers, including *Boston Globe* columnist Ellen Goodman, often focused on the novelty of the 2002 gubernatorial recall in California in commenting on or covering the election. The theme of the recall circus—as a laughable chapter in the state's political history—was a consistent one in coverage of state politics in the summer of 2002. The infrequent use of the statewide recall even where it is available, the success of recall organizers, and the large number of replacement candidates all contributed to the perception in many circles, or rings more appropriately, that the October 2002 election was a chaotic circus. As the quotation from Bernie Schroer's letter to his newspaper's editorial page suggests, however, this view was not universal.

A number of scholars have taken an interest in how framing affects political decision making and opinion formation (for example, Nelson, Oxley, and Clawson 1997). A frame is a "central organizing idea for making sense of relevant events and suggesting what is at issue" (Gamson and Modigliani, 1989, 57). Our interest here lies in understanding more about the conditions under which news organizations frame a story in a particular way and, in this chapter, we investigate news organizations' use of circus imagery as a frame for covering the recall. We analyze news stories from the eight weeks leading up to the recall election and show that the image of the recall as a circus—and hence that it should be dismissed as a trivial, unimportant, or possibly mischievous event—was invoked frequently throughout the campaign. However, there is interesting systematic variation in the use of language, suggesting the recall campaign was marked by hysteria or novelty. In particular, we find that the characterization of the recall as a circus was sensitive to specific events during the campaign: The circus imagery was triggered by events and not simply used as a blanket term. That said, national news organizations were much more likely to indulge in the circus frame than state organizations: For those outside the state, the recall may have been a circus, but for Californians, more serious political issues were at stake.

This chapter proceeds through four sections. First, we examine media coverage of the recall and initial scholarship on the role of the media in the recall campaign. This work establishes the salience of the recall to media actors and audience members alike, and asserts candidate Arnold Schwarzenegger's dominance over the recall campaign story. Beyond that however, it remains for scholars to examine patterns in recall coverage across the state and differences between national and state recall news stories. Research on the broader question of the news media's coverage of instruments of direct democracy principally has focused on how frames and ballot structures affect choices, as well as how interest group cues affect voter opinions.

For the remainder of the paper, we focus on news reporting on the recall that we identify as "circus" coverage—that is, news stories that characterize the recall as unduly novel or circus-like. We elaborate on our interest in the "circus" frame used to cover the election. Then we compare coverage of the recall in the national and state media, relying on a convenience sample of computerized and text-searchable news content available from the Lexis-Nexis searchable news article archive. Using Lexis-Nexis archive stories about the recall, we compare patterns of coverage in state newspapers and national media outlets, including major broadcast networks, 24-hour cable news channels, and newspapers with national audiences. We also examine patterns of recall coverage within California, relying on our own sample of newspaper stories from across the state. Finally, we discuss the implications of our findings for the study of media and politics.

REPORTING THE 2003 CALIFORNIA RECALL: COVERING RECALLS AND OTHER POPULAR DEMOCRATIC FORMS

Two major insights have emerged thus far among social scientists interested in media coverage of the recall campaign. First, scholars continue to describe it as a "circus" (for example, Bowler and Cain 2004) and even as a "feeding frenzy" (for example, Schecter 2004). These scholarly assessments are based primarily on the volume of interest the recall generated: reporters mobbed the recall story. Second, news about the recall was dominated by stories focused on candidates rather than issues (Fuller 2003). In this vein, more than any of the other replacement candidates or any candidate in recent California elections, Schwarzenegger dominated the recall story (Schecter 2004) and almost faultlessly managed the state's mainstream political press (Gerston and Christensen 2004; Kerns 2004).

On the first point, the salience of the recall and the attention paid to it, we attempt a quantification of the abnormal attention to the recall. What exactly does a feeding frenzy look like? How do we know a feeding frenzy when we see one? Anecdotally, we agree with other scholars who assert that the recall generated a great deal more coverage that other campaigns, but no systematic comparative research has supported this assertion. We have no reason to doubt this; however, as social scientists, we are interested in characterizing interest in the recall relative to other campaigns. We follow Fuller in trying to get a better sense of recall coverage using counts of news stories. Using guided text searches of the Lexis-Nexis news database and the online archives of the *Los Angeles Times*, Table 11.1 charts the number of news stories about the 2003 recall election and the number of stories about the 1998 and 2002 gubernatorial elections during the final eight weeks of each campaign for each of the following three news organizations: Associated Press, *Los Angeles Times*, and *San Francisco Chronicle*.

We delimited an appropriate date range for the last eight weeks of each election and requested from each database a list of all stories containing the words California and election along with the names of either of the two top vote-getters.[1] The counts from these searches are the cell-entries in Table 11.1. For the recall race, we searched the database in two ways, each of which are reported on the table: considering Schwarzenegger and Governor Gray Davis to be the top two vote-getters, or alternatively considering Schwarzenegger and Cruz Bustamante the top two contenders. To keep the searches as comparable as possible, we did not use a more complex search using more names. Clearly, Lexis-Nexis and the *Los Angeles Times* have far more news stories about the recall election archived than either of the earlier elections.

Despite some obvious limitations,[2] this story-count method suggests that, indeed, the recall generated substantially more media interest than the previous two gubernatorial elections combined, at least among leading news

TABLE 11.1   Comparing coverage of the 1998, 2002, and 2003
California gubernatorial races.

	1998 DAVIS/ LUNGREN	2002 DAVIS/ SIMON	2003 SCHWARZENEGGER/ DAVIS	2003 SCHWARZENEGGER/ BUSTAMANTE
Associated Press	206	245	652	581
Los Angeles Times	74	165	664	576
San Francisco Chronicle	96	171	506	432

organizations. These news organizations have archived more than five times the number of stories on the recall than the 1998 election—an open-seat race for governor that saw a then-record $51 million dollars in direct spending by the candidates—and about three times the number of stories on the recall than the 2002 election with perhaps as much as $130 million spent directly and indirectly . While it is possible that between 1998 and 2003, both online archives began more aggressively uploading a more complete subset of their news stories, it is unlikely that the dramatic spike in coverage of the recall suggested here is attributable solely to changes in procedure. The recall generated a great deal more interest than previous gubernatorial contests.

The most detailed study of newspaper coverage of the recall publicly released thus far speaks more directly to Schwarzenegger campaign's dominance of media attention surrounding the recall (the second major point of this paper). A team of researchers at Policy Analysis for California Education counted stories with more than 250 words in the *Los Angeles Times*, *San Francisco Chronicle*, *San Jose Mercury News*, and *New York Times*, between August 6 and October 6 (Fuller 2003). They focused on the appearance of candidate names and references to major issues (for example, the state budget, education, and child health insurance). They found that in the 1,525 news stories they collected and coded, Schwarzenegger's name appeared in more than three-quarters of stories, while any discussion of the campaign's most prominent issues, the budget, was featured in about 16 percent of the stories.

Fuller's team also found that Schwarzenegger benefited from more "lop-sided" coverage in the national news media, with the *New York Times* as their exemplar, than in state coverage. For example, in the *New York Times*, Schwarzenegger was mentioned in about two stories for every one story that Lieutenant Governor Bustamante was mentioned. That ratio reduces to just below 1.6:1 in the *Los Angeles Times*. Schwarzenegger was covered more than the other replacement candidates within the state, but the disparity was somewhat smaller outside the state.

CIRQUE DU CALIFORNIA: FRAMING THE RECALL AS CHAOS

We investigate other differences across news organizations in their coverage of the recall. In particular, we are interested in understanding why news organizations framed the recall as a circus. We have already referenced the Gamson definition of a story frame—a central organizing premise that defines the issue under discussion. Beyond this, Entman underscores the importance of emphasis in framing, noting that a frame highlights aspects of an issue and makes them more salient (1993, 52). Again, here we are not interested in explaining how framing affected public opinion or how people learned about the recall. Instead, we are interested in understanding more about how news organizations choose frames for stories.

We identify the recall-as-circus as a common frame for news stories about the recall. While we focus primarily on news coverage, columnists provide the most vivid examples of what we consider the circus frame. Reporters and writers using the circus frame emphasized the novelty of the recall, as well as the uncertainty and chaos surrounding Davis, replacement candidates, and voters. For example, political scientist Larry Sabato wrote a column expressing his strenuous criticism of the recall as "a zoo with the cages of the animals pushed wide open. Every stereotype of the Golden State has been validated, from its regrettable obsession with superficial Hollywood celebrity to its arms-wide-open welcome for, well, unusual people" (Sabato 2003). He goes on to characterize California as a "mob-ocracy." George Will (2003) called it a "riot of millionaires masquerading as a 'revolt of the people.'" *Los Angeles Times* columnist Peter H. King complained the state will be "perceived as the next banana republic" (King 2003).

This was, of course, not the only way to think about the recall. In contrast, Daniel Weintraub of the *Sacramento Bee* reviewed the California state librarian's evolving acceptance of the recall as "a legitimate citizen movement reacting to a disconnect between the governors (not just Davis) and the governed" rather than a "petulant partisan jihad" (Weintraub 2003). Bernie Schroer, Escondido resident and reader of the *San Marcos North County Times*, characterized the recall in his letter as "courageous" opportunity to "take a stand" (2003). In addition to the circus frame, and the citizen-movement/direct-democracy frame, many news organizations focused on the same things we've grown accustomed to in coverage of any political campaign—the horserace, big campaign donors, debates, and even issues.

We think that the choice of a story's frame reflects not only how journalists think about an issue but also how they think their colleagues and readers think about it. After all, reporters are trying to explain events to their readers using language and images their readers understand. Furthermore, news reports and analysis are based on actual events—representing interpretations of things that happen. Consequently, a reporter's choice of frame in covering a story related to the recall should reflect events, as well as the predispositions of reporters and the perceived predispositions of readers. We offer a preliminary investigation of the use of the circus frame for covering the recall and find that, in fact, the use of circus and chaos imagery was greater when the recall was at its most tumultuous; however, we also find a much greater propensity to use this chaotic imagery outside the state than within it, and a greater tendency for journalists writing for audiences with higher support for the recall to minimize circus coverage.

STUDYING THE CIRCUS

At the beginning of August 2003, we retained a professional news clipping service, Allen's Press Clipping Bureau of Los Angeles, to send us all newspaper articles about the recall. We selected 20 daily newspapers[3] based on geography (representing six areas of the state), size (large dailies with circulation greater than 100,000 and medium newspapers serving 25,000 to 100,000 households), and politics (areas leaning Democrat and areas leaning Republican). The result was more than 7,000 individual newspaper articles about the recall—news stories, opinion columns, editorials, special interest stories, letters from readers, comics, and photographs. Perhaps we would have structured this differently if we had known the recall would turn into the aforementioned "feeding frenzy" it became. For this project, however, we were left (as many social scientists find themselves) trying to cope with a tremendously complex source of data.

We used two sources of news coverage about the recall. One was this unique collection of local newspaper articles on the recall. To simplify the task of analyzing this wealth of news articles, we took samples from the clips we collected using procedures discussed below. However, in addition to the articles we clipped, we also use Lexis-Nexis to study recall circus coverage as well, because this database allowed us to compare in-state and out-of-state news stories in easily searched newspaper stories. We remain cautious about the inferences we developed using this resource, particularly given the limitations of using computer databases of news content (for example, Kaufman, Dykers, and Caldwell 1993).

THE CALIFORNIA RECALL IN STATE AND NATION

We compare state and national news content archived by Lexis-Nexis during the eight full weeks leading up to the recall election, August 10 through October 4, 2003. We examine all California news sources[4] and compare the recall coverage from these organizations with reports in selected sources whose principal audiences are outside the state. We include both national television networks and newspapers.[5] We are particularly interested in how the recall was framed in the state versus how it was discussed in media directed outside of the state, with particular interest in "circus" coverage.

The dependent variable we examine is the percentage of stories about the recall, from a given news outlet, which include language identifying the recall campaign as a circus. We define each news organization's population of news stories about the recall as those containing the words *California, recall, and election*. Across the forty state and national news organizations we examined using Lexis-Nexis, we find 6,575 news stories about the recall using these criteria during the eight weeks leading to the vote. We define circus coverage as all stories about the recall (containing words *California, recall*, and *election*) that also use the words *circus, chaos*, or *chaotic*. With these criteria in mind, we find 801 stories that we can characterize as using the circus frame in covering the recall, 12.2 percent of all stories about the recall.

These circus stories are distributed across time and news organizations in some interesting patterns. Figure 11.1 graphs the percentage of news stories in national and state news sources describing the recall as a circus. Two features of this data are immediately recognizable. First, the recall was more clearly associated with circus imagery in national coverage—broadcast television, cable television, and newspapers—than in local California reporting. In the major national media reports archived with Lexis-Nexis, 17.4 percent of the stories about the California recall referred to the state's circus or chaos. In state news, the percentage of stories with circus language was 10 percent.

The second identifiable characteristic of the graph is that the characterization of the recall as a circus, both for state and national news, varied over the weeks. During the first couple of weeks in the recall campaign, state and national reporters were more likely to use the circus frame than they were later in the

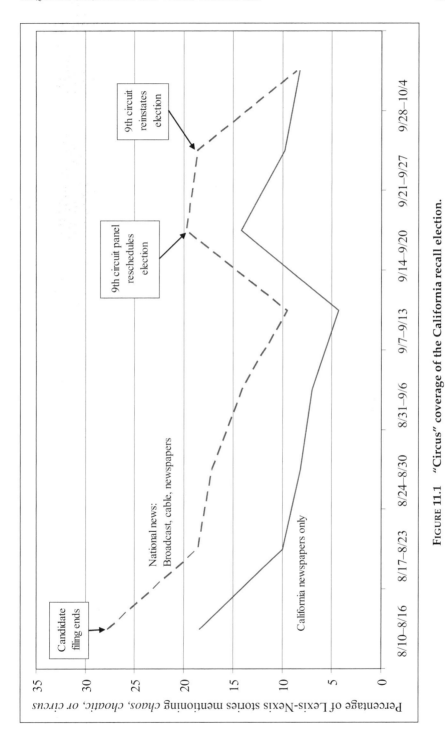

FIGURE 11.1 "Circus" coverage of the California recall election.

SOURCE: Lexis-Nexis Academic Universe News Search story counts.

campaign. There are, however, bumps in circus coverage late in the campaign. State reports are less likely to frame the recall as a circus, but there seems to be some underlying common source of coverage about the recall as a circus.

Figure 11.1 notes some important events in the recall campaign we suspect may have affected circus coverage.[6] During the first week of August, just before the graph's timeline begins (August 10), Schwarzenegger announced his campaign (August 6) as did dozens of potential replacement candidates. Candidate filing ended August 9, with 247 filed candidates and 135 qualifying for the ballot. As we might expect, this phenomenon appears to be associated with the greatest amount of characterization of the recall as a circus observed during any point of the recall campaign.

Circus coverage abates during the next few weeks. However, there is a spike in state and national circus coverage during the weeks of September 14 and September 21. On September 15, a three-judge panel of the Ninth U.S. Circuit Court of Appeals rescheduled the recall election for March 2004. One week later, the full Ninth U.S. Circuit Court of Appeals overturned this decision and restored the October 7 election date. The flurry of circus characterizations during these two weeks likely had something to do with these events.

Consequently, we cautiously draw two lessons from Figure 11.1 and the story counts that underlie the graph. Characterizations of the recall as a circus were inspired by real events—the qualification of candidates, legal excitement surrounding the special election, and other elements of the story. However, national rather than local reporters drove the story of the recall as a circus. We suspect this was the case for a couple of potential reasons.

Californians—including reporters and other media decision makers—may be more familiar with the implements of direct democracy and special mechanisms of citizen participation, such as the recall, than residents of other states. The California recall election seemed like less of a circus to Californians than it did to New Yorkers, Virginians, and residents of the District of Columbia, in part, because they experience this less often than Californians. Thus, the recall seemed less novel or circus-like to Californians than to others sent to the state to pile on to the media frenzy.

Another possibility, however, is that the national attention to the circus frame is also evidence of ideological reporting—the dreaded liberal media bias. In fact, at least one observer, *Orange County Register* columnist Steven Greenhut, clearly saw the hand of journalistic liberalism in various circus appellations for the recall, naming the "depiction by the liberal media of the recall as a circus" as number four in his top ten stupid recall tricks list, and noting that "these elites largely ignored the real frustrations that drove the recall" (2003). Assuming this is true, we should see some sort of association between news organization liberalism and use of the circus frame in discussing the recall. To investigate this, we examine patterns of coverage within the state.

RECALL HEADLINES ACROSS THE STATE

We make an important assumption in our investigation of patterns of local coverage: that news organizations write for and to their audiences. Thus, across news organizations and communities, the ideological orientation of news organizations should correlate with the ideological orientations of communities. Simply put, a newspaper in a more conservative part of California will be more conservative than a newspaper in a more liberal part of California. If this is the case, and covering the recall as a circus is evidence of liberal reporting, then we should see more circus coverage in newspapers serving more liberal (or Democratic) communities and less circus coverage in newspapers serving more conservative (Republican) communities. This does rest on a couple of large assumptions, but it provides us with an interesting and testable hypothesis.

We have an alternative expectation as well. We anticipate some kind of comfort level with the recall process that should vary by community—a propensity to view the recall of Davis as an oddity. In areas of the state more friendly to recalling the governor, we should see less circus coverage, and in parts of the state less friendly to the recall, newspapers should be more likely to view the recall as a chaotic mess.

To investigate patterns of use of the recall frame in local political news coverage in California, we draw a sample of the news clips we assembled during the recall campaign from 20 state newspapers. The particular sampling strategy we follow is to use a constructed week of news clips from each newspaper. A constructed week is a stratified sample of news coverage assembled by selecting from the population of dates a random Sunday, a random Monday, a random Tuesday, and so on for each day of the week. This sampling strategy is more efficient and reliable than simple random sampling (Riffe, Lacy, and Fico 1998).

We draw a constructed week for the eight weeks leading up to Election Day, August 5 through October 7.[7] Table 11.2 provides the number of news stories we selected for each newspaper in our study. In addition to taking an interest in the population of news clips, which includes everything the clipping service sent us, we are also interested in two subpopulations: all news and opinion articles (excluding letters readers sent to editorial pages) and news articles only (excluding reader letters, editorials, and opinion columns). The frequencies of each of these subpopulations are included on Table 11.2 as well.

Instead of focusing on stories containing various keywords, we concentrate on headlines here, counting the number of headlines in each news organization that evoke our circus frame. Granted, this has a qualitative component, but headlines were characterized as communicating the circus frame by one of the researchers, who analyzed all headlines using the same criteria of language suggesting chaos, uncertainty, or historic singularity. An Appendix includes several examples of headlines evoking the circus imagery. In the 710 news clips identified by our sampling technique, 57 (8%) include headlines we considered to be indicative of the circus theme.

We are interested in comparing the importance of local political ideology with local support for the recall. We examine the correlation between the percentage of stories with circus-oriented headlines for each newspaper in our sample and the percentage of registered voters the California secretary of state reports are registered Republican in the county served by that newspaper. We also examine the correlation between and the percentage of stories with circus-oriented headlines for each newspaper in our sample and the percentage

TABLE 11.2   Number of news articles in California newspaper,
constructed week sample.

CALIFORNIA NEWSPAPER	TOTAL	NEWS, OPINION	NEWS
Bakersfield Californian	36	18	15
Contra Costa Times	31	29	20
Desert Sun	11	11	10
Enterprise Record	17	15	14
Fresno Bee	43	42	26
Long Beach Press-Telegram	26	26	18
Los Angeles Times	84	81	63
Modesto Bee	15	13	7
North County Times	26	21	14
Orange County Register	64	62	43
Palo Alto Daily News	9	9	8
Redding Record Searchlight	17	17	15
Sacramento Bee	58	56	41
San Bernardino Sun	24	20	13
San Diego Union Tribune	12	11	7
San Francisco Chronicle	71	63	48
San Jose Mercury News	49	45	38
Santa Barbara News-Press	36	28	21
Santa Rosa Press Democrat	47	45	38
Stockton Record	37	33	25

of registered voters the California secretary of state reports provided valid
signatures petitioning Davis' recall.[8] In Table 11.3, we examine the correlation
between county Republican registration and county recall petitioning, and
the three populations and subpopulations of recall headlines identified
above—all news stories, all news and editorial opinion, and news only.

TABLE 11.3   Circus headlines, county Republican registration,
county recall petition signing.

	TOTAL	NEWS, OPINION	NEWS
Percentage of registered voters Republican [13.1–52.0]	$r = -0.27$, NS	$r = -0.34$, NS	$r = -0.29$, NS
Percentage of registered voters signing recall petition [0.0–20.5]	$r = -0.34$, $p = 0.14$	$r = -0.40$, $p < 0.10$	$r = -0.44$, $p < 0.10$

Note: NS, not significant.

We find that circus coverage of the recall is more strongly and robustly related to support for the recall in California counties than to Republican registration. The negative correlations suggest that, as each Republican registration and support for the recall increase, the characterization of the recall as a circus is less likely in California counties. The correlations are not particularly strong, but the correlation coefficients for the circus story percentages and recall support are slightly higher and reach conventional levels of statistical significance ($p < 0.10$) in two of the three populations or subpopulations we study here. In counties with greater support for the recall, there is less circus coverage. However, we have insufficient observations ($n = 20$) to support an assessment of the independent effect of each of these variables, given their close relationship.

We also compare circus headlines from our sample in counties whose support for the recall petition is greater than the state average of 8.9 percent of registered voters signing recall petitions with counties whose support for the recall is lower than the state mean. Table 11.4 reports the mean circus recall headline use for each group for our three populations and subpopulations of news clips, as well as t-tests comparing these groups. Looking at all news clips we obtained, 8.9 percent of the clips in the low-recall support group had headlines echoing the circus theme. Among newspapers serving communities with higher levels of recall support, an average of 4.5 percent of stories focused on chaos or novelty. These differences are statistically significant ($t = 2.0$, $p < 0.10$, two-tailed test).

Differences are even greater when we restrict our consideration to news and editorial opinion articles. In the low-recall support communities, an average of 9 percent of recall headlines across newspapers featured circus themes, while in high-support community newspapers, an average of 3.5 percent of recall headlines noted the chaos ($t = 2.1$, $p < 0.05$, two-tailed test). Looking only at news stories, 9 percent of stories in low-recall support communities featured circus language, while 4.1 percent of recall stories in high-support communities had circus headlines ($t = 1.9$, $p < 0.10$, two-tailed test). This further illustrates one of our important conclusions: Where readers had a greater support for the Davis recall, editors were less likely to characterize the elections and stories about it using images of chaos, a circus-like atmosphere, or the historic precedence of the special election.

DISCUSSION

In sum, we find that the characterization of the recall as a circus was driven by events. That said, given their unfamiliarity with the recall, the national news conveyed the sense that the recall was chaotic or unprecedented much more than local news organizations. While some observers suggested that liberal media bias drove circus coverage, we find it is more likely that support for and familiarity with the recall process among California readers, rather than political ideology directly, affected circus coverage. Where readers were friendlier to the recall, their news providers were less likely to characterize the recall as an oddity.

TABLE 11.4   Percentage of news stories featuring "circus" recall coverage and local recall support.

CALIFORNIA NEWSPAPER	COUNTY	TOTAL	NEWS, OPINION	NEWS	% OF VOTERS SIGNING RECALL PETITIONS
Palo Alto Daily News	Santa Clara	0.0	0.0	0	5.6
Contra Costa Times	Contra Costa	3.2	3.4	0	4.7
San Jose Mercury News	Santa Clara	8.2	6.7	5.3	5.6
Long Beach Press-Telegram	Los Angeles	3.8	3.8	5.6	7.1
Santa Rosa Press Democrat	Sonoma	8.7	8.9	7.9	4.3
Los Angeles Times	Los Angeles	9.5	9.9	7.9	7.1
San Francisco Chronicle	San Francisco	14.1	15.9	14.6	1.0
Stockton Record	San Joaquin	18.9	18.2	16.0	8.6
Santa Barbara News-Press	Santa Barbara	13.9	14.3	19.0	4.4
Weak Recall Support Group Average:		**8.9**	**9.0**	**8.5**	
Enterprise Record	Butte	0.0	0.0	0.0	8.9
North County Times	San Diego	7.7	4.8	0.0	12.8
San Diego Union Tribune	San Diego	0.0	0.0	0.0	12.8
San Bernardino Sun	San Bernardino	4.5	5.0	0.0	15.3
Bakersfield Californian	Kern	2.8	0.0	0.0	16.0
Desert Sun	Riverside	0.0	0.0	0.0	11.2
Orange County Register	Orange	3.1	3.3	2.4	14.7
Redding Record Searchlight	Shasta	5.9	5.9	6.7	15.4
Sacramento Bee	Sacramento	6.9	7.1	7.3	10.6
Fresno Bee	Fresno	11.6	11.9	7.7	13.7
Modesto Bee	Stanislaus	6.7	7.7	14.3	10.3
Strong Recall Support Group Average:		**4.5**	**4.1**	**3.5**	
Group Difference of Means t-test		2.0*	1.9*	2.1**	

Note: **p < 0.05, *p < 0.1 (two-tailed tests). This table reports the percentage of stories with headlines emphasizing the comical, chaotic, or historic nature of the recall in a constructed week sample of news stories about the recall in each newspaper listed. We examined the percentage of "circus" headlines as a percentage of all newspaper articles coded (total), as a percentage of the total excluding letters from readers (news, opinion), and as a percentage of the total excluding all opinion pieces as well as reader letters (news).

This suggests that reporters are sensitive to the communities they serve when developing their coverage of news events. Political scientists may profitably explore similar tendencies in framing and emphasis in the coverage of social and political issues—such as the subjects of initiative and referenda campaigns—and candidates.

BIBLIOGRAPHY

Bowler, Shaun, and Bruce Cain. "Introduction—Recalling the Recall: Reflections on California's Recent Political Adventure." *PS: Political Science and Politics* 37 (2004): 7–10.

Entman, Robert M. "Framing: Toward Clarification of a Fractured Paradigm." *Journal of Communication* 43 (1993): 51–58.

Fuller, Bruce. "Media Coverage of the 2003 Governor's Recall Campaign: Assessing Balance and Substance." Policy Analysis for California Education Working Paper Series 04-4. University of California, Berkeley and Davis, Stanford University, 2003.

Gamson, William A., and Andre Modigliani. "Media Discourse and Public Opinion on Nuclear Power: A Constructivist Approach." *American Journal of Sociology* 95 (1989): 1–37.

Gerston, Larry N., and Terry Christensen. *Recall! California's Political Earthquake*. Armonk, NY: M.E. Sharpe, 2004.

Goodman, Ellen. "The Cirque du Sacramento Is, In Some Ways, an Inspiration." *San Jose Mercury News,* September 3, 2003.

Greenhut, Steven. "The Top 10 Stupid Recall Tricks. *Orange County Register,* October 5, 2003.

Kaufman, Philip A., Carol Reese Dykers, and Carole Caldwell. "Why Going Online for Content Analysis Can Reduce Research Reliability." *Journalism Quarterly* 70 (1993): 824–32.

Kerns, Jeff. 2004. "Beat the Press" *Sacramento News & Review,* May 6, 2004. http://www.newsreview.com/issues/sacto/2004-05-06/cover.asp (accessed May 24, 2004).

King, Peter H. "Oranges or Bananas?" *Los Angeles Times,* October 5, 2003.

Nelson, Thomas E., Zoe M. Oxley, and Rosalee A. Clawson. "Toward a Psychology of Framing Effects." *Political Behavior* 19 (1997): 221–46.

Riffe, D., Lacy, S., & Fico, F. (1998). *Analyzing media messages: Using quantitative content analysis in research*. Mahwah, New Jersey: Lawrence Erlbaum Associates.

Sabato, Larry J. "Tyranny of the Mob, Recall, Initiatives Rule California." *Los Angeles Times,* August 22, 2003.

Schecter, David L. "Two Peas in a Pod: The Media Frenzy and the California Recall." Paper presented at the Southern Political Science Association annual meeting, Hotel-Intercontinental New Orleans, Louisiana, January 7–11, 2004.

Schroer, Bernie. 2003. "Laughingstock label is getting old." San Marcos North County Times, September 8, 2003.

Smith, Mark A. "The Contingent Effects of Ballot Initiatives and Candidate Races on Turnout." *American Journal of Political Science* 45 (2001): 700–06.

Weintraub, Daniel. "Historian Revises Opinion on California's Recall." *North County Times,* September 6, 2003.

Will, George. 2003. "A Conservative Travesty." Washington Post, October 9, 2003.

NOTES

1. We searched the *Los Angeles Times* online archive and used Lexis-Nexis for the Associated Press and *San Francisco Chronicle* from September 8, 1998, through November 3, 1998, for stories containing the words California AND election AND (Davis OR Lungren), referring to candidates Davis and then-Attorney General Dan Lungren. We searched each organization from September 10, 2002, through November 5, 2002, for stories containing the words California AND election AND (Davis OR Simon), referring to candidates Davis and Republican businessman Bill Simon. Finally, we conducted similar searches for recall election stories August 12, 2003, through October 7, 2003, containing California AND election AND (Schwarzenegger OR Davis) and, alternatively, California AND election AND (Schwarzenegger OR Bustamante).

2. Kaufman, Dykers, and Caldwell (1993) raise concerns about the reliability of using computerized databases to study news content. In particular, they note concerns about the consistency of results obtained even within the same database using the same keyword searches, as well as issues like the scope of news articles uploaded to an online data source from a given news organization. They recommend using both original hard copies of newspapers and electronic sources.

3. *Bakersfield Californian, Contra Costa Times, Desert Sun, Enterprise-Record, Fresno Bee, Long Beach Press-Telegram, Los Angeles Times, Modesto Bee, North County Times, Orange County Register, Palo Alto Daily News, Record*

Searchlight, Sacramento Bee, San Bernardino County Sun, San Diego Union Tribune, San Francisco Chronicle, San Jose Mercury News, Santa Barbara News-Press, Santa Rosa Press Democrat, and Stockton Record.

4. Lexis-Nexis does not archive California-specific television or radio news content. California news sources on Lexis-Nexis include Alameda Times-Star, Argus (Fremont), Associated Press State and Local Wire, California Business Press, Cal-OSHA Reporter, California Journal, California Supreme Court Service, City News Service, Daily News of Los Angeles, Daily Review (Hayward), East Bay Express, Inland Valley Daily Bulletin (Ontario), LA Weekly, Long Beach Press-Telegram, Los Angeles Times, Marin Independent Journal, Metropolitan News Enterprise, New Times Los Angeles, Oakland Tribune, Pasadena Star-News, Press-Enterprise, Recorder, San Bernardino Sun, San Francisco Chronicle, San Gabriel Valley Tribune, San Jose Mercury News, San Mateo County Times, SF Weekly, Tri-Valley Herald (Pleasanton), and Ventura County Star.

5. We used the following national news organizations: ABC, CBS, NBC, Cable News Network, Fox News Network, MSNBC, New York Times, Washington Post, and USA Today.

6. Gerston and Christensen (2004) provide a thorough timeline of the recall campaign.

7. The days for our sample of each newspaper's coverage were selected at random, stratified by day of the week. The specific dates in 2003 used were Sunday, October 5; Monday, September 8; Tuesday, September 30; Wednesday, September 3; Thursday, August 7; Friday, August 22; and Saturday, September 6.

8. Republican registration and recall support in California counties are related, but they are not perfectly correlated ($r = 0.76$, $p < 0.001$).

Appendix. Examples of Headlines Evoking Circus Themes

7-Aug	Fresno Bee	Utter chaos
7-Aug	Los Angeles Times	California's crazy quilt of politics frays
7-Aug	North County Times	State is out of bread but holds a circus
7-Aug	Orange County Register	Get ready for a spectacle
7-Aug	Sacramento Bee	In Kansas, at least, they aren't laughing about 'wacky' California
7-Aug	San Bernardino Sun	Recall madness: Holding election so soon problematic
7-Aug	San Francisco Chronicle	Some laughing all the way to polls: Madcap race viewed as good, bad, ugly–but never boring
7-Aug	Santa Rosa Press Democrat	Recall risks: As the circus begins, a moment to consider Feinstein's warning
22-Aug	Fresno Bee	Tyranny of mob, recall, initiatives rule California
22-Aug	Sacramento Bee	Recall dynamic changing daily in unprecedented drama
22-Aug	Santa Barbara News-Press	Some of the candidates are a little bit 'diff'rent'
6-Sep	Stockton Record	Recall doubts, fears, angst
8-Sep	Los Angeles Times	California recall is talk of the Nation, Even in Congress
30-Sep	Redding Record Searchlight	Wild Cards: With a full deck of candidates, companies cash in on recall

Appendix—continues

Examples of Headlines Evoking Circus Themes - continued

5-Oct	*Contra Costa Times*	Media have hard time covering the ridiculous
5-Oct	*Los Angeles Times*	Accusations make for a turbulent week
5-Oct	*Los Angeles Times*	Oranges or bananas: To some, California is as unstable as a Third World country
5-Oct	*Sacramento Bee*	Casting recall vote in not easy for the queasy
5-Oct	*Sacramento Bee*	CA poised for expedition into the political unknown
5-Oct	*San Francisco Chronicle*	2-ring circus, no real ringleader
5-Oct	*San Francisco Chronicle*	From porn stars to teacher, eclectic crop crowds the field: 135 candidates represent wild cross section of California
5-Oct	*San Jose Mercury News*	A Race like no other
5-Oct	*San Jose Mercury News*	Historic recall election is down to the wire
5-Oct	*Santa Barbara News-Press*	Historic vote nears finale: Readers on recall; most are opposed, but voting for Bustamante or McClintock
5-Oct	*Santa Rosa Press Democrat*	Trainer actor helped disrupt Nazi rallies; Romney calls of trip to back Schwarzenegger over ' sideshow politics'
5-Oct	*Stockton Record*	Recall: historic hysteria; Arnold goes on offensive

12

THE CALIFORNIA RECALL
PUNCH CARD LITIGATION:

WHY BUSH V. GORE *DOES NOT "SUCK"*

RICHARD L. HASEN

LOYOLA LAW SCHOOL, LOS ANGELES

The unprecedented California recall election of 2003 also spawned an unprecedented amount of litigation over the rules for the recall itself. Much of that litigation was patently frivolous, an attempt to throw up as much as possible against the recall to see what would stick in the interest of delaying or scuttling the recall. The recall litigation became part of what I have termed election law as political strategy (Hasen 2003a; see also Garrett 2004).

But some of the litigation had merit. One such example is litigation over the rules for nominating petitions for candidates to replace Governor Gray Davis on part 2 of the recall ballot. California Elections Code section 11381 provides that the rules for nominating candidates for part 2 of the recall generally shall be made "in the manner prescribed for nominating a candidate to that office in a regular election ..." But those usual nomination provisions explicitly state that they do *not* apply to recall elections (California Elections Code, section 8000(a)). California's secretary of state nonetheless applied those rules, thereby allowing anyone with 65 signatures and $3,500 a place on the recall ballot. The California Supreme Court refused to consider whether to overturn the secretary's decision or defer to his administrative judgment. The result was a ballot with 135 potential replacements for Governor Davis.

This chapter focuses on a different meritorious case, that is, litigation over the use of punch card ballots in Los Angeles and a handful of other California counties in the recall election. The argument advanced by the American Civil Liberties Union (ACLU) in *Southwest Voter Registration Education Project v. Shelley* (2003) was that the selective use of punch card voting technology, with its extraordinarily high error rates, violated the equal protection rights of voters under the U.S. Supreme Court's decision in *Bush v. Gore* (2000). Bush v. Gore was the case that ended the recount of votes in Florida following the November 2000 presidential election.

A federal district court judge rejected the argument, but a three-judge panel of the Ninth Circuit accepted it, ordering a delay in the election until the counties could replace their punch card machines with other technology. A larger (en banc) panel of the Ninth Circuit quickly reversed the panel ruling, and the recall election took place as scheduled.

Professor Vikram Amar has been critical of the original Ninth Circuit panel's decision to delay the recall, and even more critical of the Supreme Court's decision in *Bush v. Gore*. Indeed, in a recent roundup of the top ten lessons of the recall, Amar lists "Bush v. Gore sucks" as his number 1 lesson about the recall: "the Supreme Court senselessly chose not to be explicit about things in *Bush v. Gore*," thereby allowing courts, such as the Ninth Circuit panel, to "dubious[ly]" interpret the decision as a reason to delay the recall election (Amar 2004, 955–58; see also Lowenstein 2003).

In this chapter, I take issue with Amar. Far from "sucking," the *Bush v. Gore* opinion had the salutary purpose of focusing the attention of the public, elections officials, and—as in the case of the recall—the courts on important yet neglected issues of the nuts and bolts of democracy. The debate the case has spawned, and the reforms it has started in motion, have thus far had a salutary effect on the nation's democracy, even if that may not have been the intent of the Supreme Court justices who decided the case.

In the first part of this chapter, I describe the California punch card litigation in the context of the *Bush v. Gore* precedent. In the second part, I defend the original three-judge panel's opinion as a permissible application of *Bush v. Gore*, and I explore more generally how *Bush v. Gore* has affected the debate over the nuts and bolts of our democratic process.

THE RECALL PUNCH CARD LITIGATION AS A *BUSH V. GORE* SEQUEL

BACKGROUND: THE *BUSH V. GORE* DECISION

This is not the place to rehash the entire history of *Bush v. Gore* (for a brief history, and review of the literature, see Hasen 2004b), but some background on the case puts the recall punch card litigation in context.

In the days before the 2000 election, everyone recognized that George W. Bush was locked in an extremely close race with Al Gore. In fact, the election was so close that the final outcome depended on the results in Florida, where the initial count showed Bush leading by 1,784 votes out of millions of votes cast in the state.

Following an automatic machine recount of votes mandated by Florida law, as well as some selective recounts requested by Gore during the "protest" phase for Florida election disputes (which further narrowed the vote difference between the parties), the Florida secretary of state certified Florida's electoral votes in favor of Bush. Gore then filed an election "contest," asking for a selective manual recount of nearly 10,000 undervotes from Miami-Dade County and approximately 4,000 votes set aside in Palm Beach County where their legality was in dispute. (Undervotes are ballots that fail to record a valid vote for any candidate.) The trial court held that Gore failed to meet the statutory standard for a contest, and Gore appealed to the Florida Supreme Court.

The Florida Supreme Court reversed the trial court. The court held that the trial court had applied the wrong legal standards in judging the merits of Gore's claim. The Florida Supreme Court ordered that certain recounts, conducted after the deadline it had set in an earlier case, be included in the totals and that a manual recount of undervotes go forward. The court held that all Florida counties—and not just the counties singled out by Gore—had to conduct manual recounts of the undervotes.

The court further held that, in examining the undervotes to determine whether the ballots indeed contained a valid vote for a presidential candidate, the counters should use a "clear intent of the voter" standard, as indicated in Florida statutes.

While a state court judge organized the recount process, Bush took his case to the U.S. Supreme Court. Within four days, the Court granted a stay of the recount process, agreed to hear the case, considered briefing and oral arguments, and issued an opinion reversing the Florida court and ending the recount. Five justices joined in a per curiam opinion reversing the Florida Court on equal protection grounds (*Bush v. Gore*).[1] Four justices dissented.

The Court majority held that the recount mechanism adopted by the Florida Supreme Court did "not satisfy the minimum requirement for nonarbitrary treatment of voters necessary to secure the fundamental right" to vote under the Equal Protection Clause of the U.S. Constitution for four related reasons:

1. Although the Florida court had instructed that the individuals conducting the manual recounts judge ballots by discerning the "intent of the voter," it failed to formulate uniform rules to determine such intent, such as whether to count as a valid vote a ballot whose chad is hanging by two corners.

2. The recounts already undertaken included a manual recount of all votes in selected counties, including both undervotes and overvotes, but the new recounts ordered by the Florida court included only undervotes.

3. The Florida Supreme Court had ordered that the current vote totals include results of a partial recount from Miami-Dade County. From this fact, the U.S. Supreme Court concluded that the "Florida Supreme Court's decision thus gives no assurance that the recounts included in a final certification must be complete."

4. The Florida court did not specify who would count the ballots, forcing county boards to include team members without experience in recounting ballots. Nor were observers permitted to object during the recount.

The U.S. Supreme Court then declined to remand the case to the Florida Supreme Court to order procedures that satisfied these concerns, as Justices Souter and Breyer urged. The Court held that the Florida Supreme Court had recognized the Florida legislature's intention to participate fully in the federal electoral process. Under a federal statute, 3 U.S.C. section 5 (designated a "safe harbor" provision by the Court), states that designate their electors by a certain date—in this election, by December 12—cannot have their choice challenged in Congress when Congress later counts the electoral votes.

> That date [of December 12] is upon us, and there is no recount procedure in place under the State Supreme Court's order that comports with minimal constitutional standards. Because it is evident that any recount seeking to meet the December 12 date will be unconstitutional for the reasons we have discussed, we reverse the judgment of the Supreme Court of Florida ordering the recount to proceed (*Bush v. Gore*).

The majority opinion contained both broad and limiting language in describing its equal protection holding. Broadly, the Court held that "[h]aving once granted the right to vote on equal terms, the State may not, by later arbitrary and disparate treatment, value one person's vote over that of another." It also declared that "[t]he press of time does not diminish the constitutional concern. A desire for speed is not a general excuse for ignoring equal protection guarantees." On the other hand, the Court declared that "[t]he question before the Court is not whether local entities, in the exercise of their expertise, may develop different systems for implementing elections." It also stated that "[o]ur consideration is limited to the present circumstances, for the problem of equal protection in election processes generally presents many complexities" (*Bush v. Gore*).

POST-*BUSH V. GORE* RESEARCH AND LITIGATION

In the United States, the choice of voting technology falls to state or local governments, and the choices range from paper ballots to lever machines, optical scanners, punch card machines, and electronic voting devices.

The issue of voting technology was not on the public's radar screen before the 2000 presidential election. In the course of the 2000 election controversy, a great deal of evidence emerged regarding disparities in the accuracy of the various vote-counting technologies. Particular concerns were raised about punch card machines. In his dissenting opinion in *Bush v. Gore*, Justice Stevens noted that "[t]he percentage of nonvotes in this election in [Florida] counties using a punchcard system was 3.92%; in contrast, the rate of error under the more modern optical-scan systems was only 1.43%."

A number of post-Florida commissions recommended changes to voting technology (as well as to ballot design). The influential Caltech-MIT report (2001) concluded that hand-counted and optically scanned paper have had the lowest rates of unmarked, uncounted, and spoiled ballots in presidential, senate, and gubernatorial elections over the last 12 years. Punch card technology was among the worst technologies. The study estimated that between 4 and 6 million votes for president were lost for a variety of reasons, including faulty equipment and confusing ballots (1.5 to 2 million votes), registration mix-ups (1.5 to 3 million votes), polling place problems (up to 1 million votes), and absentee ballot problems (number of lost votes unknown).

Under public pressure and, in some cases, facing litigation, many states began phasing out punch card technology. Litigation in Illinois led to one of the first district court decisions applying *Bush v. Gore*'s equal protection holding to punch card voting machines. In rejecting the state's motion to dismiss a lawsuit challenging the use of punch card voting as violating equal protection under *Bush v. Gore*, the court held,

> That people in different counties have significantly different probabilities of having their votes counted, solely because of the nature of the system used in their jurisdiction[,] is the heart of the problem. Whether the counter is a human being looking for hanging chads in a recount, or a machine trying to read ballots in a first count, the lack of a uniform standard of voting results in voters being treated arbitrarily in the likelihood of their votes being counted. The State, through the selection and allowance of voting systems with greatly varying accuracy rates[,] "value[s] one person's vote over that of another," *Bush v. Gore*, even if it does not know the faces of those people whose votes get valued less. This system does not afford the "equal dignity owed to each voter." *Id.* When the allegedly arbitrary system also results in a greater negative impact on groups defined by traditionally suspect criteria, there is cause for serious concern.
>
> The Court is certainly mindful of the limited holding of *Bush v. Gore*. However, we believe that [the] situation presented by this case is sufficiently related to the situation presented in *Bush v. Gore* that the holding should be the same. This holding is also consistent with the overarching theme of voting rights cases decided by the Supreme Court—that theme being, of course, "one man, one vote." Any voting system that arbitrarily and unnecessarily values some votes over others cannot be constitutional. Even without a suspect classification or invidious discrimination, "[t]he right of suffrage can be denied by debasement or dilution of the weight of a citizen's vote just as effectively as by wholly prohibiting the free exercise of the franchise." *Reynolds*. Therefore, Plaintiffs have sufficiently stated a claim against the Defendants for violation of equal protection (*Black v. McGuffage*).

The Illinois litigation settled after the state agreed to phase out punch card voting technology.

On May 8, 2002, California's punch card litigation ended with a settlement under which the California secretary of state agreed to decertify punch card machines in time for the March 2004 elections (*Common Cause v. Jones*; see *Southwest Voter Registration Education Project v. Shelley*, District Court opinion: 1135).

THE RECALL PUNCH CARD LITIGATION

When the parties settled the California punch card litigation in 2002, no one expected that a statewide election would again take place in California using punch card ballots; the next scheduled election was March 2004, the date by which the machines would be decertified. Once the recall qualified for the ballot in a special election in October 2003, some questioned whether it was constitutional for the vote to take place using punch card voting machines in some, but not all, California counties.

Governor Davis himself first raised the question whether the use of punch card voting machines in only some California counties raised an equal protection problem under *Bush v. Gore*. The California Supreme Court summarily denied his writ raising this and other issues, a decision that was not on the merits (*Davis v. Shelley*).

The ACLU, on behalf of a coalition of voting rights organizations, then filed suit in federal court arguing that the selective use of punch card voting machines violated both the Equal Protection Clause of the U.S. Constitution and section 2 of the Voting Rights Act (*Southwest Voter Registration Education Project v. Shelley*).[2]

The district court denied the ACLU's request for a preliminary injunction. On the question of the equal protection claim, the district court stated that *Bush v. Gore* "strongly hinted that rational basis review might be appropriate to claims of marginally disparate error rates among varying voting technologies" (*Southwest Voter Registration Education Project v. Shelley*, District Court opinion: 1140). Under such review, the state could well "adduce sufficient justifications" for the use of punch card machines.

The district court acknowledged that an elevated standard of review could apply under the case, although "there are many reasons to believe that the *Bush* Court's analysis was limited to its unique context." The court concluded that, even if the state could not in general justify the use of punch cards under a more stringent review, it could "undoubtedly ... adduce sufficient justifications for their use *in this election*" given that

> [a]lternative technologies will not be available in several of the affected counties in time for the October election. Because the State cannot under its own constitution conduct the election later than the date currently set, and short of a court order compelling something different, the State's choice is between using punch-card machines in several counties and using nothing at all in those counties. The State clearly has a compelling interest in not disenfranchising the voters of at least six counties, and the limited use of punch-card voting in this election is a narrowly tailored means to achieve that end (*Southwest Voter Registration Education Project v. Shelley*, District Court opinion: 1141).

On September 15, less than one month before the election, a three-judge panel of the Ninth Circuit reversed the district court. The court characterized the equal protection issue as a "classic voting rights equal protection claim":

> the weight given to votes in non-punchcard counties is greater than the weight given to votes in punchcard counties because a higher proportion of the votes from punchcard counties are thrown out. ... [T]he effect ... is to discriminate on the basis of geographic residence (*Southwest Voter Registration Education Project v. Shelley*, Panel opinion: 894–95).

The court characterized plaintiffs' claim as "almost precisely the same issue as the Court considered in *Bush*, that is, whether unequal methods of counting votes among counties constitutes a violation of the Equal Protection Clause." The court stated that, like the Court in *Bush v. Gore*,

> "[t]he question before [us] is not whether local entities in the exercise of their expertise, may develop different systems for implementing elections." [Citation.] Rather, like the Supreme Court in *Bush*, we face a situation in which the United States Constitution requires "some assurance that the rudimentary requirements of equal treatment and fundamental fairness are satisfied" (*Southwest Voter Registration Education Project v. Shelley*, Panel opinion: 895–96).

After a lengthy review of the evidence, the court concluded that the use of punch card voting in the recall election failed to meet even rational basis scrutiny. Finally, the panel called California's interest in having the election held within the time frame set by the California Constitution "weak":

> Indeed, had the recall petition been certified just a month and a half later than it was, the recall election would have been scheduled to take place not within sixty to eighty days as provided in the California Constitution under [one provision], but instead in March 2004 under [another provision]. That exception provides for the efficient consolidation of a recall election with an upcoming regularly scheduled election (*Southwest Voter Registration Education Project v. Shelley*, Panel opinion: 900).

A majority of Ninth Circuit judges voted to have a larger eleven-member (en banc) panel rehear the case and, on September 23, just a few weeks before the election, the en banc panel reversed the original panel decision in a brief opinion. Its entire analysis of the equal protection issue was as follows:

> We have not previously had occasion to consider the precise equal protection claim raised here. That a panel of this court unanimously concluded the claim had merit provides evidence that the argument is one over which reasonable jurists may differ. In *Bush v. Gore*, the leading case on disputed elections, the court specifically noted: "The question before the court is not whether local entities, in the exercise of their expertise, may develop different systems for implementing elections." [Citation.] We conclude the district court did not abuse its discretion in holding that the plaintiffs have not established a clear probability of success on the merits of their equal protection claim (*Southwest Voter Registration Education Project v. Shelley*, En banc opinion: 918).

Although the en banc panel remarked that plaintiffs made a "stronger showing" on the voting rights claim, the panel concluded that the district court did not abuse its discretion in concluding that the public interest weighed in favor of holding the election:

> If the recall election scheduled for October 7, 2003, is enjoined, it is certain that the state of California and its citizens will suffer material hardship by virtue of the enormous resources already invested in reliance on the election's proceedings on the announced date (*Southwest Voter Registration Education Project v. Shelley*, En banc opinion: 919).

The court left open the possibility of a postelection challenge.

DEFENDING THE NINTH CIRCUIT PANEL DECISION
AND *BUSH V. GORE'S* OPACITY

DEFENDING THE PANEL'S APPLICATION OF *BUSH V. GORE*

Amar calls the Ninth Circuit's three-judge panel decision "dubious" because *Bush v. Gore* "cannot stand for" the proposition that "the Equal Projection Clause of the Fourteenth Amendment invalidates any statewide election where different kinds of voting machinery throughout the state may lead to nontrivial differential error rates across counties" (Amar 2004, 955; see also Lowenstein 2004). To Amar (and Lowenstein), the *Bush v. Gore* Court's admonition that the case did not decide "whether local entities ... may develop different systems for implementing elections" precludes such an application of the Supreme Court precedent to the recall facts. Amar instead reads *Bush v. Gore* as standing for the proposition that "giving discretion is dangerous when people might be trying to steal elections" (Amar 2004, 958), with the intimation that because the punch card controversy did not involve such discretion, *Bush v. Gore* was inapplicable.[3]

Amar misstates the ACLU's position. The ACLU did not claim that a state necessarily acts in an unconstitutional manner if it conducts a statewide election using voting machinery with different error rates. Instead, the ACLU argued that a state had to come up with a strong justification for using voting machinery with different error rates when their use would result in systematic geographic disparities in the ability of voters to cast a vote that would actually be counted.

Amar nonetheless advances a plausible "due process" reading of *Bush v. Gore* that could cause courts to reject the ACLU's claim, properly understood. Under the "due process" reading of *Bush v. Gore*, the Florida Supreme Court's failure to enunciate a uniform standard for the recounting of votes would have led to an arbitrary outcome in the recount, because different vote-counting officials, within and across counties, could apply different standards to the same question. These "due process" scholars emphasize that recount decisions were to be made initially by partisan decision makers rather than by neutral election-law officials, by judges elected on nonpartisan ballots, or by machines. (For other scholars endorsing this view, see Elhauge 2001; Greene 2001; and Schotland 2002; but also see Tokaji 2003, 2487 [reading the *Bush* precedent more broadly in this tradition].)

But the due process reading of *Bush v. Gore* is clearly not the only reading. Some scholars have read the case as a one-day-only ticket with no precedential value (Dworkin 2002), the product of a disingenuous Supreme Court aimed at assuring that Bush rather than Gore would be the next U.S. president. Under this interpretation too, the ACLU's claim should fail.

But others have read the case as stating an equal protection principle that the nuts and bolts of election systems must now assure a roughly equal chance for all people to cast an effective vote. The state "may not. . . value one person's vote over that of another" through its voting rules or machinery without a good enough reason (Hasen 2002). As *Black v. McGuffage* shows, this equal protection reading of *Bush v. Gore* was certainly within the range of acceptable jurisprudential decision making before the recall controversy.

Indeed, *Black v. McGuffage* was a rather straightforward extension of the principle of *Bush v. Gore* read as an equal protection case, even if the *Bush v. Gore* Court did not go so far as to hold that systematic geographic disparities in voting machine technology may create an equal protection violation. The settlement of the California *Common Cause v. Jones* litigation similarly suggests that an equal protection application of *Bush v. Gore* to punch card challenges was both reasonable and plausible.

The idea that like cases should be treated alike is essential to the rule of law, and it was certainly reasonable to read the punch card suits as presenting similar enough issues to the *Bush v. Gore* case to provide for an equal protection remedy. Thus, *Bush v. Gore* opened a window for plaintiffs seeking voting reforms to use social science to force jurisdictions to make certain changes in their voting rules or equipment (Hasen 2004a; see also Mulroy 2002).

What made the punch card recall litigation so controversial, therefore, was not *Bush v. Gore* 's application to systematic geographic disparities in error rates in voting systems, but the fact that it was being used to delay an ongoing, highly salient, and controversial election.

By the time the Ninth Circuit en banc panel considered the issue in late September, California voters indeed had strong reliance interests to have the vote take place as scheduled (see Lowenstein 2003). The question of delaying the election was thus difficult by the third week of September, when the en banc court finally heard the case; however, it was not difficult on August 7, when the ACLU first filed the lawsuit in district court. Back in early August, the reliance interests of going forward arguably were outweighed by the constitutional problems. Certainly the three-judge panel should have balanced these issues more carefully, but it not clear whether the panel reached the wrong conclusion.

Ultimately, the en banc court faced a profoundly different balancing question than the question faced by the district court or even by the three-judge panel. By September 23, California's reliance interests make the en banc decision reasonable. Still, it is troubling that the en banc court was willing to risk providing no remedy for the disenfranchisement of voters, allowing a suit after voting if necessary to reconsider the issues.[4]

Fortunately for the courts, and for California, the lopsided final counts on both parts 1 (should Davis be recalled?) and 2 (who should his successor be?) of the recall ballot allowed California to dodge a bullet. Given the large margins on both questions of the recall, there was no need to do a recount and further explore problems with California's voting system in the context of litigation.

Litigation would have revealed some troubling facts. Brady (2004) reports that the nonvoting rate in counties using punch cards was more than 5 percent, with Los Angeles coming in just below 9 percent (compare this with a nonvoting rate of 0.74 percent in Alameda County, a county using electronic voting) (Brady 2004). To prove, however, that voting technology was responsible for a difference in the nonvoting rate would require a statistical study that controls for other factors.

For example, voters in counties with punch cards might have been more likely to have deliberately abstained in part 1. But this explanation seems unlikely, especially given exit polling data showing similarly reported non-voting rates across voting methods in California (McDonald 2003, 3). Common sense also suggests rejecting the idea that voting technology has nothing to do with the variance in nonvoting rates. After all, Los Angeles and Alameda counties are fairly comparable counties in terms of political leanings and ethnic makeup, but the disparities in nonvoting on the first recall question is huge. The idea that nearly 9 percent of Los Angeles voters would go to the polls in this highly salient election and willingly not cast a vote on the question of recall is preposterous.

DEFENDING THE OPACITY OF *BUSH V. GORE*

Amar, like others, is critical of the Supreme Court's failure to clarify its equal protection holding (see also Overton 2002, 93 [the Court "left lower courts and others without manageable tools to determine equal protection violations in the political context"]). He seeks to explain the Court's opacity on the basis that "an honest discussion would have impugned the participants in the Florida debacle, and the Court wanted to avoid personalizing the case" (Amar 2004).

I am critical of many aspects of *Bush v. Gore*, including the Supreme Court's decision to take the case, and given that the Court took the case, its decision not to remand the case for a statewide recount in line with uniform recount standards (see Hasen 2003b). But the opacity of the opinion is something to be praised, not condemned.

Now, as myriad cases—including punch card cases—make their way through the federal courts raising a *Bush v. Gore* equal protection claim, the courts will try different approaches to deal with the claims. *Bush v. Gore* will be viewed by lower court lenses in Rashomonic fashion, and the Supreme Court will eventually sort out the scope of the decision. If the Court does its job well, it can refine its new equal protection standard in light of what works and does not work in the lower courts (see Hasen 2003b).

The Court was right to articulate a murky standard, because its holding was unprecedented and not in line with any social consensus about the proper standards for the recounting of ballots, an issue about which the public had no opinion before the 2000 controversy. Opacity made sense.

In the meantime, even without clear guidance from the Supreme Court, the *Bush v. Gore* decision has focused attention on the dire need for voting technology reform. Without the case, who knows when California, Florida, Georgia, and Illinois would have phased out the punch card systems? Congress likely would not have passed legislation funding the upgrade of voting technology had it not been for the Florida debacle and subsequent litigation.

Through its murky *Bush v. Gore* opinion, the Supreme Court has provided a window of opportunity for voting rights advocates to push voting reform in the courts. It has infused people with a healthy skepticism about the devices of democracy. It has engaged a significant portion of the public with concerns about the functioning of our democracy's mechanics. This may not have been the Supreme Court's intent when it decided *Bush v. Gore*, but it has been the result of the decision.

That's something to be celebrated—not something that sucks.

Bibliography

Books and Articles

Amar, Vikram David. "Adventures in Direct Democracy: The Top Ten Constitutional Lessons From the California Recall Experience." *California Law Review* 92 (2004): 927–58.

Brady, Henry E. "Postponing the California Recall to Protect Voting Rights. XXXVII." *PS: Political Science and Politics* 1 (2004): 27–32.

Caltech-MIT Voting Technology Project. *Voting-What Is, What Could Be*, July 2001 rep. http://vote.caltech.edu/Reports/2001report.html (accessed January 2005).

Dworkin, Ronald. "A Badly Flawed Election: Debate Bush v. Gore, the Supreme Court, and American Democracy." *The New Press* (2002).

Elhauge, Einer. "The Lessons of Florida 2000." *Policy Rev. Dec.* 1 (2001): 15–36.

Garrett, Elizabeth. "Democracy in the Wake of the California Recall." *University of Pennsylvania Law Review* 239 (2004): 153.

Greene, Abner. *Understanding the 2000 Election: A Guide to the Legal Battles That Decided the Presidency*. New York: New York University Press, 2001.

Hasen, Richard L. "After the Storm: The Uses, Normative Implications, and Unintended Consequences of Voting Reform Research in Post-Bush v. Gore Equal Protection Challenges." In *Rethinking the Vote: The Politics and Prospects of American Election Reform*, edited by Crigler, et al., 185–99. Oxford University Press, 2004a.

_____. "Bush v. Gore and the Future of Equal Protection Law in Elections." *Florida State University Law Review* 29 (2002): 377–406.

_____. *The California Gubernatorial Recall Debate and the Courts: Why Litigation Has Begun (and Likely Will Continue)*. Findlaw, July 22, 2003a. http://writ.news.findlaw.com/commentary/20030722_hasen.html (accessed December 2004).

_____. "A Critical Guide to Bush v. Gore Scholarship." *Annual Review of Political Science* 7 (2004b): 297–313.

_____. *The Supreme Court and Election Law: Judging Equality from* Baker v. Carr *to* Bush v. Gore. New York: New York University Press, 2003b.

Lowenstein, Daniel H. "An Irresponsible Intrusion." *The Forum* 1, no. 4 (2003): Article 4. http://www.bepress.com/forum (accessed December 2004).

McDonald, Michael P. "California Recall Voting: Nuggets of California Gold for Voting Behavior." *The Forum* 1, no. 4 (2003): Article 6. http://www.bepress.com/forum (accessed December 2004).

Mulroy, Steven J. "Lemons from Lemonade: Can Advocates Convert *Bush v. Gore* Into a Vehicle for Reform?" *Georgetown Journal of Poverty Law & Policy* 9 (2002): 357–77.

Overton, Spencer. "Rules, Standards and *Bush v. Gore*: Form and the Law of Democracy." *Harvard Civil Rights-Civil Liberties Law Review* 37 (2002): 65–102.

Schotland, Roy A. "In *Bush v. Gore*, Whatever Happened to the Due Process Ground?" *Loyola University Chicago Law Journal* 34 (2002): 211–43.

Tokaji, Daniel P. "First Amendment Equal Protection: On Discretion, Inequality and Participation." *Michigan Law Review* 101 (2003): 2409–524.

Court Cases

Black v. McGuffage, 209 F.Supp.2d 889, 899 (N.D. Ill. 2002).

Bush v. Gore, 531 U.S. 98 (2000).

Common Cause v. Jones, 2002 WL 1766436 (C.D. Cal. Feb. 19, 2002).

Davis v. Shelley, 2003 Cal. Lexis 6103 (No. S117921, Cal. Aug. 7. 2003).

Southwest Voter Registration Education Project v. Shelley, 278 F.Supp.2d 1131 (C.D. Cal. 2003) (District Court opinion).

Southwest Voter Registration Education Project v. Shelley, 344 F.3d 882 (9th Cir. 2003) (Panel opinion).

Southwest Voter Registration Education Project v. Shelley, 344 F.3d 914 (9th Cir. 2003) (En banc opinion).

Statutes

California Elections Code section 8000(a).
California Elections Code section 11381.

NOTES

1. Three justices issued a concurring opinion that decided the case under Article II of the Constitution. The concurrence's theory was that the Florida Supreme Court's recount standards constituted new law, in derogation of the exclusive power granted by Article II to the state legislature to choose the rules for selecting presidential electors.

2. This chapter does not discuss the merits of the voting rights challenge raised in this suit, and it does not consider the *res judicata* issue, namely whether the earlier California punch card litigation precluded the second suit seeking additional relief.

3. Amar "read[s] the Ninth Circuit [en banc ruling] necessarily as having rejected on the merits the ACLU's legal argument that *Bush v. Gore* makes any nontrivial intrastate discrepancy in vote counting attributable to the use of punch-card machinery a per se violation of the Constitution" (Amar 2004, 936). Amar is incorrect because the en banc Court did not reach the merits of the *Bush v. Gore* question. Look carefully at the three sentences of the Court on the issue quoted above in the text. The first sentence states that reasonable jurists could con-clude that there was an equal protection problem under *Bush v. Gore*. The second sentence quotes *Bush* dicta, suggesting that the case does not apply to punch card disparity litigation. The third sentence simply concludes that the district court did not abuse its discretion in deciding there was no *Bush* violation. Whether or not the en banc court should have deferred to the district court's understanding of *Bush v. Gore* (on this point, I concur with Amar at 936 that deference was inappropriate), the en banc court did *not* state that the three-judge panel's decision incorrectly decided the issue.

4. Whenever possible, it is always better to remedy an election problem before an election. Think of the 2000 butterfly ballot. Imagine if someone went into a court in Palm Beach County before the 2000 election, claiming voters would be confused by the format. It surely would have been better for the judge to scrap the format then and order a new ballot produced. After the election, there was no way to know whether all of those votes for Pat Buchanan were really intended for Al Gore.